CW00410248

Fashion and Textiles
Business Entrepreneurship
with Information Directory

The definitive guide for fashion and textile
entrepreneurs, artists, designers, lecturers, teachers,
craftsmen, students, fashion and textile enthusiasts.

1 - Photo credit: Matthew Andrew

2 - Photo credit: Emma Andrew

3 - Boutique Mahali (Designer).
Photo credit: Karlton Chambers,
Courtesy of Africa Fashion Week,
London

4 - Photo credit: Anna Tryntja

5 - V. K Wise (Designer).
Photo credit: Karlton Chambers,
Courtesy of Africa Fashion Week,
London

6 - Photo credit: Anna Tryntja

7 - Photo credit: Heather Bostock

8 - Photo credit: Anna Tryntja

9 - Photo credit: Heather Bostock

Published in 2015 by
Raven House Studios
PO Box 1286
Lincoln
LN5 5QW
www.ravenhousestudios.com

Typeset and printed by elpeeko Lincoln, UK

A catalogue record of this book is available from the British Library.

ISBN 978-0-9934114-0-3

Author:

Carol Brown is a senior academic and is widely recognised in the field of fashion and textiles. Throughout her career she has worked as a practising designer and writer. Her work has been published in a wide range of national and international magazines and journals. Authored books include Knitwear Design, Laurence King Publishing (2013); Fashion and Textiles: The Essential Careers Guide, Laurence King Publishing (2010); The Fashion and Textile Information Directory (2000-2001) and the Fashion and Textile Suppliers Directory, FATEC Publications (1999). She has also contributed essays to The Encyclopaedia of Contemporary Designers: A Survey of Style from 1945 to the Present, Thames & Hudson Ltd, (1997) and Contemporary Fashion, St James Press (1995). She has worked at a number of institutions including University of Lincoln; University Campus Suffolk (UCS); University of Northampton; De Montfort University, Leicester.

Cover and back panel: Artwork by Raven House Studios and Elpeeko Ltd

Contents

Bora Aksu collection on the catwalk, Autumn/Winter 2015
Photo credit: catwalking.com

Introduction

Welcome to the **Fashion and Textile Business Entrepreneurship with Information Directory.** This is an easy to read book that is comprehensive in providing valuable information, references and practical guidance relating to entrepreneurship in the fashion and textile industry. The book is aimed at entrepreneurs, artists, designers, and fashion and textile enthusiasts. It will also be a useful reference for graduates, students, lecturers, teachers and business advisors. It offers contacts and resources, and is a necessity for anyone who is interested in establishing their own business and working in the world of Fashion and Textiles.

The book is divided up into five sections:

Sections 1 – 4   provides information about starting up and establishing a business, discussing business ideas, marketing and promotion to business growth. Each section features inspirational quotes and interviews with fashion and textile designers, agents and business entrepreneurs providing valuable insight into their businesses and careers. Supporting each section is a list of *Useful Websites and Resources* for specific topics referenced and a book list of *Further Recommended Reading.*

Section 5   *The Fashion and Textile Information Directory* provides an excellent resource listing over 1000 essential references offering contacts and opportunities. The Directory is divided up in to the following categories:

Fashion and Textiles Organisations; Guilds and Associations; Museums and Research Centres (featuring many of the best collections of costumes, fashion and textiles in the United Kingdom); Exhibition Organisers; Fashion and Textile Consultancies and Recruitment Agencies; Legal Support; Major Fashion and Textile Trade Fairs; Research and External Funding Opportunities; Trend Forecasting Services.

When setting up in business we all have different aims and aspirations. For some, it is making sufficient money to support a family with the convenience of working from home. Whilst for others it may be developing a business that allows you to work the hours you want, when you want, or turning a pastime or interest into a successful business venture.

Whether you are a new start-up, a small business with plans to expand or someone who wants to escape from 9-5 employment to live the dream of working for yourself, doing something you love, always have belief in yourself and your ideas. So, with each stage of the process, from researching your initial idea to setting up, developing and growing your business - I wish you every success in the future.

Carol Brown

1 - Photo credit: Matthew Andrew

2 - Vintage Vixen. Photo credit: Heather Bostock

3 - Raven House Studios

4 - Photo credit: Anna Tryntja

5 - Mannequin. Photo credit: Emma Andrew

6 - Photo credit: Matthew Andrew

7 - Vintage fabric, Vintage Vixen.
   Photo credit: Janie Lismore

8 - Textile Design, Raven House Studios

9 - Photo credit: Anna Tryntja

Section 1

Starting in Business

Britain has always been renowned for its creativity, innovation and entrepreneurship, and this has been reflected in the growth and development in the number of successful start-ups in the creative design sector. According to the Department of Business Innovation and Skills 'there were a record 5.2 million private sector businesses at the start of 2014, the first time the business population has exceeded 5 million'.

Many people dream of starting and running their own business, and being their 'own boss'. Traditionally people would often have a job or work in the same industry for all their working life. Whilst today the job market has changed significantly, with greater variation in employment contracts from full and part-time to temporary contracts often offering greater flexibility but which also can result in employment insecurity. Nowadays many jobs involve lengthy commutes, costly travel to and from work with many jobs having limited career progression and prospects. With greater access to network services, and technological advancements, many people have become more resourceful, and in today's employment climate they question the work life balance and want greater flexibility and control throughout their working life.

Today, many new ventures are being set-up and launched by young school leavers, college students and undergraduates during their studies at college and university, and also many others including significant numbers in the creative arts sectors all with the aim of working for themselves. At the opposite end of the sector, there has been a substantial increase in entrepreneurs' aged 50+ setting up new ventures and becoming self-employed. This is often due to changes in employment, taking early retirement, redundancy or due to the lack of opportunities available for their age group. Many realise the potential of a good business idea combined with a desire to use a lifetimes worth of experience to invest in their own entrepreneurial venture. There are no limits to the age of the new entrepreneur as can be seen in the Office for National Statistics, who are the largest independent producer of official statistics, and the recognised national statistical institute of the UK.

Why Start Your Own Business?

Starting your own business is without a doubt very challenging, it may mean forfeiting a stable income, job security, and adaptability. Therefore, before starting out on your business venture you should question your motives, and ask yourself some tough questions, which need to be considered and answered, if you are going to be successful. Starting your own business and working for yourself may be a case of wanting to take greater control of your life rather than life taking control of you. You have choices but sometimes making them can be difficult. To achieve anything in life it usually means hard work, commitment, self-motivation, flexibility and 'thinking outside the box', but the rewards can be life changing, and very exciting.

There are many reasons why people establish their own business, which include:

- Having a great business idea, and seeing a gap for a new product or service in the market
- An instinct and vision, and feeling passionate about an idea and acting upon it
- Personal satisfaction and the challenge of running and managing a business
- Excitement, enthusiasm, motivation and drive

- Long term job security and controlling your own future

- Financial security and the earning potential

- A response to redundancy and unemployment

- Wanting greater flexibility in your working life with the freedom to make your own choices, working the hours that you want and when you want, fitting your work around family or other commitments

- Wanting an alternative lifestyle

- The opportunity to use your previous experience and to learn and develop new skills

If thinking about starting a business whether as a sole trader, a limited company or as a cooperative or any other business model, consider and analyse the reason why you want to have your own business. For business success you need to consider the aims and objectives of the business, the business ethos, the business goals and how you are going to succeed and make the business viable.

What Makes a Successful Profitable Business?

In establishing a new business, everyone's experiences are very different and unique to them personally, but ask any successful entrepreneur what makes a profitable and thriving business and they will include several of the following in their answer:

- A great idea or initiative, and having a vision

- Thorough knowledge and awareness of the selected market sector

- Long hours of hard work, commitment and perseverance

- Forming a strong support network

- Access to the right business advice and training where and when necessary

- Belief in your business idea and concept, but adaptability to change as required

- Importance of learning by your mistakes and by your own experience, and subsequently adapting and evolving

- Continuing to expand and develop knowledge, learning and thinking

- Being receptive to new ideas and transforming thinking patterns

- Energy to grow and develop the business

- Diversification when and where necessary

- A base of loyal and regular customers

- Surrounding yourself by the right people for support, encouragement and guidance

There are many very positive reasons to start a business but to be successful you must be aware of the reality of self-employment, and what it means to you. Many businesses are set up each year. According to the Office of National Statistics, 346,485 new enterprises were set up in 2013 in the UK alone. However, statistics state that after two years many new businesses will have ceased trading. This is due to a number of reasons including lack of reality and understanding of the hard work and stamina required to run a business and the financial implications such as lack of revenue, cash flow and profitability. To establish a successful business it is important to fully understand why businesses fail, and to analyse any potential pitfalls that could possibly lead to business failure.

Why do so Many New Businesses Fail?

Thorough research and investing time in the business idea is essential to really understand the potential and future of the proposed venture. If you are aware of problems that you may encounter, then you can think and plan ahead, and consider ways to cope and manage.

 Many business fail due to:

- Lack of any real knowledge of the market and an unrealistic vision
- The realisation of the level of commitment required in time and energy to establish the business
- The lack of breadth of skills at the outset of the business
- Lack of knowledge and understanding of managerial and business skills
- Hiring and employing the wrong people for the business
- Loneliness and isolation, and absence of a support network
- The stress of the responsibility of setting up and running the business
- Insufficient funds to expand and to keep the business afloat during the financially difficult times
- The inability to make the transition from financial security of paid employment
- The lack of understanding of the USP's (unique selling point) and branding of the business
- A lack of understanding and awareness of changes in the environment both economically and within the industry that will impact on the business
- Lack of adaptability

Knowledge of the Market Place

Whether creating a new fashion or textile label, setting up an online retail business or establishing yourself as a freelance stylist, writer or journalist, the job of building a business can be exciting, but there are also many risks involved. For that reason it is essential to research your target market thoroughly, helping you to make informed decisions. There are many sources of information that can be accessed to help in researching and understanding your market sector. Sources include referring to statistical data relating to business population estimates for the UK, published by The Department for Business Innovation and Skills (BIS); data and information relating to the economy, population and society at national, regional and local levels, collected and published by the Office for National Statistics. This information includes data and intelligence on the population, age structure, the economy and labour market including trade and industry structures, growing sectors, consumer spending and the quality of life. The Mintel Group provides expertise relating to market research and analysis, consumer research, competitive analysis, and data relating to products, services and product innovation. There are many useful references at the end of this section and in Section 5: Business Support Services which will help in accessing the information you need for researching your business idea. For your business to succeed, thorough research is essential. Hard facts and detailed research are needed to provide knowledge and understanding of your market sector in the planning of your business.

What type of Business?

Once you have decided on your business idea, consider the legal structure of your business and how you want your business to be set up. There are several different business structures, which include sole trader, limited company, 'ordinary' partnership and franchise.

Sole trader: As a sole trader you are classed as self-employed and must register your business with HM Revenue and Customs (HMRC). Full details of the responsibilities of a sole trader are available on the HMRC website, along with details of registering for self-assessment, keeping records, self-assessment tax returns, paying income tax and national insurance, and registering for VAT. As a sole-trader, you are still able to employ others in the business, but you alone are solely liable for the business, which includes being responsible for any financial losses arising from the business.

Limited Company: A business can be set up as a limited company, which is structured as an organisation with members who own shares in the company, and so, any profits made are owned by the company, but this means that all the finances are separate to the owners' personal finances. Full details of the legal responsibilities of a limited company are available on HM Revenue and Customs (HMRC) website, which provides a complete overview and the details involved in setting up a limited company from the appointment of directors and company secretaries, to shares and shareholders, issuing initial shares to statuary accounts, to the company's tax responsibilities.

An 'Ordinary' Partnership: A business can be formed as an 'ordinary' partnership, where more than one person forms a business, and the name of the partnership and the business is registered with HM Revenue and Customs (HMRC). In a partnership both or all partners are personally accountable for all financial risks and responsibilities of the business. Full details of tax responsibilities including the partnership, and the legalities of partnerships are available on HM Revenue and Customs (HMRC) website.

There can be many advantages in setting up a partnership, such as the sharing of responsibilities, bringing specialist skills to the business, moral support, and the development of ideas. However, a partnership must be considered carefully. Problems that may arise could include financial difficulties and disagreements, or differing thoughts on how the business should be managed, including contributions and responsibilities to the business within the partnership. Other points and complications which need to be considered could include a difference of opinion about future developments of the business, or dilemmas may arise if one partner wants to leave the business, as this may lead to huge financial implications and how the business would be managed in the future.

If establishing a partnership it is essential to seek legal advice from a solicitor. This will allow you to talk through various situations and scenarios, and legal agreements can be drawn up between partners, which will then help to avoid potential pitfalls, and future problems involving the partnership and future expectations.

Franchise: A franchise is a business operation which has been registered and is then licensed from one person - the franchiser to another. A successful franchise business will be established with a successful record of trading and have a reliable trading name. Rather than the business growing and expanding in the usual way, the business is licensed out allowing a person to buy into the franchise and trade under the company name, but operate the franchise as their own business. The cost of buying into a franchise varies depending on how long the business has been trading, the size and type of business and how well it is established. Other factors include the setting up costs, what the franchise package consists of, including any training required, and the level of guidance and support given by the franchiser to the franchisee. If you are interested in buying into a franchise, then the British Franchise Association (bfa) provides valuable information on the franchising industry and also about joining and operating a franchise. The bfa website lists the availability of franchise opportunities, and details of future franchising events, which, if you are considering buying into a franchise operation are well worth attending.

What is Your Business Name?

Once you have a business idea and the business structure, consider the business name, which needs to be memorable and distinctive. The name can be descriptive, for example, the Umbrella Store, which easily characterises the trade, or alternatively you may pick something quirky, where it becomes significant in creating and building your brand and in developing future marketing campaigns. Once you have researched and decided on a business name, check that the name is available and there are no other businesses using the same or similar name. You can do this by accessing and searching the National Business Register, which is easily accessible online and free of charge or Companies House, which provides full guidance for limited companies, partnerships and other company types. When checking your selected business name, you also need to check that there are no legal restrictions, such as including the words Institute, Council, Royal/Royalty or British in your business name. In February 2015 an updated document was released Incorporation and Names, last published 2013, which provides information and advice about choosing a company name including the controls and restrictions.

Any mistakes in copying another businesses name or trade mark can turn into a very costly error and run into copyright problems resulting in huge legal expenses. Once you have checked your selected business name on the National Business Register you can then register it, to secure and protect it as yours.

Do You Want a Trade Mark for Your Business?

When establishing your business, you may want to create a trade mark, which is a recognisable symbol, logo or design used in business, which is registered to differentiate a brand, product or service. If you choose to have a trade mark for your business, you will need to check and ensure that it is available and legal to use, and then register it to protect it, to guarantee it is unique to your business. The HM Revenue and Customs (HMRC) website provides clear guidelines advising what can be used as a trademark and what is acceptable and unacceptable, and provides details for registering a trademark both in the UK and overseas. The benefits of registering and securing your trade mark includes having the sole right to use your mark for distinguishing your goods or services, and it also allows you to place the symbol ® next to your chosen trademark to prevent others from using it.

When is a good time to start a business?

Is there a good time to start a business? The answer to this question is totally dependent on circumstances and personal to you, as we all have different needs and aspirations. Many people choose to keep earning and getting paid, at the same time as planning and setting up their business. Whilst doing this they gradually reduce their employed contracted hours, providing sufficient time to plan, set-up and establish the business. Alternatively others decide to give up well paid jobs to focus fully on their business plans - jumping in with both feet, and others start due to unforeseen circumstances, such as loss of employment or redundancy.

Writing a Business Plan

To be successful and to turn your business dream into a reality you will need a 100% belief in what you do. Any new start-up should have a business plan. Writing a business plan and setting yourself achievable goals, helps you to appreciate and understand the realism and financial implications involved in starting and launching a business.

There are many sample business plans and business step-by-step interactive templates available online, which are easily accessible to download and will support you through the process step by step. Writing a business plan helps in analysing the challenges of running your own business in an attempt to prevent many of the obvious pitfalls such as managing the business and the financial essentials and considerations. A business plan should not be a stagnant document but a working document that is frequently referred to and adapted as the business develops and grows. This will help you to keep sights on your aspirations and goals.

When writing a business plan it should be comprehensive in providing trading details listing the business name and address; the type of business; the management structure; the aims and objectives of the business; the business goals; analysis of the market sector; a marketing plan; operational details; legal issues and requirements; the management of staff; the finance (start-up costs; personal survival budget; cash flow management and financial forecast); details of premises and a SWOT analysis.

Carrying out a SWOT Analysis will help you to assess and evaluate the Strengths, Weaknesses, Opportunities and Threats of your business plan, and will help you to understand and analyse what is needed to improve the viability of the business to achieve success. Consider what the possible threats are that could have an effect on the business causing it to fail and how any potential threats can be reduced or removed, and how to be practical in dealing with any problems which may arise.

Completing a Business Plan

When writing a business plan you need to identify the type of business it is, whether you are a sole trader, a limited company, a partnership, or a franchise, clearly defining the aims and objectives of the business. Outline what the business is about, your vision and aspirations for the business and what you want to achieve. State what is unique and niche about your business, product or service. It could be the standard of craftsmanship, the uniqueness of materials and fabrics used in a collection or product, for example, the unique selling point (USP) of a designers label may be the use and combination of new and interesting eco-friendly fabrics or 100% pure new wool hand-spun and dyed in Britain. When analysing your idea consider what the USP is going to be, is it the price, the quality or the originality of the idea.

BUSINESS PLAN

Name of the Business	
Business Owner Name	
Trading Details	This should include full business address, phone/ mobile phone number and email address.
Introduction	Define what the business is, the market is and why the business should succeed. Gather information and outline what you want to achieve. State the motivation as to why you want to set up your own business.
Table of Contents	Include a table listing the content of your business plan with page numbers for easy reference.
Type of Business	Identify the type of business it is: Self-employed, partnership, franchise or limited company. Details of the product or services.
The Management/Key People	Identify the management and organisation of the business, outlining roles and responsibilities of key people in the business, supported by CV's (Curriculum Vitae's) identifying the business owners experience, skills and knowledge. The management of the business may include any business partners or people who are going to contribute to the business. Identify any further training if required.
Network Support	Identify network support such as business mentors and specialist associations.
Aims and Objectives of the Business	Provide details of the aims and objectives of the business, identifying the idea for the business, stating the unique selling point (USP) of the product or service. For example, are your designs exclusive limited editions produced in cashmere for a selected market, or is it the standard of craftsmanship?
Business Goals	In this section outline the short, medium and long term goals for the business, identifying what you want to achieve, and a timescale.
Analysis of Market Sector	Analysis of your market sector needs to be outlined, identifying your target market and providing any statistical data and evidence of the market demand for the product or service, and identifying the potential for growth. Provide details of your competitors, for example where they are located, what they offer and how your business differs in product or service.

Marketing Plan (For further guidance see Section 3: Marketing the Business)	The marketing plan should outline the objectives of your marketing and promotion strategy, providing a detailed analysis identifying: • the unique selling points (USP's) of business, the product or service • how you are going to market your business • details of your marketing budget • a breakdown of the marketing strategy identifying specific marketing campaigns • the timescale and estimated cost for each activity • the method you will use to monitor the results of each marketing activity
Operational Details	Identify and explain how you are going to operate the day-to-day business providing details relating to staff (roles and responsibilities), dealing with suppliers, production, purchasing, sales, payment methods and terms, distribution and transportation.
Management of Staff	If you intend to employ staff either full or part time, or on a freelance basis it is useful to identify this in your plan, noting any additional training or development required.
Legal Issues and Requirements	In this section, provide details of the legal structure and the registration of your business and trade mark, data protection and all insurances required. Examples may include public liability, health and safety issues, provision for illness, to employment laws if you are intending to employ staff.
Finance	The finance section of your business plan can be broken down into several areas covering start-up costs, personal survival budget, cash flow management and your financial forecast. This should include a projection and monthly breakdown analysing your sales within the first trading year, identifying any seasonal trends.
Start-up costs	These costs should be broken down into start-up assets and start-up cost.
Personal Survival Budget	Personal expenditure.
Cash Flow Management	Analysis of cash flow, turnover and profit.

Financial Forecast	The financial forecast section should include a detailed breakdown of all costs including the start-up costs, the business turnover and profits. From this you will then be able to calculate how much money you need to break even, and how much profit you need to survive and grow by investing profits back into the business.
Premises	Provide details of the location of the business.
SWOT Analysis	Carrying out a SWOT Analysis will help you to assess and evaluate the Strengths, Weaknesses, Opportunities and Threats to your business plan, and will help you to understand and analyse what is needed to improve the viability of the business to achieve success.
Additional Information	
Appendices	It is useful to include a copy of your own CV and any other relevant business partners CVs in the Appendices, providing details of all relevant work experience, skills and knowledge, and proving your credibility and skills to run and manage a business successfully.

Management of the Business

During the business planning stages, define your business strategies, setting realistic and manageable goals. Many businesses develop an excellent product but fail to be successful due to lack of management, organisational and marketing skills, and the general lack of understanding of the administration and financial aspects of the business. There are many software packages available on the market designed and created specifically for the small business enterprise, which can be useful. Learn from the experts, and gain as much experience as possible. Business advice is readily available in books, on the internet, through business support networks and from business mentors. Take advantage of all opportunities available and all information that is easily accessible to achieve your goals. If you are a lone worker or a small team who need to be adaptable in taking on greater responsibilities within the business, be innovative in your approach and be team players working together to create a supportive team and adaptable working culture.

Plan and manage each day, so your day-to-day work runs as smoothly as possible. You may be able to multi-task, but there comes a point when you may need to invest in skills and knowledge by employing and training staff who can assist in the smooth running and the development of the business by bringing in expertise and specialist skills to the venture. If you employ staff it is important to have a team of trustworthy, highly motivated and supportive people around you who believe and bring confidence to the business, who are team players and who will work and strive towards the same goal, contributing to the teams and company's success.

If employing staff there are employment regulations you need to abide by. Full details are available on the HM Revenue & Customs (HMRC) website, which has a useful section, 'Employing Staff for the First Time', and also provides details on PAYE, payroll for employers, registering an employee, employment allowances, employment status and much more.

Marketing and Sales Strategy

Thorough market research is vital in making sure there is a market out there. Question, analyse and identify who your clients are, and who your competitors are, for as the saying goes, 'without a market you don't have a business'. When planning the launch and success of a business be aware of the importance of having a strong marketing and sales strategy, promoting your business at the right time and in the right place. For further information relating to marketing and promotion see Section 3: Marketing the Business.

Legal Requirements

Legal regulations vary depending on the type and nature of your enterprise, so when planning and setting up your business you need to check through all legal regulations carefully, which may include several of the following:

- Notification of tax if the nature of your earnings have changed
- Registering the type of business: sole trader, limited company, partnership or franchise
- If a sole trader - Registering for Self-Assessment with HM Revenue and Customs (HMRC)
- Copyright, if required for patents, trademarks and domain name to protect your ideas
- Checking and registering the business name, and any domain names
- Checking and registering a trademark
- Checking data protection
- Intellectual property rights
- Insurance: Employer's liability insurance, motor insurance, professional indemnity, loss of money, goods in transit, product liability and legal expenses
- Tax and VAT
- Health and Safety
- Employment regulations, if employing staff
- 'Performing Rights' – Fashion Shows/Events

Finance

Financing a start-up business can vary in cost depending on the type of business you intend to run; that's why completing a business plan is useful in breaking down costs and understanding the financial implications, providing an analysis of the full costs of setting up and also giving a realistic financial overview of the short to long term prospects. This should include details of cash flow and what money is available for investment. This may include purchasing or hiring new equipment, new materials or maybe paying for the service of freelance specialists or employing additional staff to help the business survive and grow.

Many new businesses often tend to waste money on elaborate items that they do not really need, and taking too much salary in the initial start-up years. When planning your business, you will need to accurately calculate your start-up assets, your start-up costs, your personal living costs and the cash flow of the business, which are all essential for the sustainable financial viability.

Start-up Assets

Be realistic about what you really need to start-up. Many businesses are launched from a home office or spare room and therefore often need minimum financial outlay. Depending on the type of business, start-up assets may include for example, the fitting out of an office, desks, chairs and office furniture, machinery, computers, printers, equipment, sewing machines, lockstitch and other manufacturing equipment. These assets need to be calculated and costed in to the equation, and records kept for your business accounts.

Start-up Costs and Business Expenditure

Start-up costs include rent, business insurances, legal support, research and development of the product/service, accountancy fees, internet connection, advertising details (brochures, postcards, printing, and development of a website/blog). A clear financial breakdown should include the above and also any funding, grants or initial set up support received.

Raising Finance for Your Business

Some businesses start with very little capital whilst others need substantially more. Raising finances for your business may involve using any savings you may have, receiving financial support or backing from friends and family, banks, crowd funding, investors or sourcing a start-up grant or accessing a start-up loan to support your business initiative. See Section 5: Awards and Funding for useful contacts and information relating to the availability of funds, grants, awards and investor companies available for projects and for new and developing businesses.

Personal Survival Budget

When calculating the initial start-up costs you need to consider your own personal survival budget, and calculate how much you realistically need to live on to cover your own personal overheads each month. This budget may include payment such as mortgage/rent, council tax, household bills (water rates, gas and electricity), saving plans and general living expenses. You may need to add additional categories depending on your personal circumstances and requirements. Once you have calculated the start-up costs, the business expenditure and your own personal survival budget this will give you a breakdown of the finances required to set up and start the business, and provide you also with something to live on.

Cash Flow, Turnover and Profit

Cash flow is central to your business succeeding. Many businesses have more than one stream of income, due to diversification of services and products. In business, as in most new ventures there will be quiet times when the business has to survive on perhaps fewer orders or clients, resulting in less income coming in. Through careful planning and a realistic approach you will be able to analyse potential sales through a cash flow forecast, giving you greater understanding of the responsibilities of financial planning. For example, loan repayments need to be manageable and realistic. If the sales of goods or services plummet through a recession or due to sales changing through seasonal product demand, consider whether you will have sufficient funds to

Start-up and Business Expenditure	Outgoings	Personal Survival Budget	Expenditure
Rent/Mortgage		Salary	
Business Rates		Mortgage/Rent	
Gas		Council Tax	
Electricity		Electricity	
Water Rates		Gas	
Telephone/Mobile/Fax		Water Rates	
Internet Connection		Household Repairs	
Business Insurance		National Insurance	
Maintenance/Repairs		Other Insurances	
Lease Agreements		Pensions	
Legal Support		Subscriptions	
Transport/Petrol		Transport/Petrol	
Car Insurance/Tax		Car Insurance/Tax	
Stationary		Memberships (Gym, clubs and groups)	
Advertising			
Promotional Material		Clothing Allowance	
Subscriptions		Telephone/Personal Mobile	
Loan Repayments		Entertainment	
Wages/Salary		Personal Spending	
Accountancy Fees			
Postage			
Production			
Printing			
Stock			
Consumables			
Total		Total	

keep abreast of any repayments, and have sufficient funds for the business to survive during the difficult times, and to keep on managing and growing the business.

You may have a very desirable product/service and be extremely successful in marketing and selling, but you also need to make sure the pricing of your product or service is right, as you will need to cover all your overheads and make a profit. This entails receiving payments on time to maintain a healthy cash flow. It is essential to understand the difference between turnover and profit, the business costs and margins. A company or business can make a huge turnover but it is the amount of profit, which is essential and the important factor for maintaining the sustainability of the business. Therefore, calculating the cost of sales, and regularly monitoring your incomings and outgoings is crucial to your business financial viability and growth.

Finances need to be checked carefully, keeping your overheads to a minimum. Learn to shop around finding the best deals on insurances and the best suppliers. Contacts are crucial in building up, establishing and maintaining a good reputation, arranging the best business payment terms with suppliers and contractors. For example, always try and negotiate the very best payment and trading terms, which may result in cutting costs. Consider your pricing strategy, making sure you get the pricing of your product or service right, ensuring you cover all costs, making a profit and meeting your financial targets.

For prompt payment on items sold, always send out all invoices punctually, checking the name of the company/business is correct and despatching invoices to the correct department for prompt payment, requesting to be paid by a specific date. It is essential to keep the cash flowing, to avoid running into any financial problems, and any difficulties, it is critical to face up to the truth and seek help if necessary. Try and resolve any problems as quickly as possible, before they spiral completely out of control resulting in the business failing.

Most banks and building societies offer business banking, which is usually available 24 hours a day offering flexibility, and the support necessary. There are many business accounts on offer presenting various start-up packages that include banking advice support, business and marketing planning software, software skills training, cash flow management software, and business start-up publications. Many banks and building societies offer added incentives such as free start-up extras, which initially sound fantastic. However, it is important to look into, and check out the best banking deals before being persuaded or tempted with lots of additional extras that you do not need. You will no doubt be paying for these extras somewhere, somehow.

When opening a business bank account look for the best deals, checking out the number of years you get free banking and what this actually entails, as it can vary from as little as zero free banking to twenty four months. Compare business bank account overdraft facilities, the cost of account transactions and always read the small print checking that you get the full deal on any offer.

Financial Records

All businesses are required to keep records of their accounts, which either you can manage or you can employ a bookkeeper or an accountant to manage. Company accounts and records need to be kept for the duration of at least six years. Besides managing your books, an accountant or bookkeeper will be able to provide monetary advice and also oversee financial records for payment of tax and national insurance, and for completion of your annual self-assessment tax returns. For further details of registering for VAT, calculating the VAT taxable turnover of your business, visit the HM Revenue and Customs (HMRC) website: https://www.gov.uk/vat-registration.

If you are planning to handle the day-to-day bookkeeping yourself, specialist software is available on the market that is useful in helping to monitor and control the financial running of a business. Bookkeeping software can be used to record money going in and out of your business bank account, daily transactions and help in paying bills, monitoring standing orders, checking balances and transfers, and also in creating your own profit and loss accounts.

Location of the Business

Many businesses are set up and run from a dedicated workspace in the home, a spare room or the garden shed avoiding costly overheads and saving time and money on commuting. Laura Ashley and the Body Shop are two very successful businesses along with Virgin Group founded by Sir Richard Branson, started in this way. Working from home offers you the freedom, flexibility and mobility of work today. Many initial start-ups only need access to online technology, providing the freedom and choice to work anywhere such as in cafes, libraries, business hubs where internet access is available, improving efficiency and productivity, saving time and money.

If you choose to set up a business working from home and have expensive business stock then you need to consider your insurance policy and check your insurance cover is sufficient. Taking out the right insurances for your business is important, for example, if you employ staff you will need to take out Employers' Liability Cover. If you have customers calling at your home or you hold business meetings in your home studio or office you will need to have public liability insurance, as you are the one responsible for their health and safety, but you also need to cover yourself, making sure you are fully insured in case of any problems. There are several excellent publications available that you can download free from the website: www.hse.gov.uk - Homeworking: Guidance for Employers, which are worth reading, and which provide the latest regulations.

Units/Studio and Office Space

If working from home is not the answer for you, there are many very successful initiatives, developed to help business start-ups through local government, councils and education institutions. These include registered business start-up units and studio spaces available offering managed office space and to rent with low business overheads and high speed internet access. Often the units offer additional managed areas such as receptionist facilities with postal and administration support, a telephone messaging service, access to conference rooms and boardroom facilities for business meetings with partners and clients, cafes, kitchens and additional communal amenities.

A lot of business employability hubs are also known as business incubators and innovation centres, which have been established specifically for small to medium size start-ups. Many offer additional services such as hot desks or alternatively virtual office space for micro-businesses or businesses that do not need a physical space, but require a business postal address and a link to their website. This can then be linked to your business website and other social media networks, giving a professional image to your business.

Working in a managed space such as a start-up incubator unit often provides the advantage of being part of a creative and supportive community environment, working in proximity with like-minded entrepreneurs. This can be very advantageous in sharing knowledge and exchanging skills. Depending on the centre, additional benefits and services offered may include the availability of regular business support seminars and workshops from industry experts speaking about varying aspects of business including business planning advice and the opportunity to attend networking events.

Some business units offer specialist employability mentoring schemes, and one-to-one business support sessions with a qualified business support advisor. Having a dedicated mentor who understands what you are going through and who is able to offer valuable advice and support in helping to resolve any problems you may encounter, could make the difference between your business failing or your business surviving, flourishing and expanding.

Business Support

There are many business services locally, regionally and nationally that have been specifically established to support the small and medium enterprise (SME) such as the Regional Development Agencies, Learning and Skills Council and privately run business support lines. There are networks of business advisors and experts offering valuable advice and help, who will have access to all the latest business information in specialist fields required for new start-up businesses, to support in assisting businesses in dealing with day-to-day problems and concerns and to also advise on business growth.

Consider joining a business group to make new contacts and for the exchange of ideas. Many cities and towns have established local business groups or clubs who meet regularly. They often have very specific agendas with discussions and presentations by sponsors, updates of relevant forthcoming events and even offering prestigious annual business awards.

There are many excellent business courses on offer from short intensive start-up programmes from under a week, to longer full-time accredited programmes such as degree, postgraduate and MBA's to open learning courses or individually designed programmes. There are many short practical courses and flexible learning opportunities, designed for those embarking on a new business and small-to-medium businesses. Many of these courses comprise of training to support the development and writing of a successful business plan. Topic areas may include business management training, strategic planning, costing, finance and cash flow, accounting, marketing, branding and brand management, sales and legal requirements including intellectual property rights and all copyright laws. It is important to gain as much knowledge as possible and complete as much research to help your business succeed. Find out what is out there and what is on offer.

Many local County Councils receive government funding to offer business support facilities and short courses relevant to businesses, such as Support for the Digital and Creative Businesses; Technology for Businesses, as well as with drop-in centres, which you may find a useful resource. Help and support for businesses is also available from HM Revenue and Customs (HMRC), who offer lots of useful business information through their website, YouTube videos and through their live online webinar presentations, which you can sign up for and join in with.

There are many associations, societies and guilds, who offer support and guidance in helping you to make the right business decisions by gaining valuable advice from industrial experts. Many associations and groups also offer networking events, entrepreneurial and business support help lines and mentoring programmes. The programmes have been established for students, graduates, young and developing enterprises to gain support from industry professionals in building and establishing their idea and in understanding the potential of the business. Support such as this, can have real impact on the potential success and growth of the venture. Having a business mentor can be the difference between the business succeeding and failing.

A good business mentor must have belief in your venture and have the experience to direct and assist you when required. Some businesses seek mentors to invest financially in their business. It is useful to find out what opportunities are available from linking with a business hub; consider attending and contributing to business workshops and conferences which will help you in understanding the business planning stages, from your initial ideas to writing a business plan and launching your business. Many events are free and occasionally funding is available to attend various conferences that are on offer, as there are many people out there who want you to succeed.

> *It is useful to include a copy of your CV (Curriculum Vitae) and any other relevant business partners CVs, in the appendices of your business plan giving details of all relevant work experience, skills and previous knowledge.*
>
> **Quote: James Innes – Founder of the CV Centre**

Writing a CV (Curriculum Vitae)

A Curriculum Vitae (CV) is a record of a person's professional work history and experience. It is used to market their knowledge and skills, and can be used for various purposes. For example, a targeted CV can be sent in response to a specific job advertisement with an attached covering letter or for applying for work experience, for cold canvassing purposes when making speculative approaches to a business, or for inclusion in a document such as a business plan. A CV provides details such as a personal introductory statement, summary of your education, qualifications and relevant training courses attended, past and present employment, internships or work experience summarising duties and the position involved, and includes any relevant additional skills, achievements and interests.

Writing a successful CV takes time and effort and should not be rushed. A CV needs to be relevant to the job or situation. If applying for a job, a CV may form the basis of the interview and during the interview you may be asked to talk through it. With every job advertised in the Creative Industries sector be assured the competition can be tough, as employers are usually inundated with applications, so your CV needs to be focused and stand out from the crowd. To be successfully shortlisted for an interview, this means your CV standing out for the right reasons, and meeting the criteria of the job description. If using a CV to apply for a design position it is acceptable to include an additional page providing visual examples of your work.

An effective CV should be relevant in content to the position or company applied to, or appropriate to the plans for your business. It should be professionally presented, and the usual rule is a maximum of two sides of A4 quality paper or equivalent, which is considered sufficient length to include all information required. The content should be concise and informative, well organised and logical in content, professionally presented in an easy to read format. It is useful to divide the content into manageable sections using clear sub-headings, with all information listed in chronological order, starting with the most current and up-to-date first. Consider using an easy to read font choice and font size, such as Ariel or Tahoma in font size 10 or 11 with a slightly larger size for headings. This will make your CV much easier to read. Always proof read your CV and any legal documents, checking for any spelling mistakes and errors before sending.

> *"Effective CVs are concise but compelling; they attract the attention of recruiters with their professional layout and the quality of their written content."*
>
> **James Innes, Founder of CVCentre.co.uk**

If using a CV for the business or for applying for a new job then it should be reviewed and tailored specifically for the job in hand. It is useful to keep your CV up to date listing any newly acquired skills, jobs and experiences, and then adapt and tailor your CV for the purpose you need it for. If you need help in writing your CV, student services, career units and business mentors are usually able to offer support, and there are many CV templates available online.

CV Example Guidelines

Full Name

Address   (Provide your full postal address including postcode)

Telephone   (Include both your landline and mobile phone number)

Email Address

Personal Profile
A personal profile gives a very brief summary of you and your abilities, relevant to the situation
Example profile: A professionally qualified digital marketing designer who has extensive experience working on a wide range of creative marketing campaigns, who is dedicated, highly motivated, adaptable and enthusiastic, and enjoys developing new concepts increasing sales and enhancing the reputation of the company.

Skills
Identify skills relevant to the position, for example:
• Ability to work on own initiative, and ability to motivate and lead a team
• Good communication skills and commercial awareness with the ability to negotiate new contracts
• Ability to manage time effectively, working across a range of projects, and prioritising tasks to meet all deadlines

Employment
Provide details of your employment to date, listed in chronological order, starting with your most recent, for example:

2012 – present   Marketing Assistant, XXXXXXX, Lincoln, UK

Responsibilities include:
• Production of all in-house marketing materials and promotional literature including liaising with printers
• Experience creating online adverts
• Maintaining and updating mailing database and supporting Marketing Manager and other colleagues

2011 – 2012   Trainee Design and Marketing Assistant, XXXX, Leicester, UK

Responsibilities included:
• Writing and posting press releases onto the company website and intranet, and assisting with the delivery of social media campaigns
• Designing and distributing e-bulletins
• Assisting with marketing and general all round office duties
• Assisting with the organisation of events and exhibitions

Work Experience

Provide details of any internships, voluntary work, work placements, artist in residency positions that you have completed with dates, for example:

2012 Marketing Assistant, XXXXXX, Sheffield, UK

- Training received on design software Adobe Photoshop and InDesign.

Responsibilities included:

- Creating leaflets, providing digital artwork for online advertising including social media, blogs, websites and updating the company's website and being responsible for all social media: Facebook, Twitter and other major social platforms

Education and Qualifications

List details of any academic qualifications achieved with a brief summary of specialist areas studied, listed in chronological order, for example:

2012 – 2015 BA (Hons) Marketing Design, University of XXXXX, London

Subjects studied: Advertising and Digital Marketing, Branding and Identity, Consumer Behaviour, Photography, Digital Photography (Studio and Location), Image Manipulation

Additional Courses Attended

List details of any additional courses attended, giving dates of attendance, for example:

2013 Photo Editing course using Adobe Photoshop and other similar design packages (2 days) attended at XXXX

2012 Photo Editing and Digital Print course (1 week) attended at XXXXX

Additional Skills

In this section include any additional skills, for example:

- Languages: Fluent in French and Italian, and good conversational Spanish
- Advanced in Microsoft Word, Excel skills, Adobe Photoshop, InDesign and Illustrator, After Effects, 3D Cinema
- Full current clean driving licence

Further Information and Achievements

- Associate member of the British Web Design and Marketing Association (2011- present)
- Elected as Final Year Student Representative on the BA (Hons) Marketing Design Course, working with both staff students and students, and representing the year group at University Student Consultative Committees

Interests Include any extracurricular activities and interests

Reference In this section list details of your selected referees: name, position held, and full address details, telephone/mobile number and email address, or alternatively it is quite acceptable to state 'references available upon request'. This gives you time to contact your referees and check they are happy to support you and agree to give you a reference.

"Originality makes an effective CV; showcase what makes YOU different and what value YOU can bring to a company"

James Innes, Founder of CVCentre.co.uk

Time Management

The challenges presented in establishing and running a business are demanding, it can be both exhausting and exhilarating, but it is important to enjoy the experience, however hard it is at times. Be organised, be proactive, be flexible and learn to balance your time in running the business in the most efficient and effective way possible. Remember why you started the business, keep healthy and positive, taking time out to achieve a good work life balance. Consider time management, taking time out to learn new skills and utilise existing ones. Learn what works for you.

Business Success

To establish a successful and sustainable enterprise you will need to frequently consider your business plan. This should be seen as a strategic, analytical and a developing document which helps to monitor and scrutinise the business, and which can be adapted and updated when and where necessary. A successful business never stays static. There are always new enterprises being launched, with newer and fresher ideas, so it is essential to step back, review, reflect and respond in evaluating the business. You cannot afford to put 'your head in the sand' and ignore changes or problems, whether day-to-day operational troubles or long term difficulties. For success, you need to be adaptable, making adjustments, and be proactive and reactive where and when necessary, in responding to changes within the world of business and the ever-changing economic climate.

Full analysis of the business is needed on a regular basis. It is essential to revisit and revise the business plan, looking at the business from all perspectives, judging what is, and is not working. Consider what needs more attention, checking you are meeting your financial forecasts and your business objectives. Some enterprises fail due to the constant slog of hard work with very little recognisable gain, with the founder questioning – 'Is it really worth this?' They do not enjoy it, usually due to starting the business with an unrealistic view of what running a business really entails, and rather than looking at the positives, they look at the negatives. Other businesses fail due to no real understanding of the market and not being adaptable to change. The first few years in business usually involves long hours and exceptionally hard work, and can be very challenging, and at times very daunting, but it can also be a very exciting time. Most successful entrepreneurs surround themselves with a supportive and positive network of like-minded people, who are able to offer knowledge and help. The real entrepreneur never gives up, and will work through the tough times and work through any disappointments, moving the goal posts until they hit on the right product or service and achieve their dreams.

In running a business you are going to make mistakes, but learn from them. Problems will arise in all areas of the business, and there will be many trials and errors in solving them. With hard work, realistic goals, lots of energy and enthusiasm, a well thought through business plan - pushing you to achieve your goals and potential, a supportive network, the development of appropriate skills which can take the business forward – 'ANYTHING IS POSSIBLE'. For business success, you need to believe in your business idea and to believe in yourself. You need to keep healthy and stay fit, organising and structuring your day to meet set goals. Knowledge and planning are essential, and most importantly holding onto your passion and enjoyment of what you do.

Useful Websites and Resources

This section includes useful resources for setting up in business from writing the business plan and CV writing to resources offering legal guidelines and support. See also section 5: Fashion and Textile Information Directory for additional resources.

British Franchise Association (bfa)
Website: www.thebfa.org

Business is Great
Website: www.greatbusiness.gov.uk

Business Innovation and Skills (BIS)
Website: www.gov.uk/government/organisations/department-for-business-innovation-skills

Business and IP Centre
Website: www.bl.uk/bipc

The Business of Fashion (BoF)
Website: www.businessoffashion.com

Companies House
Website: www.companieshouse.gov.uk

CVCentre.co.uk
www.cvcentre.co.uk

Department for Business, Innovation and Skills (BIS)
Tools and guidance for businesses
Website: www.gov.uk/government/organisations/department-for-business-innovation-skills

Drapers Online
Fashion industry news and trend information
Website: www.drapersonline.com

Enterprise Nation
Website: www.enterprisenation.com

Fashion Capital
Website: www.fashioncapital.co.uk

Federation of Small Businesses
Website: www.fsb.org.uk

Gov. Homeworking: Guidance for Employers.
Website: www.hse.gov.uk

HM Revenue & Customs (HMRC)
Website: www.hmrc.gov.uk

Local Enterprise Partnerships
Website: www.bis.gov.uk/polices/economic-development/leps

Mintel Group Ltd
Website: www.mintel.com/contact-us

National Business Register
Website: www.start.biz

National Federation of Artists' Studio Providers (NFASP)
Website: www.nfasp.org.uk

Office for National Statistics (ONS)
Website: www.ons.gov.uk

The Prince's Trust
Website: www.princes-trust.org.uk

The Princes Youth Trust
Website: www.princes-trust.org.uk

PRIME
The Prince's Initiative for Mature Enterprise, which helps people over 50, set up their own businesses
Website: www.prime.org.uk

Prospects
Website: www.prospects.ac.uk

Shell LiveWIRE, UK
Website: www.shell-livewire.org

Trading Standards Institute (TSI)
Website: www.tradingstandards.gov.uk

UK Intellectual Property Office (IPO)
For information on intellectual property, trademarks, patents, copyrights, designs, law and practice
Website: www.gov.uk/government/organisations/intellectual-property-office

Further Reading

Jackson, Tim & Shaw, David, *The Fashion Handbook.* Oxon: Routledge, 2006

Vaughan, Evans, *Financial Times Essential Guide to Developing a Business Strategy: How to Use Strategic Planning to Start Up or Grow Your Business.* Harlow: Financial Times Publishing International, 2013

Williams, Sara, *The Financial Times Guide to Business Start Up 2015: The Most Comprehensive Annually Updated Guide for Entrepreneurs* (The FT Guides). Financial Times Publishing International, 2014

palmer//harding. Spring/Summer collection 2015

Section 2

Business Entrepreneurship

The fashion and textiles sector lends itself to business start-ups and attracts many creative entrepreneurs working as sole traders, limited companies and partnerships. New businesses are starting up every day. Launching a fashion or textile business offers exciting opportunities to use existing and new skills to create a strong and sustainable business in a competitive global market. For any creative business to be successful whether in design, retail, illustration or product development, ingenuity must be fully combined with sound business knowledge and excellent management skills, along with resourcefulness leading to business success.

If planning to start your own business, one of the first questions to ask yourself is, what sort of business do you want? This may be determined by your existing skills, knowledge and experience. You may have worked in one industry for many years, and be setting up an independent business in the same industry, or alternatively you may decide on a complete change of direction based on a hobby or interest you have pursued for years.

This section discusses some ideas for business ventures, and also presents profiles and interviews with successful fashion and textile designers and business entrepreneurs from the creative industries.

Business Ideas in Fashion and Textiles Include:

- Designer: fashion (women's, men's, children's wear), knitwear, sportswear, swimwear, lingerie, bridal wear, eveningwear, maternity wear accessories, footwear, millinery
- Designer of printed, woven or embroidered textiles for the fashion market or the interior and product market
- Sample designer
- Fashion / textile consultant
- Yarn spinner / manufacturer
- Pattern cutter / pattern grader
- Sample machinist
- Fashion / textile photographer
- Fashion / textile photography archivist
- Fashion stylist
- Fashion illustrator
- Writer / journalist
- Fashion editor
- Trend forecaster
- Product manufacturer
- Event's organiser
- Mystery shopper
- High street retailer
- Pop-up store retailer
- Market trader
- Online retailer
- Fashion/textile blogger
- Fashion/textile vlogger
- Digital business
- Fashion/textile workshop trainer

......the list is endless

Whatever the business, for success you need to enjoy it and be excited by the idea and the principles of the venture, as you will need to be highly motivated to succeed, working long hours, coping with the difficult times as well as the times of productivity, profitability and reward. Entrepreneurs usually have lots of ideas for business and are more often than not risk takers, but for the business to succeed the risks need to be considered and carefully calculated and this is done by carrying out thorough research and thinking laterally. Lateral thinking is a termed coined by Dr. Edward de Bono, regarded by many as the leading authority in the field of creative thinking, innovation, and the direct teaching of thinking as a skill. He describes the process of 'thinking outside the box', thinking creatively solving problems through an indirect and creative approach to generate new ideas.

Once you have an idea for your business, research is essential for success to develop your ideas, product or service before launching your venture. It is helpful to search online for similar businesses and compare what they are offering, where they are located and assess how your ideas differ.

Listen, touch, smell, see and taste: Use your senses and memory, as a guide to help you interpret, gather and make connections.

Experiment, play and have fun: We should all allow ourselves time for nurturing the child within us. This will generate seeds for wonderful ideas.

Past, present and future: Whatever your project or business idea, do look at the concept from all angles. Your research will benefit from this process.

Think human and be a weaver of stories: Create a visual language with meaning. Use beautiful words and images to connect with your consumer.

Have conversations with people who sit outside of your subject area: Innovation and magic happens when unexpected paths cross and different disciplines collide.

Francesca Coombs –
Lecturer in Fashion Marketing and Promotion, University of West London

The Designer

If establishing a design label and launching a collection consider the sourcing of fabrics, yarns and trims and the importance of the manufacture and production of your product range. This will involve developing networks and forming excellent links with suppliers of fabric, yarns and trims, packaging suppliers and manufacturing units. Once you have designed your product or range, you need to consider the practicalities and challenges of manufacturing, producing and selling your designs.

Many design enterprises start out by creating and producing items, but realise that in the long term, the level of production required is unsustainable. This is usually due to insufficient knowledge of industrial production methods and lack of specialist equipment and machinery available to ensure consistency in the quality of finish in producing samples and in the final production of the range. To improve efficiency, most designers outsource to production units.

A garment production unit may offer a complete service from pattern making to cut, make and trim (CMT), toiles, sample making, grading and production runs, and have the expertise to work with a wide range of fabrics. Problems arise when designers struggle to find suitable UK manufacturers, particularly outside London who deal with small orders. Small orders usually result in high costs and overheads, and therefore many tend to outsource the production of goods to cheaper manufacturing producers abroad, but this requires responsibility and careful monitoring for quality control, efficiency of service, and ensuring that workers are not exploited. For further information visit the website for The Ethical Trading Initiative (ETI) www.ethicaltrade.org.

If producing in the UK, it is much easier to monitor the whole process from design to manufacture, checking that the manufacture and production meets the standards required for your market sector. There is nothing worse than commissioning work and then when produced the standard of workmanship is sub-standard, and does not reflect the quality of design, the brand and also your aspirations. If produced in the UK, your product will also have the added bonus of supporting British Industry and having the 'Made in Britain' label. Many of the trade associations listed in Section 5 have links and networks to industry specialists who will be able to offer you advice, contacts and support. Many association websites list specialist UK and international fashion and textile trade shows and events dedicated to specific markets and disciplines.

Production

Whatever your specialist design area, whether in fashion or textiles, bespoke design - making to your client's individual requirements or mass manufactured, knowledge about all the manufacturing and production processes utilised will help you in working efficiently with factories and manufacturing units. This will help you to get the best results at competitive prices and produced on time, ensuring the viability of your product and business. If involved in the manufacture and production of merchandise, you need to calculate the costs and the work load involved in producing and managing the orders, along with the cost of fabric, marketing the collection, distribution and transportation of goods, to work out your pricing policies and your profit margins. When working with a manufacturer you need to check that they are able to meet your terms, producing the goods at the right price to the correct quality and on time. Questions to ask; Do they have the correct machinery to deal with the fabrics and trims you are using or are they going to outsource which will add to the costings? Do they have the experience necessary to complete the order and have they a good history of reliability.

Financial acumen is essential in keeping your overheads as low as possible; learn how to negotiate the best possible payment terms with all suppliers you use and request wholesale terms to get the best deals. This will reduce costs and help in managing your cash flow. Careful calculation on the payment terms and payment methods needs to be considered, as cash flow is key to your success. Keep a close check on stock control, and track all orders, giving you full understanding of what you are selling and to whom, analysing and monitoring sales and sales data.

Labelling Garments and Textile Ranges

When producing a garment or textile range it is essential to include full and accurate details of the fibre content on all labels for garments and selected textile products. This provides customers with accurate information meeting the UK and European statutory requirements for labelling garments and textile products. Statutory requirements include identification of the products fibre content. The percentage of all fibres should be listed in descending order, for example 90% cotton, 10% elastane. The Department of Business Innovation and Skills provides details of the regulations on their website providing guidance to business on the EU Regulation and the UK Regulations - 'Guidance on the Textile Products (Labelling and Fibre Composition) Regulations 2012'; the UKFT provides details 'Care Labelling: A Guide to Your Responsibilities', and GINETEX, the International Association for Textile Care Labelling has a very informative website giving information on textile care labelling and regulations worldwide.

Ciment Pleating offer a wide range of pleating services

Finding a Market for Your Work

Whatever your design specialism you will need to find a market for your work. You may be a designer who deals directly with your client, for example, producing bespoke, made to measure, one-off bridal gowns, which are all individually cut and fitted specifically to the client's measurements. Many businesses such as this often start off advertising locally and attending trade fairs and receiving new orders through recommendations and word of mouth. For other specialist fields you may choose to sell your work through an independent retailer, an online retail outlet, or at a trade exhibition or craft fair, through party plan or one of the many popular online market websites where you can have your own trading place or your own website.

Selling on business websites has become popular with, and has been the success of many start-ups. You may consider selling your designs directly to the customer, wholesale, retail or directly to the consumer/client through your own online store, through an exhibition or trade fair, cutting out the middleman. This allows you to offer your customer inside knowledge into the product development such as fabric properties and manufacturing techniques employed. On the other hand, you may consider working freelance to a commissioned brief or consider having your work stocked in an independent high street retail outlet or department store.

Approaching a Buyer

Many designers dream of selling their ranges through a department store such as the House of Fraser, John Lewis and Debenhams, but competition is very tough, as there are many new, emerging, and established designer labels all contacting buyers wanting to arrange an appointment. Buyers work in a highly pressurised, competitive environment, working with suppliers, designers, merchandisers and visual merchandisers with sales targets to meet. For success, a buyer must have excellent knowledge and understanding of their target market, the industry trends and consumer demands, making sure the right products are selected to sell at the right place at the right time, whilst operating within their financial budget. Their main duties and responsibilities are to build the outlets brand, which involves planning, sourcing and selecting merchandise and developing the product range. Before approaching a buyer, you need to have an understanding of the market to attempt to entice the buyer to select and stock your designs, to achieve positive results.

To approach and gain the interest of a stores buyer in stocking your merchandise, find out who you should contact by ringing the company and speaking to the receptionist and find out the head buyers name and full contact details including telephone number and email address. If this is not available ask for the assistant buyers details. If the receptionist is not helpful in providing this information do not give up but try again another day. Keep persevering until you have the information you need. Once you have the buyer's details send them a brief introductory letter. This could include details of your product range, identifying what you are offering and highlighting what makes your range different. Include any promotional material and copies of press coverage received, a copy of your look book and if possible, a sample of the product to attract their interest. It is important to stand out from the crowd. Follow your initial contact with an email in the hope you can get an appointment to visit and show them more of your work.

A buyer's calendar is very busy with many dates booked up attending meetings, national and international trade fairs and events, fashion weeks with designers showcasing their work, where they will be placing orders, so timing in contacting any buyer before these events is important. If the buyer is interested in stocking your designs, then be prepared. The buyer will negotiate the best price possible as they have targets to meet and have to work within their allocated budget. Be clear about your pricing, payment terms and also be realistic.

Whatever your specialist design field you need to keep focused, abreast of the market, and also most importantly establish and maintain an excellent track record of working with suppliers, manufacturers, buyers and clients, completing all commissions to contract and presenting orders on time, accurately invoicing goods to the terms agreed. Learning to negotiate, producing and meeting all contracts by delivering goods on time, to the quality required at the right price will help in establishing the success and reliability of your business and result in establishing fruitful long-term relations with buyers and clients.

palmer//harding

palmer//harding. Portrait of the design duo

*palmer // harding collection
Autumn/Winter 2015*

palmer//harding is the British fashion label founded and launched in 2011 by the successful design duo Levi Palmer and Matthew Harding. As recipients of the British Fashion Council Newgen Award, sponsored by Top Shop they have received financial support for two years running in 2012 and 2013 to establish and promote their business, and to showcase their work. The palmer//harding label was born, and has since grown and is receiving international recognition for their directional designer women's wear. Their designs comprise of timeless classics, including shirts and shirt dresses in Swiss and Egyptian cottons, constructed with flawless precision, even down to the stitch length of 18-22 stitches per inch. The emphasis is on quality and wear-ability with features of ingenious detailing. In recent collections features have included open circle shirt sleeves, shirts with contrasting fabric under layers, intricate corrugated and spiral pleating giving each design a thoroughly modern twist.

palmer//harding regularly show their collections at London Fashion Week, which has resulted in prestigious international press coverage received from American and British Vogue US, Elle, Harper's Bazaar, Hunger magazine, i-D, The Independent, Marie Claire, Paper, Tank, Wall Street Journal and WWD all acknowledging the stunning quality of their work. Their collections are now stocked in many international outlets such as Curve in New York City and Los Angles; Dover Street Market; Ikram, Chicago; Louis Boston, MA; Nitty Gritty, Stockholm; Space Mue, Korea and the Room at Hudson Bay, Canada. Further details of their latest range, stockists and press coverage can be viewed on their website: www.palmerharding.com

*palmer // harding collection
Spring/Summer 2015*

An Interview with palmer//harding

How did you get started?

We met at university at Central Saint Martins. After we graduated we worked freelance for a bit but it didn't fulfil either of us creatively so we decided to start palmer//harding.

What were your main challenges when setting up your business?

Cash flow was and is the biggest challenge for a small business, both when you start and in your first years. When we started we were lucky enough to have some savings (about £5000) and Levi had a well-paid freelance job with a 6 month contract. This saw us through the difficult first season.

What are the benefits of working in a partnership?

It's so useful to have a voice you can trust creatively. Also when one person is feeling unmotivated it's helpful to have the other person there for encouragement and support.

How would you describe your brand identity?

Emotive, intelligent, sophisticated and architectural, in our first season we launched with a collection of only white shirts, so that has been our USP from the start. Now we offer a full range, but it is the white shirt that is the star of our brand every season.

How important is technique to the creativity and success of your work?

I don't know if we have any particular technique for creativity or success. We look to fine art a lot for inspiration and individually as designers, Levi will drape and Matthew will sketch, they are our strengths. We do dip in and out of other methods of design development, but those are the methods that work best for us.

Do you outsource the manufacture and production or are all garments manufactured in-house?

We outsourced the bulk of our manufacturing from the beginning due to being such a small team; otherwise we wouldn't have been able to manage our deliveries on time. We only do very expensive items (which tend to be small units) in house.

How do you balance the creative and commercial side of the business?

That is a difficult one, so many brands start from designers wanting to focus on their own aesthetic, but once you start a label you realise that designing is only 1/5th of the work load, the rest is keeping a business afloat. It's difficult at times but we find the best way it just to make lists, make critical paths and try our hardest to delegate the less important tasks to members of our team so we can focus on the major stuff, designing.

What is your proudest achievement in business to date and why?

It has to be a tie between our first season being featured in American Vogue and our SS15 catwalk collection where one of our mentors (and 80s super model) Jan Strimple walked in our show.

What are the future aspirations of the palmer//harding label?

We are continuing to build the commercial side of our business by offering a shirt series of continual and commercial pieces that express the handwriting of the brand. Meanwhile, we are continuing to do catwalk shows which are becoming more and more directional, allowing the image of palmer//harding as leaders of directional shirting to grow each season.

What advice would you give to someone who is considering launching their own fashion label?

It is incredibly stressful and consuming to launch your own business and not at all glamorous as imagined. If you are dead set on doing so, make sure you have a good support network in place; this can include friends, family, peers, everyone who supports you. These people will offer the advice; encouragement and love that you will need to get off the ground. Apart from that have something to say, know who you are and what you want to do. With so much noise and chatter in this industry you need a clear and defined voice for your brand to be noticed, otherwise you will just get lost amongst the many other brands that are out there.

Harriet Sanders Accessories

Harriet Sanders, founder of the brand Harriet Sanders Accessories, designs and produces individually handcrafted bags from ethically sourced Italian leather. All her bags are hand finished with Harriet's distinctive style of beautiful contrasting suede linings. Colours used include leathers and suede's in scarlet, pistachio, coral, lemon, plum, chocolate, and cerulean. Styles are varied from small, neat cross over body classics to satchels, handbags, rucksacks, clutches and purses, all entitled with names such as Bella, Bloomsbury, Gladbag and Matinee. Her range is ever growing with new styles developing within the brand. Harriet Sanders designs are sold in many outlets nationally with stockists including Anthropologie, the British Museum and the Museum of London, Blackwell – The Arts and Crafts House, Cumbria, and in Crushed Chilli Gallery, Durham, and she also has a following in Japan. Harriet is constantly designing and striving to create the perfect bag for her customers, customising designs to suit their dreams. Details of her ranges, stockists, and her bespoke designs can be viewed on her website: www.harrietsanders.co.uk

An Interview with Harriet Sanders

How did you get started?

After graduating from the London College of Fashion University in Cordwainers Fashion Design Technology, I was unable to find a job within the fashion industry, as it was the start of the recession. Whilst at the job centre, I was approached by a member of the Prince's Trust who offered me a free place on a 'Get into Business' course. After producing a business plan, I opened a shop where I could sell my own bags, along with products from other artists similar to myself. However, the other artists failed to deliver and I ended up buying stock for the shop. A succession of unfortunate events (all affecting the footfall to the shop) meant that I became a shopkeeper instead of a designer. After 6 months, I decided to shut the shop and try another path.

Working from home, I handmade a collection of bags and took a stall at Old Spitalfields Market, London for three days a week, testing the market to see what sold and at what prices. After a successful year, I had earned enough money to do a trade show, where I gained my first four stockists. Demand for my bags grew and I concentrated on just selling directly to stockists and online. After 6 years of hard graft, promoting the company and building the customer base, we now have our own studio and employ two members of staff, and have a really great following stocking over 40 shops across the UK.

What is your working method?

My working method has never really fit into any sort of 'box', something I struggled with at university. The end product is more important to me than how I got there. When it comes to designing, I need to know whether the design is feasible, so I work everything out, taking bags apart and remaking them, all in this imaginary workshop in my head! I can be thinking about a design from 5 minutes to 5 weeks. Once I have figured it out I can usually cut the patterns and make the sample in one simple process.

Do you manufacture everything in-house or do you outsource any of the production?

Initially, I worked with a manufacturing factory in India, but it didn't work out, as I wasn't there to oversee the production and the finished bags were not how I envisaged them. We now make everything in-house. This helps us to respond more effectively to orders and 'trends'. It is also a really good selling point, as we are British handmade. It also allows us to offer our customers the ability to mix and match leathers to create their favourite colour combinations. If we stocked every single colour combination we offer then we would have over 45,000 bags in stock, so we make bags to order.

How important is technique to the creativity and success of your work?

Technique is very important. During my university course I trained working with leather, cutting patterns and ultimately making bags. Without these skills I wouldn't be able to do what I do now. All of my employees have some form of sewing background, and I have also trained them in the techniques used to make my bags. When making bags, the key to success is getting every stage

Designs by Harriet Sanders Accessories

Harriet Sanders, founder of the brand Harriet Sanders Accessories

of the making process completely accurate. Get one stage wrong and the entire process suffers, resulting in a bag that most likely won't pass quality control.

What is your greatest career challenge to date in establishing your own business?

Cash flow, you can plan your financial forecasts down to the last penny but unfortunately this industry is very unpredictable. When I first started the business I found it almost unbelievable that the weather could affect sales but it does. A sunny day can see a spike on our website sales, or a sudden rush for stockists to top up on their summer styles/ colours. Payments from stockists can be up to 4 months from the day they place the order, to the day they receive the order, plus they usually expect 30 days credit upon delivery of goods. It takes a lot of careful planning and crossing of fingers!

What is your proudest achievement in business to date?

In 2012, I was awarded Highly Commended Best Fashion Accessory by Attire Accessories Magazine, which was totally unexpected but very much appreciated. In 2014, Jasper Garvida asked me to collaborate with him on Ethologie's S/S15 collection, which debuted at London Fashion

Week and was featured in many magazines including Vogue. Most recently, I have been nominated as a finalist for Gloucestershire Women in Business Young Entrepreneur of the Year 2015, but ultimately, I have to say, that every time I create a design and it actually works and looks good, is a really proud achievement for me, and more so when our customers buy it!

What advice would you give to someone who is considering setting up their own business in textile design?

To only do it if you are really passionate about it. Running your own company is like looking after a child, it requires a lot of attention, and you must never lose sight of what you are trying to achieve. It doesn't mean earning lots of money, it will come, but in the beginning you'll most likely be earning less than what you predicted. Putting all of that aside, if you really love your work, it no longer becomes a job but a way of life. I love it when a customer sends me an email of appreciation, or posts a picture on social media declaring their love for their bag that has just arrived. It makes all the hard work seem worth it, knowing that something you did, made someone else, a stranger really happy.

Margo Selby –
Founder of Margo Selby Woven Textile Company

Margo Selby, founder of Margo Selby woven textile design company

Margo Selby, founder of the Margo Selby woven textile design company, trained at Chelsea College of Art and Design, and then continued her studies at The Royal College of Art. On successful graduation, she worked from home, designing and launching her first collection of woven textiles in 2003. Her collections comprise of stunning, quality fabrics using colour palettes in richly patterned, geometric designs with names such as Phoenix, Congo, Atomic, Suki, Woodstock and Dune. Her fabrics work well in both classic and contemporary interiors, and her ranges include designs for cushions, throws, upholstery fabrics, wallpapers and bespoke rugs, and have been applied to fashion and accessories.

Margo has achieved great success both as a designer of textiles and as a business woman. Her work is constantly evolving and in 2012, she authored the book Contemporary Weaving Patterns by A & C Black Publishers Ltd, which has received many excellent reviews. Alongside her design work she also offers weaving workshops for both complete beginners as well as more advanced weavers. The Margo Selby label has achieved great recognition, with her work regularly featured in many publications including Homes and Gardens, Stories Collective and Selvedge magazine, and in 2014, she was shortlisted for the 'Best British Pattern' award for her 'Dogstar' fabric by Elle Decoration. Further details of Margo's work can be viewed on her website and blog: www.margoselby.com

An Interview with Margo Selby

What are the main influences when designing and where do you get your inspiration from?

Colour is a significant motivation in my work, which I take from a wide range of sources including indigenous textiles from around the world, graphic design and architecture. Our latest collection combines inspiration from the sophistication and delicacy of Japanese textiles, with the bold and rhythmic patterns from African tribal design. I constantly gather images and ideas and collate these into cohesive groups, which can then be translated into fabric collections.

Much of my work is inspired by the process of weaving itself, and our patterns reflect the organized nature of the craft. The work of the Bauhaus designers has always been an inspiration to my design process. I am equally passionate about creating a piece of weaving which celebrates the beauty of a woven textile as an art form, as well as developing ideas in weaving which are suitable for industrial production. Weaving is my passion and starting point for all I do whether it is a one-off art piece or a commercial design. The two are intrinsically linked and symbiotic.

What is your working method?

When I create a fabric, I start by designing the warp. Into this we weave the weft yarns, which can be changeable. The warp is the backbone of the fabric and an integral part of the design, and it cannot be changed once the fabric is on the loom.

I experiment with weaving different structures and weft yarns until I have a product I am happy with. The weaving is slow and methodical and the fabric grows one row or pick at a time, giving much contemplation time for design. Once I am happy with a fabric, often after many warps developing the idea, I then explore the possibility for production with an industrial mill.

How important is technique to the creativity and success of your work?

I like to explore technical constructions on my hand-loom, combining fibres and structure to innovate new fabrics and patterns. I'm always interested in exploring new materials and techniques both in hand weaving and industrial production.

I have always been drawn to surface and texture and I enjoy mixing different fibres to see how they react with one another. I have researched fibres that would shrink when heated and have tried weaving these in combination with silk to create three-dimensional surfaces. This process led me to the silk and Lycra combinations used in my first collection. Since then I have continued to develop this concept by exploring new heat shrink yarns and combining them with more durable fibres like cotton and polyester to create stronger fabrics suitable for interior applications.

How would you describe your brand identity?

I would describe it as one of exceptional quality textile products for commercial and domestic interiors. I think people want products that add colour and texture to the home whilst investing in quality so these products become heirlooms of the future.

Where do you sell your work?

I sell my work to independent shops and retailers across the UK, Europe and the USA. Our fabrics are used by interior designers for residential and contract projects, which is an area of the business we are excited to be developing.

What is your proudest achievement in business to date?

Since I started the business eleven years ago working on a hand-loom in my bedroom there have been many achievements. My business has grown and is now a busy textile studio employing eight full-time members of staff and a team of piece workers in Whitstable, weaving bespoke textiles for a wide variety of end uses.

The hand-loom and the craft of weaving remain central to all our products. Working on flooring for the first time and witnessing both carpet and colour come back into fashion was a proud achievement. Seeing my designs, originally produced as soft silk and wool fabrics, blown up and re-coloured to make them suitable for flooring is very satisfying. We have also developed interior fabrics for contract use to be sold by the metre, and diversified our accessory range into bedlinen and towels.

What advice would you give to someone who is considering setting up their own business in textile design?

Record and archive all of your ideas as this will be an invaluable source of inspiration to you.

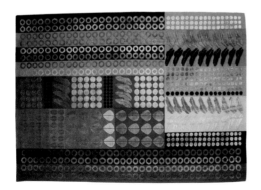

Designs by Margo Selby – Cairo Rug

Designs by Margo Selby – Jewel Rug

Laura Olivia - Textile and Surface Pattern Designer

Laura Olivia founder of Laura Olivia Printed Textile Designs

Textile and surface pattern designer, Laura Olivia specialises in designing and producing prints for the interior, fashion and stationery industries, selling her designs internationally in the USA, China and Europe. Originally from Berkshire, she trained in textile design at Nottingham Trent University, and on successful graduation, she started work in the interiors business, giving her great insight into the furnishing fabrics and wallpaper industries. After working in the industry for several years and realising that a 9-5 working lifestyle was not for her, she decided to take 'a leap of faith and follow her dream' of doing what she loved and making a living out of it.

In 2012 she launched her own business Laura Olivia designing homeware, as well as working with an agent who sold her furnishing fabric and wallpaper designs to clients around the globe. She was selected to exhibit at 'One Year On', the event for designer's in their first year of business at the 'New Designers' exhibition in London. The show was a huge success and shortly after she received commissions from the high street retailer 'Wilkinson' to design a large range of stationery that was sold throughout 250 stores with her photograph and name alongside. This resulted in further commissions working on various design projects, directly with clients based both in the UK and abroad. Clients she has worked with and/or sold work to include Arthouse, Wilkinson, Bianca Turner, Holden Decor, Ellison First Asia, Dunelm, Tesco, Morrison's, Mori Tessuti and more. She now also has a range of licensing partners including Artistic Britain, S-Blinds and Keka Case.

The label Laura Olivia has been featured in a wide range of publications such as The Independent, Northern Homes magazine, Vogue, Grand Designs and BBC Homes & Antiques. Laura continues to attract an ever growing list of clients, and recently she has launched her own brand of home accessories and lifestyle products, which can be viewed on her website and blog at www.lauraolivia.com

Printed textile design 'Lotus' by Laura Olivia

An Interview with Laura Olivia

Printed textile design 'Aeonium' by Laura Olivia

Printed textile design 'Aeonium Mustard' by Laura Olivia

What were the main challenges when setting up your business?

I would say the main challenge was getting that first client or initial sale because it takes time to get your work to a good commercial standard. Also it is difficult to sell to people when you haven't got any previous experience behind you. I overcame this by initially working with an agent, so I had already gained experience of selling my designs across the world before I approached anyone directly.

How would you describe your brand identity?

My brand identity is tropical, bohemian, exotic, floral and definitely vibrant!

How do you balance the creative and commercial side of the business?

I now have a small team behind me and so I am learning to delegate more. I now know how important it is to keep your marketing ticking along even when your project deadline seem like the most important thing in the world, as it is just as important that you have more work afterwards!

What kind of clients do you work with?

My niche is interior prints, so most of my clients are usually soft furnishing manufacturers, suppliers or large retailers. I used to be an interior designer and that is still very much part of me. It also means I know what works in interiors and what actually sells. I have also worked on beauty product packaging, stationery and fashion projects, all of which I have loved and would enjoy designing and working on again in the future.

What design services do you offer?

We offer a surface pattern consultancy, so much of the time we work to the clients own brief, as well as selling existing prints. Although I have a signature style and this is often the handwriting that smaller businesses would like to reflect in their products, we are also able to offer design work in many other different styles. This has resulted in many long term contracts with larger businesses that are very trend driven.

Can you name one of your proudest moments to date?

I think one of my proudest moments to date was the first time I walked into a major retailer and saw a whole display stand full of my own range, with my photograph besides it. I wish I could bottle that feeling and take a gulp every day!

What advice would you give to someone who is considering setting up their own business in textile design?

I would recommend going on a business course fairly early on in your career! I would also suggest trying different things but setting a time limit on when you will actually specialise in one area and make that your niche, you can always branch out later. Lastly I would say work smarter, not harder, and don't be too hard on yourself.

Retail

Retail is big business and is a highly, pressurised fluctuating industry due to the changing face of the British high street with the growth of technology, and online and mobile retailing. In recent years, the UK, high street has seen many changes with a general decline in traditional high street retail outlets, and a growth in bargain shops, charity shops, and an abundance of cafes, tea-rooms, pubs, clubs and restaurants, and social meeting places. Many of the larger retail chains continue to relocate to purpose built out-of-town retail parks, which offer a wide mix of retail chains and department stores with very few independents. This has resulted in many vacant high street shops, as noted in the 'Porta's Review', the independent review into the future of our high streets by Mary Portas, December 2011.

There are pros and cons of opening a high street retail shop. One of the most important considerations is having a prime location with excellent footfall and accessible parking. Some market towns are thriving tourist locations and are popular, progressive and continue to have large numbers of independent shops, which are in demand and expand very quickly with a growing clientele. In contrast, other retail start-ups open and close within a year. This is often due to the number of vacant high street shops and the lack of redevelopment in the area. Other problems arise due to high overheads with rent and business rates, fitting out the store and the expense of carrying and maintaining stock, as well as offering new lines and merchandise on a regular basis.

The advantages of opening a high street independent retail business in the right location include being able to meet customers and provide a personal shopping experience and service, offering a specialised product, along with expert knowledge and styling advice. If considering opening a high street outlet, do your homework researching in to any proposed developments for existing centres or new facilities, and plans to improve the amenities, accessibility and improvements to the physical environment and safety in the area.

There are many relevant reports, which are useful to read providing retail industry statistics, such as the Retail Industry: statistics and policy by Chris Rhodes – June 2014. This report is well worth reading and gives an excellent summary of the retail industry including 'key statistics of the volume of sales, the proportion of internet sales, and employment and business statistics of the retail industry'.

Before launching or going ahead with your plans, it is useful to contact your local authority who should be able to provide you with information on the diversity of the types of businesses within the proposed area, giving details of the retail outlets, street markets, cafes, the demand for retail premises and the number of vacant premises available. They should also be able to provide details of any planning policies, planned investment to the area and also if there any council run schemes, which have been established to attract new businesses into the area.

Pop-up Store

The 'Pop-up' store is a fairly new trend and is also known as 'flash retailing'. This is a term used when a store is provisionally using a retail space on a temporary basis, and is a way of rejuvenating and bringing empty shops back into use and restoring new life to the high street, and for the retailer attracting a new audience. Having a 'Pop-up' shop is an excellent way of leasing a property on a short term contract basis without the risks of taking on a lengthy fixed lease lasting several years. Many pop-up shops are seasonal based and are around the Easter or Christmas period, or alternatively a town or city festival.

Local Markets

Many cities, towns and larger villages have street and covered markets which generally offer an assorted range of stalls, adding interest and vibrancy to the local amenities within the area. Market trading is a relatively inexpensive and flexible means of starting a business and selling directly to the public, meeting both existing and potential customers. It is also a relatively cheap way of trading compared to leasing high street retail premises. As many market traders will tell you, market trading can be physically tiring with early morning starts, long hours, and with the most onerous part being setting up and taking down the stall, particularly on cold winters mornings and evenings.

To sell from a market stall you need to have a licence, which is obtainable from your local council, along with the statutory legislation for traders. Starting a business venture trading from a market stall is an opportunity for you to showcase your work, and can be invaluable in testing out the market demand for a product. Success stories include Clare Parker, founder of Vintage Vixen who started her business selling vintage fashions from a stall on the local Saturday outdoor market, who after 18 months successful trading decided to move into shop premises, and the business has continued to grow and flourish. Another success story is Harriet Sanders of Harriet Sanders Accessories who started selling her handmade leather bags from Old Spitalfields Market. Old Spitalfields and many such markets have excellent websites promoting each traders business. For further information, details and rates of trading at your local market, contact your local authority. They should be able to provide you with information relating to the diversity of the current stall holders, the dates and times of the market and any specialist events, festivals fairs or trade shows, who the weekly market is managed by, the application process, rules and regulations and charges for stall holders.

Selling at Trade Fairs

Trade events are big business, there are many local, regional, national and international fairs that are regularly advertised in specialist magazines and featured on websites. You may be a designer who produces and concentrates their trade selling mostly to individual customers attending local events such as Christmas markets, summer fetes and specialist trade fairs. Alternatively, you may be a designer/maker who would benefit from exhibiting at a larger national or international event giving you the chance to showcase your work and to receive large scale orders.

If selling products at a trade fair remember to factor in the cost of the design, build and furniture for the stand. Also consider transport, accommodation and expenditure in manning the stand, and the full expense of marketing before and after the event. (See Section 3: Marketing the Business, and also Section 5: Resource Directory – Exhibition Organisers).

Clare Parker –
Founder of Vintage Vixen,
Newark, Nottinghamshire, UK

Vintage Vixen evolved from a passion for vintage clothes. Clare Parker began her boutique style market stall selling vintage clothing. After testing the water, Clare opened her high street retail vintage and retro shop Vintage Vixen in Newark, a thriving market town in Nottinghamshire, and an area renowned for its International Antique and Collectors Fairs, the largest event of its kind in Europe. The store Vintage Vixen has an excellent customer following. Her colourful, eclectic and ever-changing stock includes vintage and re-worked vintage clothing, accessories and jewellery. Her collections include original sixties mini's and seventies dresses, eighties midi's, swing and shift

Clare Parker Founder of Vintage Vixen

dresses, tooled and fringed leather bags, stack heeled boots and a wide assortment of accessories. Clare has a full understanding of all aspects of the business, from knowledge of her stock, to her passion in locating the perfect find for her customers. Over the years many customers have become regulars to her store. She usually opens seven days a week for customers to browse, and in the evenings by appointment for a personal shopping experience. For more information on www.facebook.com/welovevintage.newark   twitter@littlevixens www.vintagevixen.net

Collections,
Vintage
Vixen

An Interview with Clare Parker

How did you get started?

I was working for a local steel fabrication company when the recession hit and many staff were put on reduced hours. I needed to earn extra cash so I bought myself a couple of clothes rails and bundled a stash of vintage treasures into my Ford KA and set up a market stall each Saturday in my local town centre.

What were your main challenges in setting up the business?

When I began the market stall I never looked any further into the future than the next Saturday! Gradually I started to get regular customers and also increase my stock. After eighteen months trading I decided to develop the business and move into shop premises. With the support of my employers, I reduced my day job to 30 hours working there three days a week, and then opening my shop Vintage Vixen on the remaining four days. I also increased the days of opening, as a friend helped, working in the shop during the summer months. This worked fairly well for a year, but it became increasingly difficult to juggle the two responsibilities, so I had to dig deep to find the confidence to give up my paid employment and jump in with both feet. I think this was the biggest challenge, it was huge!

Did you have any support to help you with the business in the initial months of setting up?

First and foremost my partner Darren has always been a fantastic support. He has always had more confidence and belief in me than I ever think I have had in myself. He didn't complain when he was helping me put up rails at 7am on frosty Saturday mornings in the market square, and he doesn't complain now when my house is overtaken with vintage laundry, as my washing machine never stops! Close friends and family have also been a huge support, but I have to mention my former employers, because when I told them of my wish they were only too willing to accommodate and adjust my working hours.

Did you seek any advice?

I didn't really seek any advice, but I had a dry run on a small scale with my market stall. I think most people thought I was crazy giving up a good job and opening a specialist shop in a small market town in the middle of a recession! Sometimes you have to trust your instinct.

How important is location to your business?

Location is very important; my shop is in the town centre but I also put up an A-board, which guides people directly to my shop, which is useful, but most vintage lovers will follow their nose! Pre-shop, we once spotted a sign whilst holidaying in the depths of Cornwall and we drove for about twenty minutes looking for this treasure trove in a barn at the end of a farm track. People will hunt you down so I think business reputation, particularly in this field is as important as shop location.

What is the best part about having your own business?

I enjoy my job immensely and I realise that I'm very fortunate. It's a great feeling to help someone choose an outfit, and for customers to come back and tell me how pleased they are with their choice, or they'll call in with a photograph or post something online, which is really satisfying, making my job even better!

Collections, Vintage Vixen

Collections, Vintage Vixen

What is the most difficult part of having your own business?

It's incredibly hard work, with long hours and very little time off, but for me, it's totally worth it. The uncertainty of business and being self-employed is difficult, but the uncertainty makes you just work harder.

How do you balance the creative and the commercial side of the business?

You have to be disciplined and learn the art of saying no. My buying decisions are primarily made with the heart, but sometimes your head has to rule. This is my business and I have to make it work, no-one else is going to do it for me.

What is the future of your business?

The next step is to launch an online store. I think the future of retail is uncertain, as shopping habits have changed dramatically. As retailers, we strive to keep our shop windows attractive, but I have to listen to what customers want, and online shopping cannot be ignored.

What advice would you give to someone who is considering launching their own vintage fashion business?

Begin with something small to test the water. Set aside a budget to work with that you are prepared to invest and that you are also prepared to lose should the business not work out, and then just set your heart on it and work at it. Be passionate about it, believe in it and smile.

Party Plan

Party plan is a form of direct selling. There are many party plan companies which have become very successful using this method of trading. Party plan involves meeting people who have gathered together in a social location and selling your products directly to them through sampling and demonstrations. Party plan can be used to introduce new product ranges and can increase sales, and offers flexible working hours. There are many established companies continually seeking representatives to sell through party plan, and who provide you with the kit, training and resources to set up.

If you have a product or range to sell, such as jewellery or accessories, direct selling at a party plan may be an option worth considering. To host a party, guests are invited to an event on a specific date and location organised to promote and sell a specific range, product or service. Usually drinks and snacks are provided. If the event is hosted in someone's home it is usual to give the homeowner a reward of a choice from the product range. During the event new contacts are made and guests are encouraged to host a similar party where you can exhibit and promote your wares. The negative side of this method of selling is that it is often seen as pressure selling. If you have attended such a party, you may have felt there was an expectation that you should buy something from the range before leaving, which could pose a risk of negativity towards your business.

Online Business

Online retail is big business and highly competitive. Due to advancements of the internet many shoppers are relying on online shopping sites, which have a global following. If you are considering setting up an online business selling directly to customers, it is essential to study the many websites out there and do some thorough market research in finding out which online market is most suitable to launch and/or expand your business.

One of the most popular online sites is eBay, the online auction site, which has approximately four million people in the UK alone selling items on its site each month. Many businesses have tested the water by trading on eBay, sourcing stock and selling online, and then progressing to, and establishing their own online eBay shop. This provides an opening to expand their product range, and then develop their business by establishing their own independent website. Successful examples of eBay entrepreneurs include the inspirational Sophia Amoruso, Founder of Nastygal. Sophia started off selling vintage merchandise on eBay, and then set up an eBay shop. Due to hard work, determination, a thorough knowledge of her customers and target market, the business has gone from strength to strength. She then launched her own successful business Nastygal.com, an online retail store NastyGal, which is now one of the most successful and fastest developing retailers in the USA.

There are many other popular auction sites which include CQUOT and eBid. Other established and popular online retail sites include Amazon, Behance, carbonmade, Crevado, Dwanda, Etsy, Folksy, Gumtree, Not-on-the-High-Street, Redbubble, Seek and Adore and Zazzle, which all have very different characteristics and styles, with each one offering a variety of services. If thinking about starting an online shop, look and compare what each site offers.

There are many online market websites, offering very easy step-by-step instructions directing you through the stages of setting up and developing your own trading place within their site. It may be advantageous to consider having more than one online shop with a direct feeder from one shop to the other, but check out if this is permissible by the websites being used.

If considering selling a product or service via an established online site or market, consider the following:

- The popularity of the site, and what sort of traffic do they get
- The appeal of the site to both national and international visitors/trade
- What businesses promote their services or products on the site?
- Is the site user friendly?
- The charges including any annual subscriptions, joining fees or administration costs, and any hidden costs
- The commission costs deducted by the site on the sale of goods/services
- The sort of payment options they accept/recommend, and the payment terms
- The community spirit between sellers

When selling online, write clear product descriptions and list under categories with supporting images in the correct format and file size, to show the product range or service off to its best advantage. When selling online, customer communication is all important to the success of your business. Many trading websites encourage customers and vendors to leave feedback reporting on the quality of the goods, the level of communication, the packing and receipt of prompt delivery. Positive feedback is vital to the success of any business and future trade. Any online queries received need to be answered quickly and orders despatched punctually. If there are any delays or problems in the dispatch of orders then customers need to be notified immediately.

The advantage of having an online business is the pace that you can react to change. Full details of the payment methods such as PayPal, Shopify, WorldPay, and credit or debit card should be listed, along with shipping prices. To be successful in online trading it is essential that you are highly organised, keeping up to date with administration, and are prompt in posting any purchased items.

If selling online consider the following points:

- The market you are catering for
- The price range
- The ability of customers to track orders
- The pricing of stock including packaging and posting

Blogging

Most bloggers start blogging as a hobby or interest, reporting on subjects that they are passionate about, adding regular items of interest to share with their intended audience. Developing a network of loyal followers is all important for the success of a blog, alongside connecting with other social networking sites. When blogging make sure you add new blog posts on a regular basis, and if possible at the same time each week. You may initially give yourself a target of three posts a week, adding to the blog on specific days, so your followers know what days you will be adding further posts. Invite guests to contribute to your blog, enhancing the appeal and the sites dynamics. Very few people initially start out making money from blogging, but there are many bloggers who develop their interests establishing a flexible internet job, working the hours they choose and want to work.

Vlogging

Vlogging, also known as video blogging is the production of online videos. This has become a popular pastime for many, but for some it has become big business with the addition of lucrative marketing and advertising deals. For a vlogger to be financially successful it usually involves many hours and hard work establishing a site, producing and presenting interesting topical content that will attract the attention of followers. Typical vlog topics include fashion, make-up and beauty, shopping, interior design, lifestyle and business. To be successful, research is central, devising new, exciting and up to date content, which is then recorded, edited and presented attracting mass followers. Companies' products and merchandise are promoted through demonstrations and endorsements and this often involves the negotiation of contracts resulting in profitable returns. Similarly to blogging, there are many easy to follow instructional videos on the internet with tutorials, demonstrating how to get started and how to edit your video for the best results.

Women's bustle skirt, sewing pattern kit – Clothkits

Scandi flower print Women's skirt, sewing pattern kit – Clothkits

Kay Mawer – Managing Director at Clothkits

Kay Mawer is the current owner of Clothkits, the company originally founded in 1968 by designer Anne Kennedy. Clothkits have become renowned for their 'make-at-home' clothing kits, comprising of easy-to-follow instructions and dressmaking pieces printed directly onto fabric without 'the fuss of paper patterns'. Due to her love of textiles and many conversations reminiscing about the Clothkits brand, Kay researched and

Kay Mawer – Managing Director at Clothkits Ltd., Portsmouth

discovered that after many years of successful trading, the brand had been bought by Freeman's, the mail order catalogue company. Freeman's had eventually absorbed the Clothkits identity into their own brand, and the Clothkits brand became dormant.

Due to Kay's interest in the brand and with great entrepreneurial spirit she approached the company, and after months of negotiations successfully bought the brand. In 2008 she re-launched the brand, applying the original concept and reworking the designs to produce a new collection of Clothkits outfits for women, girls and boys, which she sold in their original kit form by mail order. Today, Kay works collaboratively with a range of designers taking the brand into the 21st century. She has expanded the company's services offering online tutorials, workshops and also a made-to-order service. With the trend for home crafts and nostalgia, Clothkits has quickly re-established its identity, and continues to appeal to an international market particularly in the UK, Canada, Denmark, Australia and Singapore. For further information and details of Clothkits visit their website: www.clothkits.co.uk

An Interview with Kay Mawer – Managing Director at Clothkits

How did you get started?

I was always encouraged by my mum to sew and make clothes, and for many years I had thought about running my own business but not sure what in. Reminiscing with friends, the Clothkits brand came up in conversation and after lots of research I found and approached the company owners to buy Clothkits. During this period I did think about setting up a similar 'flat pack' clothing company, but I felt strongly that Clothkits had a heritage and the name, and I knew Clothkits was right for me. After 12-18 months of negotiations I bought the company, the copyright for the designs and the ownership of the brand. The bottom line was the

intellectual property (IP) just consisted of a bit of paper, so I had to start the business again from scratch.

What support did you have when first starting the business?

I am always surprised at how much goodwill and support is out there. When first starting out I had a mentor funded through a government scheme and who provided expert business advice. I also attended various Chamber of Commerce meetings, the Gatwick Diamond Business Group and I have also received government funding that helps businesses in the local area to employ staff.

What is the USP of the business?

The printed kits formed the USP of the business, as they evoke a memory, a feeling of nostalgia and a love for the brand, which really means something to people and also makes people smile. When I first started out I wasn't sure where the journey was going but as soon as I launched a webpage 'coming soon' people were logging on and showing interest in Clothkits.

How important is location to your business?

The business is based in Chichester. It has grown from cutting out patterns on my kitchen table to moving into the garage, then to a short-term leased shop, and finally I have purchased a redundant pub and moved the business there. This works really well and has given the business room to grow. The old downstairs bar is now a shop and upstairs is where we design, pack and dispatch orders. We also have a permanent room with machines and cutting tables for manufacture and workshops. There are also two spaces which we rent out to a dressmaker and someone working in alterations. What works is the diversity of the business.

How do you balance the creative and commercial side of the business?

I have enjoyed creating the business, but until recently I was still involved in the design, packaging and dispatching of orders along with dealing with administration, which was killing my creativity. I have had to learn to let go and to delegate more, allowing other people to take on more aspects of the work and also to be involved in decision making. This has allowed me to be more creative in the business and to work on future developments.

Where do you show your work?

We launched Clothkits at Kids Modern, London, launching our website on the same day. We have also shown at events such as Knitting and Stitches, Sewing for Pleasure and the East London Design Show. During the last twelve months, we have not exhibited at any events, as the business has metamorphosed with mail order, the internet and the workshops.

Is the production and distribution of kits managed at base or are they outsourced?

The production of the kits all takes place in Chichester with the exception of the printing, which is very specialist. Initially I did buy a digital printer to do all the printing in-house, but actually this was a false economy. I soon realised the importance of paying for specific expertise. The printing is now all outsourced, but the design, packaging and distribution of kits is all done in-house.

What have been the main challenges to date in running Clothkits and having your own business?

Taking on staff, moving premises and also taking on the lease for a shop were all very difficult and challenging stages in running the business. The shop was rented on a short-term lease, and on the first day the takings were £4.95. Since then we have grown (thankfully!!), expanded, and bought new premises. I have also taken on staff with the help of funding from the Business Growth Scheme, and we now have five people working in the business.

What is the future of your business?

The business is going very well and is a great formula. I have considered replicating the business in other locations and even franchising it but there is so much potential in the physical space in this building, so I may consider expanding and developing what we offer, and build a creative hub, consisting of a cafe and studios.

What advice would you give to someone setting up a business today?

Firstly, just do it – go for it! Whatever business you choose to go into, make sure that it is something that you are passionate about - it makes all the difference, and don't be afraid to ask for help, there is so much kindness out there.

Fashion Illustrator and Textile Designer

Over the decades there have been many successful illustrators who have made their mark in this very specialist field, from the stunning work of René Gruau and innovative work of Antonio Lopez to the exquisite fashion drawings, illustrations and portraiture of the internationally renowned fashion artist David Downton.

Many fashion illustrators today use a combination of techniques from traditional hand rendered skills, applying watercolour, gouache, pen, ink and collage to digital work using specialist skills, and others apply a combination of hand rendered and digital methods to create exciting results. Most fashion illustrators work on a freelance basis, producing work for specific contracts, which often include commissions for fashion and beauty for editorial and advertising campaigns in magazines, packaging, and for the gift industries, and artworks for books and manuals.

Illustrators with an established reputation will often represent themselves working directly with existing clients, negotiating contracts and payment of fees. On the other hand, most illustrators choose to use a professional agent who works directly with clients such as publishing houses and the media in representing a number of illustrators to gain commissions and in negotiating contracts and fees. Agents are always on the lookout for new, exciting and innovative illustrators. If considering establishing yourself in this field, it may be useful when initially starting out to establish work with an agent who will deal with all legal contracts and negotiate the best possible fees. The Artists and Writers Yearbook published annually by Bloomsbury, London is an excellent source of information and is described as 'the essential guide to media and publishing industries'. It provides lots of practical guidance from writing for newspapers and magazines, to publishing advice, and includes contacts for art and illustration agents and editors, and gives details of publishing and media resources.

If you choose to work with an agent, always check the commission charged, as this is usually deducted on payment. The agent will have specific procedures for the submission of commissioned work, so always read and check these guidelines carefully, and along with the terms and conditions of any contracts check all the small print before signing. See section below on Copyright Issues, Patenting your Ideas and Designs, and also read the excellent advice given to readers by Gary Assim, known as the image lawyer on social media on page 54-56.

Designs by Raven House Studios 2015

Copyright issues, patenting your ideas and designs

Whatever your trade, whether a designer, an illustrator, writer, photographer or stylist and if producing original work, you may require copyright protection preventing anyone directly copying your work. To obtain copyright you can use the copyright symbol © followed by your name and date, for example © Will Morris September 2015. This identifies who and when the original work was completed. Once you have done this you have several options including posting a copy to yourself by special delivery, which offers a secure, protected and dated service, and then safely storing the unopened copy providing evidence of when the work was completed, if required. Alternatively a sealed copy of the work can be deposited at a bank or with a solicitor for safety and evidence, identifying the date of the work.

There are always going to be people and businesses out there who copy your ideas, often producing poor imitations of the original, and likewise you must avoid copying anyone else's ideas and designs. Whatever the business idea, whether it is as a designer/maker, writer, freelance teacher, blogger or retailer it is essential that you do your research ensuring there is a market for your idea. Your business idea may be ground-breaking, state-of-the art and very inventive, or it may compete and trade in a well-tested market.

If you are the creator of a product or invention you may consider patenting your design to protect its originality from being copied and the then being exploited by others. Full details and the latest information and guidelines about patents are available on the Government Intellectual Property Office (IPO) website: www.ipo.gov.uk/patents. Information provided includes the process of searching for similar patents, guidelines on preparing and filing an application to patent your work, and the process of gaining a patent in the UK. The website also gives guidelines about protecting your product or invention in other countries by applying for a patent protection through the international legal system of the European Patent Convention and the World International Property Organisation (WIPO), which are organisations providing intellectual property services, policy details and information for protecting your Intellectual Property (IP).

Gary Assim – The Image Lawyer

Gary Assim, known as the Image Lawyer on social media, is renowned nationally and internationally for his knowledge and work specialising in image and design rights, fashion, retail and intellectual property involving the creative industries. Gary joined Shoosmiths, a major UK law firm in 1997, becoming a partner the following year. He is responsible for the firm's relationship with its international network, the World Services Group, where he is currently a member of the executive board.

Over the past few years Gary has been involved in leading cases on copyright and design rights advice. He is passionate about safeguarding and protecting consumer brands and he has advised such companies as Jimmy Choo, Chloe and Dr Martens, as well as setting up the mentoring scheme for the British Fashion Council to help their NewGen and Fashion Forward (FFWD) designers.

Gary has applied his knowledge and expertise in writing for prestigious publications such as the New York Law Journal, International Commercial Litigation and various national and international trade press. He is also a well-known commentator on television and radio speaking regularly on intellectual property rights, and also lecturing in related subjects at various universities including the University of Northampton, UK.

His expertise is recognised and has been rewarded through receipt of many international awards. In 2007 he was nominated in the Lawyers Hot 100, and in 2008 Gary was named in the Top 100 list of the Most Powerful and Influential People in Fashion by Drapers. In 2010, Gary was awarded the Intellectual Property Magazine Innovation prize, and more recent accolades in 2012 and 2013 include being named in the World Trade Mark Review's WTR 1000, a huge tribute acknowledging his work. For two consecutive years 2014 and 2015 he has been awarded with the Global Client Choice Award - Intellectual Property. The list goes on. Gary is recognised in the industry and in other sectors celebrating his dedication to his work and knowledge, working with partners and clients, advising, guiding and helping to ensure their creative property rights are protected, and protecting their business from becoming someone else's.

An Interview with Gary Assim

What do you consider to be the biggest challenges facing a new business starting in fashion and textiles today?

There are two main challenges facing running a fashion business today. First, the designers need to be left to design and not become embroiled in the day to day administration of running a business. The challenge for the designer is to find a partner who will deal with this administrative burden. The partner can be a parent, sibling or friend but the designer must trust that person so that he/she can really be free to design.

Secondly, in such a competitive marketplace the designer must be meeting the demands of an ever fickle customer base. His/her designs have to be distinctive and the sort of product people actually want to buy.

What do you think are the biggest mistakes new businesses make when first launching their business?

Many new businesses rely totally on marketing and PR, thinking that a good story and press coverage means success. Marketing and PR are great, but at the end of the day any marketing and PR received needs to result in orders, orders make sales and sales means money. You cannot live on great PR alone, you actually need to sell what you design!

What do you consider is the most common downfall of many new start-ups in the creative sector?

In my experience, although it is getting better, many designers do not understand the basics about running a business. Those that want to be the next Alexander McQueen think that by merely designing an excellent product results in success. Actually success is measured across a number of criteria including great designs, well manufactured products, supplied on time, good PR, good stockists, well managed bank facilities, a partner to deal with the business administration and a great lawyer to help them!

What types of work can be protected by the Copyright, Designs and Patents Act 1988?

Drawings, designs and written work. 2D (two dimensional) work such as drawings, written work or work typed or written/drawn on a computer/tablet is protected by copyright. This is a right which is provided automatically and as soon as the work is created. No registration is needed but most people use the copyright symbol © and their name and year to indicate that the work is protected by copyright e.g. this note © Gary Assim 2015.

3D (three-dimensional) work such as the product itself or any part of the product can be protected by design rights. These rights can be automatic or can be registered. If you rely on your automatic rights then you have a 3 year period of protection in Europe against anyone copying your design. If you decide to register your design then you may have up to 25 years protection in Europe.

There is a total misconception by many as to what the term 'public domain' means, particularly when referring to a copyright work, and in using images and information from the internet, could you advise?

The term 'public domain' really refers to the fact that the public can see the work in question whether it is written, a design or a photo. With the advent of the internet it has become much easier to state that a work has been put in the public domain. However, just because the work is available on the internet does not mean that you, or anyone else, can do what they like with it. The work is likely to be protected by copyright and unless there is a notice stating that you can use the work in any way you like you are likely to be infringing the copyright in the work by using it. Best practice is to contact the person who put the work on the internet and ask for permission to use it. In most cases you will be surprised to get a positive response.

What are the best ways a designer can protect themselves, from their work being plagiarized, particularly with reference to the internet?

Protection comes in many forms, the name of the designer and/or a logo can be protected as a trade mark, design drawings can be protected by copyright and products can be protected by design rights. When it comes to images being put on the internet by the designer or by people having taken photos from a fashion show there are a number of issues to address. In the former case the designer is probably wanting to increase awareness of the design and the fact that people may blog or use it on the internet may support the designers wishes. Of course, the designer can still prevent images from being used if it wants e.g. those being used for profit by someone else without permission. In the latter case it is more difficult since the photographer is likely to be the person who puts the image on the internet and is therefore the copyright owner of the photo.

What advice would you give a designer in confronting someone who is using their work for example, an illustration, a design without their permission?

Firstly consider, has the designer registered the design? If not, the designer has 3 years automatic protection from the date it first made the design available to the public e.g. at a trade show, on a catwalk or in a Look Book. If there is something novel about the design which would attract protection a designer could confront the person who has copied the design or he/she could go through a lawyer and consider taking legal action. If the design has been registered then the designer will have up to 25 years protection and again could contact the infringer direct or use a lawyer.

With regard to an illustration this will be a copyright work. If someone else has used the illustration or one that is substantially similar then the illustrator can prevent that person from using the illustration anywhere not just on the internet.

What is the duration of copyright for artistic work?

In the UK the duration of copyright is 70 years after the creator has died.

What advice would you give to a designer accepting and working to commission?

Be very careful! First thing before any work is commissioned, check whether it is exclusive or not, as most commissions are exclusive. Exclusive means that you can't use the work in the future, and you no longer own the rights to the work, therefore you need to charge more for the design. Look very carefully at the terms and conditions of any contracts. For example, a designer may design something very close to one of their pre-existing designs in their collection which might include the use of fabrics, the quality of a design and/or construction techniques, and if they tie themselves into a contract, they may never able to use that design/fabric/construction technique again. It is easy to be blinded by someone offering you money for your design work, but it is important to really understand what the contract involves and what you can or cannot do in the future. Alternatively, you may consider licensing your design work, which may be a better option, as this only gives the other party a licence to use your work. You still own it and can do what you want with it subject to the terms of the licence.

And finally, which one piece of advice would you give to a designer who is setting up in business to ensure their business is legally sound?

I would strongly recommend that you register your name, if this is going to be the name you want to be known by, as a trade mark both in the UK and China. Registering your name is important for the following reasons; (1) if you do not register your name someone else might do (especially in China) and this will prevent you from using your name in that particular country; (2) when it comes to an investor they will want to know that the brand is protected otherwise they may not be interested in investing; and (3) when you apply to register your name make sure you apply in your own personal name and not in the name of your limited company (if you have one). In recent years there have been several well known cases, when a business has been sold, the designer's personal name has been transferred over with the business, and the designer is no longer able to use their own name to trade. It is important to keep your name, if the company goes bust, or understand how much money you are getting for giving up the right to your name if the company is sold.

Useful Webites and Resources

ACID (Anti-copying in Design)
Website: www.acid.uk.com

Arts Thread
Website: www.artsthread.com

Blogger
Website: www.blogger.com

British Copyright Council (BCC)
Website: www.britishcopyright.org

British Fashion Council
Websites: www.britishfashioncouncil.co.uk

British Design Innovation
Website: www.britishdesigninnovation.org

The Copyright Licensing Agency (CLA)
Website: www.cla.co.uk

Craft Central
Website: http://craftcentral.org.uk

Da Wanda
Website: en.dawanda.com

Dalton's Weekly
Website: www.daltons.co.uk

Design and Artists Copyright Society (DACS)
Website: www.dacs.org.uk

Design Factory
Website: www.designfactory.org.uk

Design Nation
Website: www.designnation.co.uk

The Ethical Trading Initiative (ETI)
Website: www.ethicaltrade.org

Etsy
Website: www.etsy.com

The Fashion and Design Protection Association (FDPA)
www.fdpa.co.uk

Fashion Enter
Website: www.fashion-enter.com

Fashion Net
Website: www.fashion.net

Folksy
Website: www.folksy.com

GINETEX - the International Association for Textile Care Labelling
Website: www.ginetex.net

Institute of Patentees and Inventors
Website: www.invent.org.uk

Intellectual Property Office (IPO)
Website: www.ipo.gov.uk

Let's Make It Here
Website: www.letsmakeithere.org

Make it British
Website: http://makeitbritish.co.uk

Misi (Make It, Sell It)
Website: www.misi.co.uk

NUJ Freelance Fees Guide
Website: www.londonfreelance.org

Not on the High Street
Website: www.notonthehighstreet.com

Textile Artist.org
Textile Artist.org is a website dedicated to promoting the work of artists using textiles and mixed media techniques, as well as offering guidance on the best ways they can market themselves. The site is run by Joseph and Sam Pitcher, sons of artist Sue Stone.
Website: www.textileartist.org

Textile Source
An international wholesale textile sourcing Directory
Website: http://textilesource.com

Further Reading

Brown, C, *Fashion and Textiles: The Essential Careers Guide.* London: Laurence King Publishing 2010

Buzan, T. *Mind Maps for Business: Using the Ultimate Thinking Tool to Revolutionise How You Work.* Harlow: Pearson Education Ltd. 2014

Edward de Bono. *Lateral Thinking: A Textbook of Creativity.* London: Penguin. 2009

Rhodes, Chris, *Retail Industry: statistics and policy.* June 2014

The Writers and Artists Year Book. London: Bloomsbury Publishing (Annually Updated)

palmer//harding. Autumn/Winter collection 2015

Scoop London, 2015

Section 3

Marketing the Business

According to the Oxford Dictionary, the definition of marketing is 'the action or business of promoting and selling products or services, including market research and advertising: *the Western arts of marketing and distribution'*.

To achieve success in business, it is essential that you define what the business is all about and get the message out there, so the public know what you do. Marketing is about being proactive and raising the profile of the business, promoting the product, services and brand to an audience of both existing and potential customers and increasing sales. To be able to do this successfully, you need to be prepared to spend time researching your market thoroughly, finding out and defining your potential target market, analysing the demographic segmentation (age group, gender, income, education, occupation and lifestyle) of your customers, and calculate the size of the market through the data available. To fully understand your target market research and evaluate who your competitors are, and question how your business will differ in product, service, pricing and originality.

Who are your competitors?

To identify your competitors, research and find out the following:

- The history and the location of your competitors
- The business structure of your competitors
- The breadth of their product or service range
- The unique selling points (USPs) of their product range(s)
- The differences between your business and competitor businesses in product/service range
- The marketing strategy and where they advertise, and how they promote and market their business
- Their business presence on the internet
- Partnerships - do your competitors have partners, and if so who are their partners

Researching your competitors will give you greater insight and understanding of your niche market. Questioning how your business differs from that of your competitors will help you to recognise any gaps in the market and the USP's of your business. This will give you greater insight into the market potential and what you need to do to succeed. It will also provide the necessary information to produce a successful, targeted marketing plan to attract new customers and keep existing business, maintaining customer loyalty.

When analysing your USPs consider the following questions:

- What are the benefits of your product or service to your customers?
- What are they going to gain by buying your product or using your service?
- What business advantages do you have that are greater than your competitors?

What is Your Marketing Strategy?

A marketing strategy should be an integral part of your business in helping you to build your business reputation, which will help to increase trust in the brand, boosting business and increasing sales. Once you have designed your product or service, you need to consider your marketing plan, and how you are going to get the message out there and attract customers. Ask yourself what are the most effective forms of marketing for your business. Methods of promotion and marketing include advertising, direct marketing, editorials, e-Marketing, packaging design, press releases, business newsletters and look books to launch a collection, public relations/ PR campaigns, radio or television and social media, but this will vary greatly from business to business.

Databases of Contacts

Business connections are invaluable, and a database of contacts is an important asset and a tremendous resource to any business, and should be regularly added to and updated as the business develops and grows. Establishing a database is often completely underestimated in its value. Forming connections and developing links with other businesses, associations, and new contacts can result in the development of exciting ideas, new business leads and the sharing of knowledge and experience. It can also result in the development of collaborative ventures and mutually beneficial links. Without contacts you do not have a business. Depending on the business, a database of contacts may include the names and details of business support services and associates, details of associations, trade fair organisers, new, existing and potential customers, media contacts and suppliers.

When first starting in business consider forming a database to organise, store and record the details of relevant contacts, using either a computer database programme such as Microsoft Excel or alternatively stored as hardcopy. There are significant advantages in using a database programme, which include the easy accessibility of stored data, and the ability to categorise your contacts into various groupings or fields for easy reference. Categories may include the media, news and feature editors (local and national newspapers, magazines, free press, and trade magazines), supplier's customers/clients and potential customers. These categories can then be divided into sub-folders, forming an address book, which can easily be amended and updated. Recorded details may include information such as name, job title, postal and email address, telephone/mobile phone number and, date and details of previous orders placed in the business. Contacts listed on a computer data base can be accessed and then easily transferred and printed out onto adhesive address labels, for mail shots and for sending out press packs, and completing orders, as required.

Remember, any customer data comes under the legal obligations of the Data Protection Act, and therefore in the interest of your customers and business all details must be stored securely. Protect all data and information on your computer by having and using a good security package, safeguarding your business.

If you are not technologically savvy, setting up a data base using a database programme may initially appear difficult, but in the long run, and as the business grows and your client base expands it will save you time and money. There are many colleges in the UK offering free short computer literacy courses, providing workshops on topics such as developing databases and spread sheets, helping students to navigate and understand the business technology essentials. There are also many free online computer literacy courses available, which are easy to access.

Database of Contacts

	Title of Publication	Editor's Name	Title of Position	Address	Email	Tel. No.	Mob. No.
1							
2							
3							
4							
5							
6							

Example of database for media contacts

Business Networking

'Networking is the building and maintaining of relationships within a network of people for their mutual benefit'.
Chambers 21st Century Dictionary

Networking can be difficult, particularly if you are a relatively reserved or shy person and find it difficult to interact with people in general. However, establishing work relationships through meeting new people and building connections is essential to the development of a business in moving your business forward and expanding your thinking. Means of networking include developing your professional business contact networks and establishing opportunities to meet like-minded people who are excited by opportunities that arise. The advantages of networking can be very beneficial in forging new business through the exchange of ideas, knowledge and learning from others experiences and also in the development of new collaborative partnerships.

Businesses networks include:
- Journalists and media organisations,
- Local employers and business groups
- Other businesses and also organisations and businesses you have worked for
- Trade organisations – associations, societies and guilds
- Academic networks/researchers in institutions/educational establishments
- Friends and family
- Government departments
- Training organisations
- Development agencies

The advantages of networking include:

- Making new contacts
- Building mutually valuable business relationships
- Support and guidance
- Sharing experiences and ideas, and exchanging information
- The development of successful collaborative partnerships, ventures and/or projects
- Sharing and improving your knowledge of market information
- Training and development opportunities and/or giving and receiving expert advice
- Offering and receiving a business lifeline of support
- The generation of new business

Many new business ventures have been set up and opportunities grown through a conversation at a social gathering or business event, when two like-minded people have discussed their dreams and aspirations, and with excitement as a result of exchanging ideas, new and collaborative partnerships have formed. In the course of networking you may meet a wealth of potential contacts consisting of customers, competitors, suppliers, service providers and potential business partners who are all looking for similar benefits and to widen their contact base.

Places to meet new contacts and to meet similar like-minded people include:

- Trade fairs and exhibitions
- Organised meetings
- Conferences
- Workshops and training events
- Membership of associations and trade groups
- Organised networking and focus groups
- Social events
- Social online media: Blogging, Facebook, LinkedIn, Flickr, twitter

The London Textile Fair

Join the SOURCE community at www.ethicalfashionforum.com

Brad Burton – Motivational Business Speaker and Managing Director of 4Networking

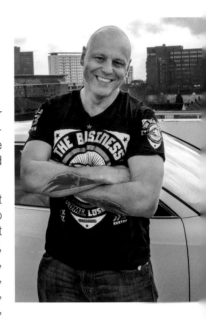

Brad Burton is a motivational business speaker and Founder and Managing Director of 4Networking, the UK's largest joined-up business network which holds over 5,000 events across the UK each year for businesses to meet, support each other and exchange ideas.

Brad was born in Salford in 1973, and as Brad describes it 'Dad left, primary school, computer games, class clown, no qualifications, shop boy, BMX bikes, girls, chalet cleaner, night clubbing, pothead, games journalist, Dad, shot at, moved away, depressed, dole, shop manager, blagged CV, head of marketing, dole, Director, dole, 3 days away from bankruptcy, father again, depressed, married, employed, self-employed, depression, skint, skint, skint, author, Dad again, stopped smoking pot, founded 4Networking and success'.

Brad has since authored three business books and is now the highest 5* rated author (with over five hundred 5 star reviews) in business books on Amazon. He is a motivational business speaker who is inspirational and who regularly speaks at conferences and business events, engaging his audience with a unique approach to business. For further information visit: www.bradburton.biz

An Interview with Brad Burton

Depression, 3-days from bankruptcy, £25,000 in debt, the dole and struggling; what were the main factors that set you on the road to success?

I was despondent, depressed and I had to stop making excuses for myself, I was a happy go lucky guy but needed to change. It is all about mind-set. I just applied all the resources I had, and looked at the world with fresh eyes, and stopped masking and putting things off. It is all about the power of self-belief, and making things happen.

Sometimes you cannot afford to do something, but sometimes you just cannot afford not to.

How did the idea for your business 4Networking come about?

There was nothing really happening to join up business networks, they were all rather main stream, and I wanted to set up something new. I wanted to steer the UK business community to a new platform, breaking the mould of the usual networks out there. 4Networking offers a support

community to businesses, it is about forming good business relationships and this was what was missing. From one group it's now grown into a completely joined-up network with over 5,000 meetings each year across the UK.

How important is networking to businesses today?

Business networks are hugely important, Twitter, Facebook, 4Networking, it's about sharing information; it's about people having a voice and building contacts.

You are the founder of the largest joined up UK business network, a motivational speaker and author, what are the motivational factors behind your success?

Yes, there is 4Networking, and I have also written three books on business, which gives greater credibility to my work. The motivation was about doing something, sharing ideas and motivating others that they can do it. They can run a business successfully, but they have got to have belief in what they are doing and to also understand why they are doing it.

What makes a successful entrepreneur?

You can't play it safe; you need to think on your feet and think fast, and use all your resources.

How do you define success?

Success to me is the ability to do what I want when I want. It's not about being hyper wealthy, and having diamonds and big cars, although I would like a Lamborghini – 'things don't make you any happier'. It's about being honest with yourself, believing in yourself and enjoying what you do.

What is the difference between a good business and a brilliant business?

A business that makes a positive difference, a business that is enjoyable to run, and being comfortable with where you are in life, it is not about money, holidays, possessions or big cars it is about enjoying your business and your life. Living the life you really want.

What are the problems for businesses today?

Legislation in business, HR rules and employment laws, most businesses suffer the same problems but just have different resources to pull on and also to deal with. I have 5 employees and 100s of sub-contractors; business laws create a culture that leads to problems in employing someone.

What do you attribute to your success?

I didn't have a plan B - I had to make my idea work, and I had to have a 100% belief in myself. I wanted to quit eleven times in the last ten years, but people depend on me, such as family, business employees, people in the network, so I had to get on with it. Important things in my business are the speed of decisions I make, my experience and competency, being confident and positive, having a vision, a desire to succeed and having a winning mind-set.

What one piece of advice would you give to someone setting up in business today?

You got to ask yourself why you are doing it, if the only motivation is money then forget it; it's not a big enough incentive. Treat everyone you meet with respect, remember everyone is human, and it's about having a 100% belief in yourself and your idea.

What do you want to leave as your legacy?

My legacy is that I have changed the way many people think about business and proved that you can make a niche for yourself. Many people are on life's hamster wheel, work, work, work, with very little return. No one owes you a living. I just looked for an opportunity, I then started 4Networking without any capital, and I have shown people that they can also do it. It's all about being optimistic, positive, and believing in yourself.

Brad Burton, Founder and Managing Director of 4Networking

Keynote speaker and motivator at Business and networking events

Business Support

When starting in business it is helpful to find out which organisations are able to offer practical help, such as, legal and financial advice, training opportunities and funding for businesses and the public sector. In Section 5: Business Support – you will find many useful references relating to business organisations and agencies listed that give advice and guidance, providing up-to-date information and keeping you abreast of the latest financial and market news in your specialist field.

Networking Online

Today, the internet plays a significant role in most people's lives, with continuous advancements in technology. In recent years we have seen a huge expansion and acceleration in the growth of online social media platforms, which used in a positive way can provide a great networking platform to share and exchange information. Online media can act as a powerful marketing tool to any business. Having a dedicated online business presence will help in raising your business profile and give your business a professional identity.

Today, social media is considered an essential and invaluable tool in marketing and in bringing your business and business activities to the attention of millions due to its global presence. Examples of social media platforms include Business Facebook, Twitter, LinkedIn, blogs, and links such as Twitter, Google+ (Google Plus), YouTube, Instagram and Pinterest, and in the exchange of emails, newsgroups and online discussion forums. For instance, Google+ is a social networking website which attracted over 540 million users in 2014. It allows you to create a user account and upload information including features such as a profile photo, profile description, school history, employment and interests. There are many additional features such as Web Circles, which provides a networking opportunity for groups to form, and share information.

LinkedIn is a recognised professional networking service, founded in 2002, and to-date has over 300 million registered users globally. Once you have registered you can then add your profile, and links to your blog, website and other social media networks, which is relatively easy with simple step by step instructions explaining how to create a professional individual or business profile or company page. The profile can be edited at any time and added to, as your business develops. At a cost, there are upgrades available that offer a higher level of membership and use of additional facilities, and can be accessed on their website.

LinkedIn has many established groups including specialist fashion and textile focus groups which you can join, offering online networks of like-minded people, knowledge and opportunities. Examples of specialist groups include Textile Professionals; KnitLinked; the Freelance Textile Designers Group; the Fashion Marketing and the Digital Media Group which has a membership of over 57,000, and the Eco Fashion and Ethical Fashion Networking Group, to name a few.

To have a successful online media presence it is necessary to keep all information up to date and easy to access. Joining in various online discussion forums can be useful in contributing ideas, knowledge and experience in a specialist field. This can result in widening your network of contacts, and in gaining new openings and exciting opportunities.

Building a Brand

'Show me a successful brand and I'll show you a company that understands the benefit of creative integrated marketing. Online and offline channels are blended to deliver contextual messages that engage audiences and drive conversion. It is the lifeblood of brands in our digital age'.

Tom Gillman, Commercial Director, Crafted, Ipswich and London

Branding a business is giving it a unique identity. Consider the name of the business. This can be checked out and registered along with a domain name at Companies House or the National Business Register. It is useful to link your business name to your domain name allowing you to trade and advertise on the internet through for example a blog or website. When registering your domain name consider registering domain variants of the name for example co.uk; .com; .net; .org; .org.uk; .info. This gives you assurance that no one else can use that name and also gives you scope to use various domain names within your business.

Branding is central to marketing and promoting, and provides a unique and recognisable concept for a business. This includes the name of the business, any logos, trademarks, letterheads, business cards, stationery, packaging, press packs, promotional literature and other individual features of the business. A brand should be easily recognisable and consistent in design. Branding links together any promotional and advertising material from online social media content, to packaging and emails, and should be appropriate, recognisable and appealing to your target market. This does not mean staying stagnant but being creative and coming up with new approaches, and presenting your ideas in new ways but still within the brand of the business.

When first setting up a business, most start-ups are working with very limited resources, so it is important to work within your allocated marketing budget. Any money spent on marketing activities, such as advertising, or printing of promotional literature must lead to results ensuring a return on your investment. In planning a marketing campaign, consider your database of contacts and networks.

'Brand equity is built with a strong vision, and in a noisy marketplace, your brand has to sing to make it resonate. You must successfully set yourself apart from competitors with a story that evokes real feelings. That's when your brand will make a connection'.

Christine Faulhaber – President and CEO at Faulhaber Communications

Business Stationery

Business stationery and any promotional material should be designed within your brand, so it is recognisable and may comprise of business cards, complimentary slips, business letterheads incorporating your business name, address and website and/or blog details, and logo or trademark. If you are a limited company remember the legal requirements and to include the company's registration number, your registered office address, and where the company is registered, making sure you identify it as a limited company on all stationery and on your website. Full details of the legal responsibilities are available on the government website: www.gov.uk/business-legal-structures/limited–company.

When designing and producing business stationery, there are many software design packages available on the market such as Adobe Illustrator and InDesign, which are useful in the creation of graphics, layout, and in typesetting documents, posters, stationery and publications. If designing your own stationery consider using a contemporary, easy to read font, rather than ornate italics that make it difficult to read. You may choose to print your own stationery, but if you are sending your finished artwork to a printer, always check which printing process they are going to use and what format they require the design work in, checking the delivery and turnaround time. A good digital camera is a fantastic resource for taking professional-looking images for inclusion in your marketing materials. If you commission a professional photographer to produce the visuals for any marketing material, make sure you fully understand the contracts and check who owns the copyright of the images, and what the costs are, if you choose to use the images more than once or as agreed.

There are many online companies who offer digital design and printing services producing business cards and stationery for minimal charges, and there are also online packages to help you to design your own, if you feel that you have the necessary design skills. If not, consider hiring the skills of a graphic design studio to help create a logo design or the brand concept of the business. However, make sure you negotiate a competitive price and that there are no hidden extra costs. If you also intend to use their printing services, this may be an added incentive to give reduced rates.

Photographing Artwork

Whether photographing garments, fabrics, accessories or other items, the photographs you make of your products reflect the care and attention to the products themselves. If you are photographing your own work the following guidelines will help you in developing your photographic skills and in developing your vision when recording work.

Selecting a camera

There is a huge choice of cameras on the market today, but almost any camera can be used for 'product' photography, from a tablet or phone camera to a Compact, 'bridge' or 'SLR' (Single Lens Reflex) camera. If choosing a 'Compact', 'bridge' or 'SLR' camera try to choose one with a 'zoom' lens, as this will give you greater control over what you frame, and how little you want to have in each shot. Wide angle lenses get more in, but can 'distort' your subjects, so it is best to try and use a 'normal' lens (or lens setting) rather than a wide angle, for a more realistic result. Cameras that have a 'macro' (close up) mode or settings are handy for close up shots focusing on detail. If you are uploading images onto the internet, choose a camera that is capable of making images as 'jpegs'. Some cameras can make two versions of the same image, one very small for web 'thumbnails', and one larger image (for web or print). Today, many people find using a phone camera or tablet sufficient, due to the ease in editing and uploading images instantly to their social media/blog for sharing with their potential audience.

Lighting

When photographing your designs or products always make sure they are well lit, by lighting your product from above and slightly in front if possible to get the best result. Having a dimly lit product will tell your customer very little about what they are buying. Unless you want to achieve a very dramatic final image, then soft light is usually better for product photography, as it produces less shadow and gives a smooth transition between highlight and shadow. Hard light tends to have strong shadows and a harsh graduation between light and dark, and it can distort your subjects overall appearance. Perfect soft light can be found outside on an overcast day. It can also be achieved by using a diffused light source. For example, try using a window, or lighting through frosted glass or a (white) sheet, or by using a 'light tent' which are available to buy online, and are useful when photographing items that are relatively small.

Flash

For products try to avoid using 'on camera' (or on tablet/phone) 'flash', as flash that originates from a camera will often overpower the subject, and make it appear flat and harsh, especially when photographing fabric. Many cameras and tablets/phones allow the user to switch the flash off. Consider using controlled artificial or daylight at an angle from the camera rather than originating from it. This will make subjects appear more three dimensional. When using artificial light, opt for 'daylight balanced' bulbs or alternatively LED's. Daylight is 'whiter' than traditional 'tungsten' bulbs, which make images appear yellow. 'Fluorescent' bulbs may make your images appear green or pink. Again, 'daylight' fluorescent bulbs are readily available and can be ideal at generating a reasonably 'soft' light.

Backgrounds

When taking photographs, it is often preferable to use simple, uncluttered backgrounds (the area behind and to the side of the item you are photographing), as this will help your audience to clearly see the product. Bed sheets or paper work well as backgrounds or there are many 'photographic backgrounds' available to buy online. When choosing a background colour, keep it simple and neutral so it is not too distracting, and avoid anything that will date quickly. Black, white and grey backgrounds are the norm. It is important that your main focus 'stands out' from the background, e.g. if photographing a white shirt, it may get 'lost' against a white backdrop.

Mannequins

If using a mannequin, again, try to choose one that is not too distracting, and won't date quickly. For this reason, I often choose a very simple (often very old) design of mannequin or tailors dummy.

Photographing garment or product detail

When photographing a blouse or shirt; consider taking one image of how the shirt looks from the front (on a mannequin or a hanger), the second image might be a rear view of the shirt. The third and fourth images could be close-up shots of specific areas of the garment such as a collar, pocket, cuff or stitch detailing that you wish to draw attention to. Remember that less is usually more. Having three or four excellent images of one product will often tell everything the audience needs to know, most people don't want to browse through dozens of very similar images of one product.

Photographing fabrics

If photographing fabric, the images need to show the pattern, colour, texture (is the fabric shiny, dull or is the fabric sheer, then you need to see that too?) and finally how the fabric 'falls' or 'drapes' over a form. This can be done in a number of ways, such as draping it over recognisable forms or get a friend to place their hand behind the fabric, as this usually gives a good indication of how sheer the fabric is.

Creating a 'studio'

A studio is simply a controlled environment where you can photograph things or people. Light could either be daylight (often from the roof in the form of skylights) or artificial. Using a fabric backdrop to give some light source will then suffice as a home studio. Lights could be a few 'daylight' bulbs in an 'angle-poise' type desk lamp, and/or a ceiling of 'daylight balanced' fluorescent lights. If you have a room with a glass ceiling (such as a conservatory), then this may be ideal to use on overcast days.

Remember; relax, have fun and experiment with different framing and lighting, gaining experience, developing your photographic skills to produce inspirational images and a record of your services and your products. If you don't want to photograph your products then hire a reputable local photographer to do it for you. Always ask to view examples of his/her previous work before commissioning.

Matthew Andrew:
Photographer and Lecturer in Photographic Practice – University of Salford, UK

Marketing and Promotional Activities

There are many methods of promoting and marketing to enhance and optimise the exposure of your business bringing it to the public's attention. Whether you are launching a new business, a new product or service or organising a business event, the results must be memorable reflecting the brand. All methods of promotion and marketing have their own distinct merits, and include the following activities:

- Advertising
- Direct marketing
- Direct sales
- Editorial
- Entering awards and competitions
- Letters and emails
- Look books
- Local, regional and national media

- Networking
- Newsletters
- Packaging
- Company labels, garment labels and swing tags
- Press releases
- Social media
- Trade events

Advertising

Advertising is a promotional activity, which includes the use of posters and adverts in specialist and trade magazines, newspapers, business and specialist directories, trade books and on the worldwide web. It also includes outdoor advertising such as hoardings, on the underground, on buses and in retail shopping malls attracting a wide audience together with commuters on their way to and from work, and the public in general.

Advertising can act as a very powerful tool and be part of a major marketing campaign used to increase sales and promote a brand. For example, a bridal wear designer may advertise their designs and services locally and regionally, such as a town journal, taking advertising out coinciding with the promotion of a local bridal wear event, where they are exhibiting. Purchases made at the event may include the receipt of a discount voucher offering 10% off any sales when visiting the trade stand at the forthcoming event. This can be then advertised on the events website, tying in all the promotional and marketing activities. Alternatively, it may be useful to invest in a major ad campaign taking out a number of ads over a period of months, for example, an eighth of a page in a specialist trade journal promoting a product. However, care must be taken that money isn't wasted, as advertising can be exceedingly expensive and unless well planned, will reap few returns.

Most national magazine publications produce media packs also known as media kits. A well planned media pack will give information listing the circulation and frequency of the publication, the demographics of readership, the terms and conditions of advertising, production specifications and, magazine and digital advertising rates. For example, Vogue Media Pack - Condé Nast, provides excellent details giving a clear view of the Vogue Portfolio, the Vogue audience, circulation and readership statistics, an overview of advertising opportunities, the distribution and production schedule, and much more.

Media packs usually list their advertising rates, but be prepared to negotiate, securing the best possible price, size, quality and placement of any advertising. Media packs will often give deadlines of the dates for submitting ads, which help businesses in planning and strategically placing advertising during specific months and linking to particular themes. National magazines usually work at least three to four months ahead of publication, therefore, in September, many publishing teams will be working on the December issue. Advertising can be a very expensive method of marketing, and is suitable for some businesses but is not suitable for all, so make sure you fully research the benefits, negotiating the best price and deal, and request inclusion on their website, and always remember to check all 'proofs' carefully before going to press.

An advertisement needs to achieve maximum attention. Therefore, when drafting an advert consider the choice of font, layout, size and the positioning of the advert in the publication, which is of prime importance and rates will vary. Keep paragraphs short, and sentences punchy, focused and to the point. People skim read, so say what you have to say in as few as words as possible. Headlines and visuals need to instantly grab the reader's interest and attention, encouraging further reading, and keeping the message clear. To understand the impact of any advertising campaign you will need to monitor its success by adding a purchase code or voucher that can be easily tracked.

Direct Marketing

A good data base of contacts is important for direct marketing. This involves promoting the business by targeting existing and potential customers, through directing information by postal mail, targeted fliers, postcards, brochures, catalogues, promotional letters, tele sales, text messaging, and emailing. As with any marketing methods, it is important to identify your target market and measure responses.

Leaflet or brochure marketing entails the design and printing of professionally presented promotional literature, and can be an effective marketing tool to increase sales. Leaflets can be as simple as a one page flier printed singularly or double sided, and can then be incorporated for a small charge as a supplementary leaflet in local or regional papers or magazines. Leaflets can be distributed in this way and targeted to specific areas and locations, even precise streets within a town, or can be targeted to cover the entire circulation area of the paper. Contact your local paper or chosen publication for costs and details. Some publications also offer a design and print service, but once again check the competitiveness of any quotes, and try and negotiate the best rates.

Purchasing Mailing Lists

There are many companies and groups which sell mailing lists and printed labels to use for direct mailing campaigns. Purchasing a specialist mailing list can save time and may be useful in providing direct contact between you and your target market. Mailing lists include retail buyers, educational institutions (schools, colleges, universities), galleries, dress agencies, fancy dress suppliers, film producers, women's and men's clothing hire, ladies, men's and children's fashion retail outlets, newspapers and magazines, soft furnishing retailers, and yarn shops to name a few.

Editorial

Editorial is usually written by an editor, deputy or feature editor, or journalist presenting their views and ideas about a product, service or concept. For example, a textile business may send the assistant editor of a lifestyle, fashion or interior magazine, samples of their new textile fabrics along with a written statement or press release informing them of an exhibition of their work in four months' time. If the editor likes the product and it fits in with their publication, then they may choose to include a brief written piece reviewing the work. This will help inform readers, reporting on the forthcoming exhibition, and also the availability of the designs or fabric collection. In the written media, most magazines and newspapers have editorial pages, specifically for this purpose. As you can imagine, editors are inundated with details of new products and services, but they are always on the lookout for that latest inspirational story, an original idea or product to generate newsworthy content.

To secure successful press coverage, you need to target your information, noting that all media has a house style and is easily recognisable, so once again think of the link between your target market and the target readership of the publication. Find out as much information as possible about the publication, such as the print and digital circulation statistics, details of readership and house style, which should all be available in the company's media pack. When sending any information to the media make sure you have the correct details and target your information sending it to a named person within the correct editorial team, using their correct email or postal address. Developing contacts with the media is essential to most businesses. If you are successful in securing any editorial always write and thank the editor showing your appreciation, and remember to add their name and contact details to your growing media database.

Press / Media Releases

Press releases are sent out to the media to inform them and provide details, and to promote any important forthcoming events. For instance, a press release could be used to promote the launch of a business or a re-launch or an expansion of a business, the introduction of a new product or service, or to promote and publicise an event, a fashion show, a trade event or a seasonal story. The aim of a press release is to provide fast fact information and up-to-the-minute news. To gain attention, it needs to be targeted and sent out to a specific list of media editors and journalists. It needs to contain all the relevant details of the event or story that an editor, journalist, radio broadcaster or television presenter can easily translate into a newsworthy story, resulting in free editorial and news copy.

When writing a press release check all the details and content are accurate and word perfect. If a press release is sent out promoting an event remember to include all important details such as the date, time and location of the event, noting any admission costs, including a map, the background and purpose of the event and also the contact details of the person handling enquiries. This helps if there are any queries or requests for further information.

Press Packs

A press pack, also known as media kit is often used to promote and market the launch of a business, a product or service or to coordinate a promotion, and can be used to target specific media attention; from editors of both online and hardcopy publications to reporters, and also investors. The contents of a press pack may vary depending on the type of business and what you are trying to promote. A typical press pack may contain details of the business and company background with a fact sheet providing the benefits of the product of service. The pack may also include a brochure and sample products, and if relevant a press release giving the date and details of a product or service launch. Press packs may also include free invites and a VIP ticket to an event, adding an incentive and drawing the media's interest. To gain maximum impact, you may include an additional sheet, which may contain quotes from the managing director, design director or founder of the business, highlighting the merits of the product or service that you are promoting. This can then be adapted by the editor and used in an article along with images that you may have supplied on a CD.

An example press statement may include a draft interview for the launch of a new label.

For example:

What is the ethos behind the label?

The label ECO-INWEAR Ltd was founded in 2014, with the ethos built on sustainability, harmony and our love of the natural world, to produce environmental-friendly fashion ranges. All our designs are produced using eco-sustainable fibres, such as bamboo, organic cottons, hemp, upcycled wools and eucalyptus benefitting the consumer but also helping the environment.

What was the inspiration behind the forthcoming season's collection?

The collection was inspired by a theme of vintage florals combined with old school stripes and checks. The collection uses a wide range of natural eco fabrics in soft, feminine, floral prints contrasting with edgier fabrics for impact, creating juxtapositions in patterning and textures.

As shown above, in the draft interview questions and responses, providing clear information saves an editor time, and also gives a good overview of the label or product. This can then be adapted to copy, with minimal editing.

At a trade event you may be asked for a press pack providing details of your business, products and services, so be prepared and have packs available to give out in response to any media requests. Also, consider leaving several press packs at the event organisers office, as the events team work to promote the event and also to promote the business of exhibiting delegates.

Packaging

Great packaging can result in improving sales. For example an ethically friendly fashion label may be recognisable for its eco-friendly packaging, reflecting the ethos of the company and has a dual purpose, which many appeal to many of the businesses target audience. Packaging, garment and gift labels, product swing tags and price labels with barcodes can be customised and designed in almost any shape, size and material reflecting the signature of your brand and product style. They can also affect the physicality and reflect the price of the product, and become collectable items in their own right. Depending on the product, packaging can play an important role forming the first impression and attracting consumer attention. It can change consumer views and promote the business and perception of the brand. There are many companies out there offering a vast range of packaging options from simple paper bags to plastic and fabric substrates, to folding cartons, ridged and flat pack boxes, including eco-friendly and customised bespoke services designed to the client's specifications and in keeping with their branding. Once again shop around for the most competitive prices for your packaging supplies, and request samples of products, checking the delivery, turnaround times and negotiate payment terms.

Trade Shows and Events

London's Scoop International Trade Fair for luxury fashion and brands

There are many specialist fashion and textile trade shows and events, which can provide opportunities to showcase your business and provide the opportunity to meet new and existing customers, for networking, brand awareness, to generate new sales, finalise contracts and attract interest in your business. People visiting a specialist trade fair have chosen to attend, making them a very receptive, accessible and focused audience who want to view the latest products and services.

If considering exhibiting at an event, look at the exhibition website for exhibitors guidelines. Event websites will usually provide exhibitor details outlining the benefits of exhibiting, including the number and breakdown of visitors expected to attend the event and the target audience.

If planning to exhibit at a trade event contact the event organisers requesting an exhibitor's pack. This will provide exhibitor information and guidelines, and will help you to determine whether the event is the most suitable for your business. Exhibitor event packs usually contain details of exhibitor regulations, a floor plan of the event identifying the position of each stand, the cost of

Checklist of Considerations When Exhibiting at an Event or Trade Fair

	Considerations	Cost	Completed
Receipt of exhibitors pack from the organisers	• Details of the location, date and times of the event • Entry for exhibitors • Entry times for visitors • The number of exhibitors' passes available, and how many you require • What is being offered by the organisers to exhibiting businesses?		
Location	• Position and the full dimensions including height of the stand • Is the event internal/external? • If the event is held externally, consider the design of the stand and how you are going to protect your stock from poor weather conditions		
Booking trade stand	• Request site plan and book stand • Receipt of contract confirming deposit/costs paid and all supplementary details		
Stock	• Prepare all stock • Decide on pricing strategy for trade/direct customers		
Design of stand	• Does the stand project the right image and does it reflect the branding of your business? • Consider the health and safety implications of the general public entering your stand, is it safe? • Check that all electrical cables and flooring are safely secured • Check the size, weight and build of the stand, if you are transporting screens and building the stand by yourself or with a team • Make sure the stand has impact and represents your business brand. Remember to check the build of the stand for ease of construction due to time limitations in building prior to the event starting		
Build of the stand	• When is access to the event available to build the stand? • How many people do you need available to build the stand? • Are carpets and fixtures and fittings included on the stand?		
Electrical requirements	• How many sockets do you need – lighting, video presentation? • Do you need wi-fi?		
Lighting	• Type and safe positioning of lighting		

Furniture	• Furniture - style, functionality and consistency with your brand. This may include desk/table, seating and display shelves • Garment/sample rails/display units It is useful to take a tool kit with you to help with the build of the stand and signage. This may include hammer, nails, double sided sellotape, drawing pins, staple gun, glue gun etc.		
Security	• Security is required on the stand for personal items such as coats, bags, wallets and purses, and this may also include lockable cupboard units for stock and admin.		
Transport	• Transport to travel to the event i.e. size of van, renting van and insurance • Where and what is the location and availability of parking for unloading stand and products during the event? • Are parking passes inclusive in the price of the booking, and if so, how many are available?		
Delivery	• Are there specific times for delivering the stand and stock to the event, and what time is available for access to build the stand? • Transportation of stock or equipment to the events hall and stand		
Staff team	• Who and how many team members will be manning the stand? • What are they going to wear, and is it going to reflect the brand for example t-shirts with the company logo on? • Do the team require any training in marketing and selling skills in preparation for manning the stand? • Do they all have full knowledge of the product/service? • Do they all have business cards?		
Invites	• Direct marketing – design, print and plan date to send out any direct invites by post or email		
Publicity	• Is your business listed as an exhibitor on the events website? • How are you going to promote your attendance at the event via your business website and social media sites: blog, Facebook, twitter, and to all relevant contacts on your database? • Do you have sufficient, relevant and up-to-date promotional material available for the event?		

Press coverage	• Preparation of press packs • Distribution of press packs before the event, and if so, what are you including, and who are you sending them out to, and when? • Will you have additional press packs available with you at the event for the press and exhibition organisers, if required?		
Sales	Are you intending to sell products from the stand, if so what payment methods are customers able to pay with? • If payment is with cash then do you have a cash float? • Do you need to price goods? • Do you have an order/receipt book?		
Event offers and promotions	• Are you intending to offer any promotional discounts to visitors to the event?		
Booking of accommodation, if required	• Is accommodation required by your team who are attending the event? • Any accommodation booked, is it near and convenient to the event for easy interaction with fellow exhibitors, which provides good networking opportunities? • Note date and receipt of booking		
Insurances	• What insurances do you need to have before, during and after the event: transport/travel, damage or loss of stock • Do you need public liability for the show?		
Follow up contacts	• How and when are you going to follow up contacts and leads after the event to maintain interest in your business? • Do you have a signing up form to receive a business newsletter informing visitors about your latest products and offers? • Have you added all new contacts to your business mailing list and database.		
Summary and outcome	• What are the overall costs to exhibit including the stand, staff costs, the stock, advertising, travel, parking, accommodation, meals and drinks, including all the additional extras, and what are your predicted returns? • Have the full costs of exhibiting been accounted and budgeted for in your marketing plan • What are the outcomes for exhibiting at the event?		

space, lighting and the availability of additional benefits including advertising, promotional listings and inclusion of your business details on their website. Website advertising can then be linked to your business website and all your social media, along with the inclusion of your business details in the event literature and information packs.

If planning to exhibit at a trade event you need to plan well in advance and book your stand early, as many companies will book their stands automatically from one year to the next to get the most prominent, visible and select pitches at the best rates. Most trade event organisers promote their fairs and events extensively and advertise using the internet, the press, radio, TV, posters, banners, and as well as magazines, trade journals, the exhibition guide and other specialist brochures. Many event organisers offer an 'early bird' booking incentive with reduced rates, so if you intend to exhibit, book early, to get a prominent and well-positioned stand in the event and also negotiate the best deal.

Some trade fairs offer exhibitors further promotional opportunities, for instance, the opportunity to sponsor part of the event through the supply of promotional bags, pens, notebooks and other promotional freebies given to visitors on arrival. Banner advertising in prominent locations within the event directing visitors to your stand is another popular method of promotion, along with the opportunity to sponsor a prize if competitions are a feature of the event. These are all methods of marketing your business. In larger national and international events there is often PR support on offer and various exhibitor package levels available from the basic and standard level to competitive package levels with an assortment of additional pre-show promotion opportunities.

When designing and planning your exhibition stand consider the message and image you want to give, and what is within your budget. Consider the design of your stand, you may choose to use a modular system that is designed to be adaptable to the space, and therefore can be used again and again in various permutations. Whether you self build or employ a company to design your stand for you, the design needs to look professional and to stand out from the crowd in a positive way, making a great first impression. When designing the stand consider the time you will have to arrive, erect the stand and get everything ready for a prompt start to the event. Keep the stand simple in build, and consider weight, transportation, portability and safety.

Exhibiting at any trade show offers great networking opportunities. They can be great fun with lots of camaraderie between exhibitors and visitors. However, attending an event over several days can be exhausting physically and mentally, so make sure you are well prepared have some sort of seating on your exhibition stand for both staff and visitors, and security for locking up any personal belongings.

Fashion Shows

Similarly to exhibiting your business at a trade event, presenting a forthcoming collection at a fashion show offers a great opportunity to showcase your work with the all-important point of achieving sales. However, participating in and planning a professional fashion show is very expensive financially and involves endless hours of planning and preparation. You may be in a position to employ an event management company who offer complete packages for anyone looking for a visual production, be it the organisation of a catwalk show or product launch from finding the right venue, to front and backstage management including the design, production and distribution of all marketing materials, tickets and brochures.

Alternatively you may be planning to organise and manage a fashion show yourself with a team of helpers, and if so, you need to plan well in advance. Consider the location and booking of the venue, the catwalk, staging and the seating arrangements, the loan of chairs, backstage and front of house, dressing rooms, the lighting and sound, the music and any licenses required,

Bora Aksu – Spring/Summer 2015 backstage

the number of models, dressers, stylists and hairdressers required. Consider your marketing strategy, how, when and to whom are you going to promote the event? Are you going to charge for tickets and what are the booking arrangements?

Are you going to present all visitors with a brochure/and or a goody bag? Are you going to organise a VIP event and who are you going to invite? Consider the costings of the event, will you seek sponsorship and will all sponsors be promoted through marketing and promotional advertising and literature? How will you document the event; will you record it using photography, video? On a practical note, to protect and give you peace of mind, consider the health and safety implications, make sure all security and insurances required such as public, property and product are covered, ensuring you guard against all eventualities and risks at the event.

A Look Book to Launch a Collection

If you are a designer of fashion, textiles or accessories, the production and publication of a look book, presenting your forthcoming collection is an excellent means of promoting your latest work with the inclusion of professionally photographed, styed images that represent your brand. The images featured, whether studio shots or taken on location, should characterise the brand, as they can also be used in your marketing campaign and can be featured in magazines, posters, prints, adverts, postcards. Look books need to be individual and can be distributed and targeted at buyers, editors and the press, to your customers and potential clients.

When producing a look book, whether it is designed to promote a range of knitwear, lingerie or a diffusion range of separates or a range of textiles, consider the layout of the publication to gain maximum impact. If photographing any designs to be included, consider using a professional, and then always make sure the cost quoted is within your budget. Before agreeing and signing, check the contract carefully for details of copyright and ownership of the images. If you intend to design and plan the look book yourself, it is useful to complete a mock up version, drafting out the format, layout and the written and visual content page by page. Remember to add in your business contact details including website and your social networking links.

Publication of a Business Newsletter, E-newsletter or Bulletin

The publication of a regular newsletter, e-newsletter or bulletin may form part of your marketing campaign, and is an excellent way of informing customers and potential clients of your business. It will keep them up-to-date about new product developments, product launches, services and business news. Newsletters are relatively cheap to produce in-house using a simple home printer or alternatively produced using a printing firm. The newsletter can also be added to your blog and other social media sites. There are many newsletter templates available on the internet, along with the availability of software packages that are on the market. Most are relatively easy to use, allowing you to add text and also drop in photographic images. Keep your newsletters brief, focused and to the point. Once produced, the newsletter can be distributed via email or traditional post, but be aware of who you send it to, what you are trying to accomplish, and encourage any subscribers and readers to give you feedback.

Public Relations (PR)

Whether in print, online or by word of mouth it is essential to the success of your business to get the message out there in building a reputable brand that people recognise and trust; and as the Chartered Institute of Public Relations (CIPR) states 'Every organisation, no matter how large or small, ultimately depends on its reputation for survival and success', which is so true. PR is about forming good working relationships and building up excellent communication with the public, the media, investors and suppliers, and becoming known and recognised for the reliability and success of the brand. Successful PR is about receiving first-rate publicity and developing brand loyalty from existing customers and getting the right message across to strengthen and develop new business.

There are many established PR companies who offer services such as media relations, media services, and who are able to help with launches and event management. If considering using a company check out their services, competitiveness, their rates, and also their success stories. Due to costs, most start-ups develop their own PR campaign establishing strong links with local media and circulating company information by word of mouth, through customer reviews and contacts with the media.

Radio and Television Coverage

The media is a very fast paced and powerful industry, and it is useful to develop your networks to include journalists, editors and reporters. This will be helpful in building up good working relationships with the press to raise the profile of the business through regular media coverage and campaigns.

Journalists, editors and presenters are always on the search for newsworthy stories that capture the attention of the public, or stories that are linked to current, topical subjects and thought-provoking features which draw the attention of the listener and appeal to the masses.

If approaching a local, regional or national radio or television station for radio or TV reportage find out who is who, and what is the best way of contacting the relevant person, and also, what is the best show that is most suitable for your business, product or service. Consider your story, what do you want people to know and why is this information of importance or interest to the shows listeners, how does it fit in with the programme and what makes it unique and of interest.

Most radio station websites have details advising 'How to contact a presenter', a 'What's On' diary giving details of forthcoming activities and events. Many local and regional stations have online forms to complete to get your event advertised online and on the radio. If you have a future event or launch consider contacting the media to receive press coverage, have your details featured on their website, and invite the local radio and television to attend the event.

Awards and Competitions

There are many local, regional, national, and international industry-recognised awards established to celebrate and mark the success and achievements of businesses. Consider entering competitions and awards, for example local, regional and national business awards, specific design awards, and awards set up by specialist associations, which if successful gives recognition, and verifies the success and reputation of your business and your work, attracting media interest.

Many local and regional business groups give annual awards to businesses in recognition for their success and enterprise, offering various categories such as Successful New Business; Business Person of the Year; Training and Staff Development; Apprentice of the Year; Employee of the Year; Lifetime Achievement Award; Excellence in Business – Small/Medium Enterprises; Excellence in Business – Large Enterprise and Customer Service Award. Annual business events are usually held to present the finalists with their awards in recognition and to showcase their work and achievements, celebrating their business success, and usually receiving substantial media coverage. There are many awards and competitions well worth entering, See Section 5: The Information Directory for further information.

Social Media

'Whilst the essence of marketing remains unchanged (communicating a value proposition with the intention to promote or sell to a relevant audience) delivery channels evolve continually. Regardless of their size, businesses are still tasked with putting relevant marketing messages in front of the right audience, at the right time and in the right place. Increasingly, that place is 'digital' in nature with a message that is personalised, contextual and delivered in a way that customers can relate to. Mobile, social, responsive, immediate, user generated, measurable, relevant. This is the language of digital and the future of marketing'

Tom Gillman, Commercial Director, Crafted, Ipswich and London

The internet, if used efficiently, has opened up so many opportunities in today's busy economy. Most businesses in today's technological age need to have an online presence of some description whether it is for example, a website, a blog, a presence on twitter, Instagram, Google+ or LinkedIn. For instance, Twitter is a very popular network, used by millions of businesses today to report the on what's happening and giving news updates, adding small snippets - 'tweets' of business information.

Having a social media presence helps to inform the public and your customers of your latest business activities, keeping your business at the forefront of people's minds for the right reasons. It also helps to monitor the level of engagement, activity and the popularity of visitors to your social media sites. If using a social media platform as a marketing tool remember to ensure that all your business and product information is kept current, relevant and consistent.

Developing a Web Blog

Blogging is big business, and can be enjoyable and fun. For most businesses today, having a blog serves as a very valuable publishing platform and can act as an effective marketing tool. A blog can be used to deliver up-to-date business news and relevant stories, featuring and promoting new products and services. It can be invaluable in offering a discussion forum, and include archives of your past blogs, and incorporate photo diaries supported by exciting images and relevant video filming discussions. A blog should be inspirational to the reader, and if used well, it can be a very powerful and dynamic means to building the business brand. It can help tell your story and is excellent for forging new social links through contact with your customers, online communities and networks.

When designing and creating a blog, it is recommended that you select a domain name that links to your business. Domain names extensions include, for example, co.uk; .org.uk; ltd.uk; plc.uk, or a country of origin .fr for France. However, if you want to attract a global following, it is worthwhile to use .com, .net and .org names. Once you have selected your domain name, you then need to find a blog host or service provider. There are many providers available to choose from on the internet, for example, WordPress is a provider that is a leading web hosting service, hosting more than 320,000 domains to date. It has easy to follow instructions, and the basic start-up offers most essential features, and the service has an excellent reputation and good back-up support.

Other popular providers include Blogger, Live Journal, Serendipity, Square Space, Tumblr, and TyePad to name a few. Many are free with additional fees for services such as added customer support services, so research and read the online reviews to find the best provider for your requirements, that is easy to manage and that you can rely on and have confidence in. Select a provider that is user-friendly and, for example, if you are producing a very visual blog and need to include lots of images choose a blog template that is designed to allow you to showcase and upload lots of images when you publish it live.

Your blog can be linked to your website and other social media platforms such as LinkedIn, Twitter, Facebook and Flickr, allowing you to develop connecting links between all your social media activities forming part of your social media campaign. Good communication makes new contacts. The size of your network can make a real difference to the level of your success. There are many blogs out there, so check out some of the more popular blogs to understand and appreciate what makes them stand out from the crowd. When writing and developing a blog it's all in the detail. Make sure the content is well researched, interesting and engaging, appealing to the audience intended, with relevant, accurate and up-to-date posts.

Keep any written content concise and to the point, making it easy to read. The layout of your blog should be reader friendly, breaking up the text using headings and subheadings supported by great images making the blog visually exciting and encouraging the viewer to visit again. It is essential to regularly update your blog, adding new posts at least once a week. Many professional bloggers are known to add new posts every day, adding to the content, keeping the information fresh, new and interesting. Consider inviting regular guest writers, who are experts in their field to contribute and add articles, and write special features adding a further dimension to the content of your site. When writing a blog, check that all spelling and punctuation is accurate, and the style of writing is in keeping with the brand.

Blogging is big business in terms of what it can do in promoting a brand, and also in terms of additional potential income revenue that can be earned. Many sites advertise and promote other company's products and/or services, and in return receive commission on the web traffic visiting their site and often receive a percentage cut for the generation of sales. If you decide to include any advertising on your site then for any real results it ought to be relevant, responsible and integrate with your business, sending out the right message to all present and potential customers.

Further possibilities include opportunities to promote your ideas, work and business through the numerous fashion, textiles and lifestyle websites and blogs by contributing as a guest writer and adding links connecting to your business website or blog.

Keeping the internet fed with relevant, current content is vital if you want your business to stand out online. Creating (and maintaining) an active company blog is a great way to boost your natural search visibility, whilst conveying the personality of a brand and communicating, why the person reading your blog should be transacting with you.

Tom Gillman, Commercial Director, Crafted, Ipswich and London

Developing a Business Website

Having a business website is considered essential in today's competitive market and global economy. Many businesses sell exclusively online and other businesses receive a high percentage of online revenue from their website. Many businesses commission an expert to design and produce their website; however, if you are technologically savvy, and consider yourself able, there are lots of online website builders, offering website templates and design tools. Popular website builders include WIX, weebly, and Squarespace. However, there are many other website builders available that are easy to use and offer design flexibility, and are relatively inexpensive.

A good well-planned website builder will direct you step-by-step through the developmental stages, providing relatively easy-to-follow instructions, guiding you through the stages in designing and operating your own website. Most website builders allow you to design, construct and customise the site through the use of templates, with the addition of extra web pages, with further options such as the inclusion of online portfolios and videos. Some website builders offer full service packages, from design through to the management of your site including support in increasing your search engine optimization, as it useful to be able to measure the success of your site by the number of hits and feedback received. Measuring the success of your site is done by tracking the number of people who visit your site and the numbers tapping into any advertising campaigns. This provides important data as to the success of your site. To further increase the hits to your site consider adding links to your other social media accounts such as Twitter, LinkedIn and your blog, and also linking your brands website with other specialist blogs.

If you are selling online, there are also opportunities to add a store or shop window, showing images of your product or service, separating products into categories, and adding a shopping cart to take orders. For receipt of online payments on your business website consider integrating a PayPal system or a system for accepting credit card payments from customers.

There are many website training courses available online or alternatively offered at local colleges. Many courses are available offering technology and web design, teaching how to develop and build a website, create web pages using basic layout methods that include text, graphics and hyperlinks. Courses on offer usually cater for the beginner to the intermediate student, offering the chance to study and use programmes such as Dreamweaver, Photoshop, Fireworks and Flash CS, using industry standard software.

"Audio Visual medium facilitates the art of storytelling a product/brand via a combination of tone, colour and sound in the fourth dimension. Giving you the greatest chance to engage with a brain by utilising as many senses as possible with current technology"

By Omar Franco - Creative Director, Evocca College, Melbourne Area, Australia

Online Sites

There are many online sites where you can promote a business, product or service. These all vary but sites to look at include ARTS THREAD, Behance, The Crafts Council Directory, Designed in England, Design Nation and Not on the High Street. For example, Design Nation is a group which supports and promotes both new and established makers through their promotional database, listing their expertise and showcasing their work.

"Social Media, I believe has been largely misunderstood by marketers. The current dismal figures of Social Media Reach and Engagement prove that it is not just another "Broadcast" channel with tangible ROI. But rather it is a dialogue platform with direct connection to the engaged customer, one which effectively hands over some of the control of the Brand over to early adopters and the devout. It is a ruthless environment that does not flourish with the old conventional hype but spreads according to peer validation and timely trends."

By Omar Franco - Creative Director, Evocca College, Melbourne Area, Australia

Writing a Marketing Plan

To launch and promote a business or new product you need to think creatively and develop a marketing strategy. Getting your message out there is probably one of the most important aspects of your business and needs thorough planning. Writing and creating a marketing plan will help in coordinating all marketing and promotional activities, from day-to-day general marketing, for example updating all social media activities, to specific targeted marketing campaigns, listing calendar dates and deadlines. Most business start-ups have minimum finance available to spend. Therefore, you need your marketing strategy to be effective and within budget, making your money work to gain maximum returns in generating excellent publicity that is positive and reaps results.

A marketing plan should include the following:

Product/Service

A) Identification of the Product or Service

B) Analysis and Details of Your Competitors

Who are your competitors? Where are they located? What do they offer? How does your product/service differ from theirs? Identify your competitors and find out as much about them and their business as possible. Identify the USP of your product or service, which for example could be lower price for a similar service or the quality of what you offer in comparison to your competitor or the level of service supplied.

C) Identify Your Marketing Goals

In your marketing plan identify your short term and long term goals, defining what your business goals are by writing a mission statement. For example: I want to sell 2000 metres of fabric in six months and a total 5000 metres in a year. Year 2 - I want to receive repeat orders and double my turnover and profit. For a lingerie designer launching a new business and collection the business goals may be to launch two seasonal collections of lingerie in the first year, and for the collections to be sold in identified major high street stores and independents achieving a turnover of £xxxxxxx resulting in £xxxxxxxx profit. The mission statement of course needs to be calculated from a financial perspective in relation to your business and financial plan, retaining and increasing profits.

Once you know what the mission of your business is, the next stage is to define what your marketing strategy is going to be, to achieve your goals, defining how, when and what is the best way to target your customers. To be able to do this you need to research and understand the role of marketing and the different ways to market and promote your business product or service. For example, advertising works to promote some products but not all. Thorough knowledge of your market will help you to develop a strategic approach and to keep your marketing materials focused, relevant and up to date. This may include a range of methods of marketing including advertising, direct marketing and sales, editorial, letters, email, packaging, press releases, online advertising, social media marketing, and radio/television campaigns. Complete a SWOT analysis defining the Strengths, Weaknesses, Objectives and Threats of your plan.

D) Outline the Actions Needed to be Taken

Devise a marketing action plan with a time frame giving you a schedule to work to. For example, if you are a knitwear designer launching a new business and collection, actions may include

- To develop and launch a website promoting and selling the collection

- To produce a quarterly newsletter available online and also hardcopy for all clients and potential customers providing business updates about your latest collections, listing any events you are showing and attending.

- To launch the spring/summer collection at a national trade exhibition

- To contact and make appointments with buyers at specific high street outlets to discuss stocking the collection

E) Calculate the Marketing Costs

When producing or updating your business plan, always calculate how much you have available within your budget for your marketing activities, be realistic, as any expenditure should be carefully calculated and should result in financial returns.

F) Marketing, Sales and Tracking Results

To understand the success of your marketing goals, helping you to track results and understand what works and what doesn't, calculating the effectiveness of your marketing activities in attracting the necessary sales for your business to survive and grow. There are many different ways of doing this through coding on adverts and mailshots, website traffic, comments received on social media, online and offline sales, sales at events and trade shows, subscriptions to newsletters and network connections, which all forms data and knowledge to evaluate the success and give greater direction to your marketing activities. A great marketing plan will ensure you get the message out there.

Business Success

Focusing on the client, valuing your customers and the customer/client experience is essential to, and should be at the heart of any successful business, along with the credibility of the product or service. Think how you are going to provide good customer service, consider each business transaction, and how it is dealt with. For example, getting all orders out in time, and ensuring customers are informed of any delays immediately. Gain customer trust and belief in the business, so that your customers will return again and again. As we all know one of the best ways of promoting anything is word of mouth.

Useful Websites and Resources

Advertising Association
Website: www.adassoc.org.uk

Advertising Standards Authority (ASA)
Website: http://asa.org.uk

Arts Thread
Website: www.artsthread.com

Blogger
Website: www.blogger.com

Chartered Institute of Marketing (CIM)
Website: www.cim.co.uk

Companies House
Website: www.companieshouse.gov.uk

Direct Marketing Association (DMA)
Website: www.dma.org.uk

Direct Selling Association (DSA)
Website: www.dsa.org

Everywoman
Website: www.everywoman.com

Instaprint
Digital Printing and design services for business and promotional materials
Website: www.instaprint.co.uk

Market Research Society (MRS)
Website: www.mrs.org.uk

Moo
Business stationery and promotional materials
Website: http://uk.moo.com

National Business Register
Website: www.start.biz

National Enterprise Network
Website: www.nationalenterprisenetwork.org

4Networking
Website: www.4networking.biz

Nominet
Website: www.nominet.org.uk

One.Com
Website: www.one.com

Typepad
Website: www.typepad.com

Vistaprint
Website: www.vistaprint.co.uk

Weebly
Website: www.weebly.com

WordPress
Website: www.wordpress.com

Further Reading

Blick, Dee *The 15 Essential Marketing Masterclasses for Your Small Business.* Capstone 2013

Brown, Eileen. *Working the Crowd: Social Media Marketing for Business.* British Informatics Society Ltd (BISL), 2012 (2nd Edition)

Burton, B. *Life. Business. Just Got Easier,* Capstone, 2013

Cooper, Ian, *Financial Times Guide to Business Development: How to Win Profitable Customers and Clients.* Harlow: Financial Times/Prentice Hall, 2012

Everett, Judith C & Swanson, Kristen, K. *Guide to Producing a Fashion Show.* New York: Fairchild Books, 2013 (3rd Edition)

CIPR (Chartered Institute of Public Relations), Solis, B (Foreword by). *Share This Too: More Social Media Solutions for PR Professionals.* John Wiley & Sons, 2013

O'Reilly, Tim, & Milstein, S. *The Twitter Book.* Sebastopol, CA: O'Reilly Media Inc., 2012 (2nd Edition)

Townsend, Heather. *The Financial Times Guide to Business Networking: How to use the power of online and offline networking for business and personal success* (The FT Guides). Harlow: Financial Times Publishing International, 2014 (2nd Edition)

Bora Aksu collection on the catwalk. Autumn/Winter collection 2015
Photo credit: catwalking.com

Section 4

Expanding the Business

For any business to survive, grow and mature, requires in-depth understanding and knowledge of the business and market. Many businesses fail during the first two years due to concentration on the creative side of the business, developing the product and service, and have insufficient business acumen needed for the business to develop and grow.

When initially starting out, many will write a complex business plan, enthusiastically and creatively outlining their aims and objectives, marketing strategies, and complete a financial forecast. However, once the business is launched they concentrate on the creative elements of the business, which is only a percentage of the work required to succeed. They think about the business in the short term, but do not fully envisage and understand the importance of long term goals in building a substantial, financially viable and sustainable business – a business which has a real future.

Why grow the business?

Building the business is important in maximising turnover and profit, ensuring you meet your financial targets year on year to thrive and grow. As stated previously, many creative businesses have a great product or offer an excellent service but fail to understand the importance of the operational side of the business, but if this is managed well and you are ambitious, analytical and receptive in your thinking, and understand your market then the business will be successful rather than stagnate and fail. For a successful business, you need to be constantly reviewing existing markets, to be reactive, to be able to adapt to change, and be open to new opportunities to really appreciate the potential and the future of your business.

In today's global market place, businesses are constantly changing and developing due to economic factors, technological advancements and changes in trade within the industry. For example, a company making jeans from traditional blue vintage denim may have to reconsider their product, if demand for such denim exceeds supply; and therefore becomes too costly a product for the specific target market. The company may have to consider using an alternative fabric, and launch a seasonal brand-new collection, marketing the collection as a special edition range, or it may involve launching a completely new line or expanding the product or service range to attract new markets.

To develop and expand your business it may be a case of increasing your product range and/or service or diversifying into other areas, by looking for fresh opportunities which complement the existing business. This may involve growing and expanding your customer base by finding new markets or improving productivity levels and entering into the wholesale market, or entering an international market and exporting. Survival of a business may involve completely changing the direction of the business. The important point is to be able to analyse your market, review, and respond quickly to change. Most entrepreneurs are constantly thinking of new ideas, new products and new services, but the realism needs to be thought through. For success, you need to establish your brand with care and consideration, develop a reputation, and provide a high level of customer care to achieve trust amongst existing and future customers.

If the business is stagnating or failing, then to survive and prosper you have to adapt, change and evolve and be open to new opportunities, developing new markets to stimulate growth, As discussed in Section 3, marketing your business is essential to the enhancement of your brand, helping to improve and raise activities to increase your turnover. Along with the advantages of expanding the business, the pace of change, development and growth needs to be thought through and increased strategically at a manageable pace that allows for a sustainable level of growth to maintain the profitability of the business.

All successful companies regularly review and constantly update their business plan, whether this is through their annual review evaluating the management, marketing and financial structure and accounts of the business. The annual review should provide a full breakdown of the business performance. You may have a great product or service that is in demand but if you have incorrectly calculated production costs and your overheads are too high, then you have not got a sustainable business. It is not about turnover, but the profit. The business could grow in size, increasing the number of employees, and expand production, but if the profits stay the same then there are difficulties afoot.

Exporting

Due to the advent and power of the internet and social media platforms, many businesses are now gaining access to new markets and successfully expanding into a global economy. If you are planning to expand your business by exporting, there is information, help and advice readily available on the Government UK Trade and Investment (UKTI) website. Advice includes training and support for exporters providing help for new SME's who want to start exporting, providing insight and encouragement for business growth. The website also includes details of Government schemes, and the support available from International Trade Advisors to 'assess company's readiness for international trade, and start exporting'. Other advice available from the UKTI is assistance in researching new markets through their Export Marketing Research Scheme, their Overseas Marketing Introduction Scheme, and their Trade Show Access Scheme. If considering expanding into the export or import market, the UKTI website is well worth looking at, as it is informative, offering detailed reports and guides giving advice on export finance and insurance, transporting and shipping goods, and importing goods.

Finance

Ambitions for growth need to be calculated, developed and implemented alongside strategic business planning considering the short and long-term benefits. It is essential to be in control by understanding day-to-day cash flow of the business and awareness of budgets, bank statements and expenditure, saving money where possible, getting the best deals, negotiating costs, which in the long term will help you to develop a financially viable and successful business. With business growth extra finance is usually needed to help manage the cash flow to grow and expand the business. Expanding the business may entail investing in additional business equipment, such as buying a business car or van, upgrading manufacturing or IT equipment or it may mean employing more staff or specialist services.

Additional finance may be sought from family and friends or by applying for funding through a grant scheme that supports new and developing initiatives and projects such as the government initiative of the Growth Voucher Programme. Other options include applying for a traditional business loan from a bank or building society. If applying for a loan or overdraft you need to think about the risks associated with additional lending and how long you need the loan for. For example, financial investment can be ploughed into a business for the upgrade of equipment, the purchase of new stock, a marketing campaign, the making of new products, a new collection or range; however, you may not see the benefit or return on the investment for many months, which needs to be calculated into the financial forecast.

Look around and compare the best financial deals making sure you get the very best possible option that suits your cash flow needs. Look at the flexibility of pay back terms, the interest rates and any additional charges or penalties incurred for early repayments, as loan pay back terms need to be factored into your business accounts. Failure to pay back a loan or overdraft and defaulting on payments will lead to all sorts of problems including damaging your business reputation, and possible bankruptcy. The first few years of establishing a business are usually very difficult financially. However, they can be very rewarding, challenging and exciting, but do not expect huge pay-outs in salary during the first few years. To build a successful and sustainable organisation, any profits need to be invested and reinvested straight back into the business.

Investors

There is continued interest in investing in the Creative Industries from many different sources. For additional funding, consider applying for local financial support such as the Regional Growth Fund (RGF), an initiative established by the Department of Business, Innovation and Skills to support the local economies, or the Governments Start-Up Loans Finance Scheme, providing business loans and advice through their mentoring activities to startup businesses.

Besides the Government schemes, there are also many established networks of investors, who are interested and involved in programmes and associations to help new and developing businesses expand and grow. Investors are usually business experts who are able to provide specialist knowledge in the development of business planning, offering guidance and financial investment, and introducing new contacts with the aim of expanding the business further. In return the investor usually seeks a return on their investment within a set number of years. Many business partnerships are developed by pitching an idea to an investor and successfully continue to flourish and grow achieving great success.

Investors include groups and individuals, for example Angels Den, Find Invest and Grow (FIG) and Business Finance for You, along with many other groups who offer a resource of financial business support for both new and established businesses. Full details of Angel investing are given on the UK British Business Angels Association website, which also provides excellent details of the work of the Association, the Angel Investment market, and the key factors to consider. The website also gives details of the regulatory framework, formed to protect both the Angel investor and the entrepreneur, in addition to useful resources and links.

'Taking on an investor is like being married; choose your partners very carefully, as you may be with them for a very long time'.

Gary Assim – The Image Lawyer

Crowdfunding

Crowdfunding is a further way of raising capital for a business, project or venture. It is a means of generating money from a range of people who are interested in what you are promoting, and then choose to invest in the venture usually by means of the internet. Crowdfunding attracts investors who are interested in advertised projects or schemes, and as a consequence choose to invest into the venture. There are many crowdfunding sites to choose from that include Crowd Funder, Crowdrise, Funding Circle, Indiegogo, kickstarter, Rocket Hub, Seedrs, to name a few.

There are different types of Crowdfunding investment such as donation, where the investor will donate money out of pure interest in the project and in return receive updates about the project, samples of merchandise, or perhaps receive tickets to an event you are raising money for. For example, you may be raising money to exhibit and showcase your work at a fashion show which requires a large input of funds to pay the cost of hiring the venue, the catwalk, models and the development of a collection, music and the overall organisation of the event. Other crowd funding investments entail the outlay of finance, and if the project is successful the money is then returned with interest, or thirdly the investor is buying into the project through investment and in return receives shares. Details of each scheme are usually available on their individual websites, often with case studies of successful funded business stories, which make interesting reading.

Additional Training and Development of New Skills

To expand a business it may mean you need additional training to develop your expertise such as building up digital skills, or to employ staff or hire professional support in a specific area of expertise. For example, you may need the specialist skills of a web design developer, a computer programmer, an administrator to deal with orders and invoices and a technologist and sampler to produce a range of sample garments or accessories. Whatever it may be, in the long term it may save you money and time, and makes sense to employ specialist support. In business - time is money, and every hour is important. Many small companies tend to outsource work. Contracting work out to others is now considered a popular way of hiring assistance, for as many hours, as required, from one-off jobs to regular part-time support. Having additional support in the day-to-day running of the business is usually more efficient and cost effective, allowing you to concentrate and hone your specialist skills, whilst outsourcing other work to avoid turning it away due to insufficient resources.

Hiring a Virtual Assistant

Hiring a virtual assistant (VA) is a flexible and popular method of outsourcing work. Contracting work out on a freelance basis without the costs or legalities of employing someone on a part-time or full-time contract is particularly useful for small start-up businesses, when you need specific skills or general support and when money is at a premium. There are many professional self-employed freelancers who work as virtual assistants (VA's) offering their services such as general administration work, managing clients, handling accounts and bookkeeping. A VA usually charges an hourly or daily rate and can be employed through an agency or employed independently. Depending on the type of work, they are usually able to work anywhere in the country, as many VA's work from their home or independent offices, and work is usually organised and sorted out through phone calls, emails and skype. There are many independent virtual assistant agencies established in the UK, as advertised on the internet.

The Association of Virtual Assistants has a website with an online Directory of Virtual Assistants, listed county by county throughout the UK, and with some VA's located oversees. As the business grows and the work load increases, it may be more cost effective to employ someone on a fractional or full time contract who actually works alongside you in the office.

Recruiting Staff

Employing staff for the first time can be a huge learning curve. Finding the right staff to join you or a team can be difficult, but when recruiting new staff it is important to know exactly what you need and want from the employee. Before advertising, write out a clear job description outlining the roles and responsibilities of the position. List the main responsibilities, essential skills, the hours involved and the salary on offer. Draft out an advert listing the details of the position, requesting a letter of application, a full CV and contact details of their referees.

Many staff are recruited to small businesses through recommendations or by word of mouth. Other ways of recruiting staff include advertising the position online, on your business website and also on other online job websites where you can often advertise a position very reasonably or for free. Other places to advertise the post include your local paper, specialist trade journal or the local job centre, depending on the job role and the specialist skills required. Alternatively, many businesses choose to recruit staff using an established recruitment agency that is available to support you through the recruitment process.

Recruitment and Employment Agencies

Recruitment and employment agencies act as a resource matching up the employee with employer, and helping businesses find the right applicant for the job. Agencies usually deal with a wide range of contracts from permanent to temporary to contract staffing. A good agency will have industry expertise, and will be able to support the businesses in the recruitment process in finding the right person for the job. There are thousands of established recruitment and employment agencies throughout the UK that work across a range of industry sectors, and some with cross-sector expertise, working in areas such as Human Resources (HR), administration, retail and sales, and the media, digital and creative industries.

If considering using an agency, check out the agency making sure they have a reputable background. Check who they recruit for, and what industry sectors they specialise in, their fees, and most importantly if they abide by the government guidelines for employment agency rules, restrictions and responsibilities. Guidance is available on employment agencies and business on the government website: www.gov.uk/employment-agencies-and-businesses.

If searching for a job, many recruitment agencies can be helpful by offering valuable careers advice, and guidance. Agencies are always seeking out potential applicants for various posts. A good agency will have a vigorous approach to interviewing potential candidates, checking their details before adding them to their books and adding their CV to their database. Many recruitment and employment agencies offer other services that include careers advice and guidance, training, consultancy and 'job boards' – the advertising of jobs on the agency's website.

Employing New Staff

After the interview and before employing a new member of staff always check the interviewees references from either their previous employer or a person of standing who has worked in a professional position such as a teacher, a lecturer or project supervisor.

If you are expanding and employing staff you need to consider the employment laws and legal implications from the written contract and employer's liability, including the employee's right to work in the UK, as if not, this could result in huge fines. One of the best sources of information is the Gov.Uk portal, which provides full guidelines and details, from recruitment, hiring and employing staff and apprentices, to contracts of employment and working hours.

Interviewing and Appointing New Staff

When interviewing and appointing new staff to join your team, you need to be fully aware of the aims and aspirations of the business. For an effective team, employees need to be committed, enthusiastic, loyal and trustworthy. They also need to understand what their role will be, how their role fits in with the team dynamics, and what skills they bring to the business. Clear parameters within working teams help to build a skilled work force who are able to work together with adaptability, flexibility and efficiency.

For success, and a happy, supportive work environment, employees need to feel they belong, that they have something to offer, and are recognised for their work. Each person in a team needs to have full understanding of how their position fits into the bigger picture. They need to understand the aims and objectives of the business, where all employees are working together towards the same goal. There are only so many hours in a day, and as a founder of a business you will need to concentrate on what the business is all about, making business decisions. Therefore, it is essential that you are able to delegate and trust people, and to rely on employees expertise.

If employing staff, look at the management structure within the business, and question the feasibility of it. Does the present structure offer an efficient, supportive and motivated working environment? Is there a mentoring scheme in place to help and support new employees in settling in to the company and in understanding their role? Investment in staff training for employees to learn and develop new skills is a great motivational factor for most people in understanding that the business is prepared to invest money in further training and their personal development. Businesses need employee's skills to develop and grow with the organisation in line with the future needs and productivity of the business to manage business growth.

Apprenticeships

Many employers are now taking on apprentices on schemes that are giving the apprentice the opportunity to study a trade. This provides the apprentice with on-the-job training, real work-life experience, improving their career prospects, combined with study and the development of new skills that help to support the needs of the business. The National Apprenticeship Service aims to help and guide employers through the process of employing an apprentice, and has full guidelines 'Employing an Apprentice', and 'Building an Apprenticeship programme', available on the services website.

Internships

Consider offering a paid internship to an undergraduate or recent graduating student. Paid internships are usually considered as voluntary positions, and can last for anything from a few weeks to a year. A well-managed, supportive internship can be an excellent way for an intern to gain valuable insight and work experience into the world of work, enhancing their future job prospects or possibly leading to offers of permanent or paid work. If you are considering offering an internship it is important to establish that it is a genuine voluntary position, clearly defining the parameters of the role, the legalities, what costs you are going to cover, and identify what the benefits are to the intern and your responsibilities as a business employer. It is worth looking at the guidelines 'Employment rights and pay for interns' available on Gov.UK.

Business Success

Whatever you choose to do, and however large your business grows, never lose sight of the aims and objectives of the business; know where you are going and the purpose and motivation as to why you established the business in the first place. There are going to be disappointments along the way, things that don't go as well as you hoped and planned, but learn from the challenging times and gain experience. Many very successful companies have sprung up from business failure, but the difference between the average person setting up a business and the entrepreneur is that the entrepreneur never gives up, but adapts and experiments until the business model and venture is thriving and becomes a success. Business success is about perseverance, hard work and knowing when to ask for help, knowing when to delegate, being courageous, adaptable, resourceful and understanding about the potential of the business, it is about having dreams and fulfilling them.

Debbie MacBeattie – Founder and Managing Director, ROC Recruitment and temps - online Ltd

Debbie MacBeattie is founder and Managing Director of ROC Recruitment (the trading name for MacBeattie Recruitment Ltd) and Temps-online Ltd. ROC Recruitment is a traditional recruitment agency established in 1991, whilst Temps-online is an internet based business. Debbie started out in business with very little funding and she was in no doubt, the business had to make money from day one and it did! Through hard work, determination and belief in her venture she secured serviced offices in South Moulton Street, London and started ROC Recruitment, which has grown into a very successful award winning business.

The agency works with a range of organisations, from world-class companies to private individuals, working across a variety of sectors and job roles. The company specialises in a wide range of areas include administrative and support, personal and executive assistants, retail executive, area and regional managers, head office and operations, retail store management and sales, brand communication, marketing, buying and merchandising, including retail E-commerce along with other industry sectors. Through a strong work ethic, commitment and determination, and a thorough knowledge of the market, Debbie has established a fantastic international client base, and remains very involved in the day-to-day running of the business still today.

Debbie's accomplishments have been acknowledged through receipt of many national and international awards. In 2002, she represented Britain at the British Association of Women Entrepreneurs (BAWE), and was also a runner up in the Women Entrepreneurs of the World at FCEM (Les Femmes Chiefs D'Enterprises Mondiales) in St Petersburg, Russia receiving worldwide recognition for her work. This Association which has a network of five million members from the five continents, brings together like-minded women 'in solidarity and friendship', and who share a common interest in entrepreneurship, so this was a fantastic achievement. Further details of ROC Recruitment and temps-online Ltd can be viewed on the website: www.roc.co.uk

An Interview with Debbie MacBeattie

What inspired you to establish your own recruitment agency?
I was working for a company that went into liquidation, and I had previously worked in the recruitment industry, so using my previous knowledge; I decided to set up my own recruitment agency. My mission was to build a profitable business and to deliver an excellent service to our clients and candidates.

How important has networking been to the development and success of MacBeattie Recruitment Ltd?
Networking is very important to the business in building relationships and also in helping to develop our reputation. Many of our candidates have become our clients, due to establishing a high level of integrity and trust.

What are the benefits to a business of using an external recruitment agency to recruit new staff?

Recruiting new staff is a time consuming process and it is a costly resource for any business. A good recruitment agency will offer an increasing range of technology, methodology and an array of different tools and databases, as we deal with over 5000 candidates a year. We also have a whole myriad of resources and networks, to understand the requirements and recruit the right candidate to the role.

What advice would you give to a new business that is considering expanding their enterprise and recruiting new staff to join their team?

When recruiting new staff keep your costs very tight, be very clear about defining roles and how they can be managed.

What are the general costs of using recruitment agencies to find and recruit new staff?

The cost of using a recruitment agency is calculated on a percentage of the employee's annual salary.

How do companies maximise their success in recruiting the best candidates?

In recruiting the best candidate, it is important to have a very clear job specification, and a robust interview process. This may involve one interview or up to five interviews, comprising of meetings and interviews with HR, the Director, Management and various teams. Usually multiple interviews and presentations are required by the more discerning the brand are in challenging the process to get the right candidate.

In 1997 Roc was the 87th fastest growing business in the UK, and today after 24 years in business your success continues, what is the secret behind your continuous success?

Hard work, resilience, determination and tenacity.

Do you believe there is a pattern, a formula to becoming a successful entrepreneur?

I think there are definite traits in individuals who become successful business people. They usually have many similarities such as their ambitions, their leadership skills, their creativity and they are pioneering in their ideas, but of course this depends on the type of business.

What has been your greatest career challenge to date?

Surviving the last 5-6 years due to changes in business, and also the collapse of Lehman's and having to cut costs, but ROC Recruitment has still continued to grow and develop. In a recession it is always a good time for a business to grow.

What is your proudest achievement in business to date, and why?

In 1997, I received a Sunday Times/Virgin Atlantic Fast Track Award and was the 84th fastest growing company in the UK, but all things in business are important to me. I am particularly proud when ROC receives recognition from people who really value our services and the support we provide.

Debbie, you successfully founded and have run your own business from zero to a turnover of £13.5 million plus; what advice would you give to someone who is just starting out in business today?

You cannot afford to go into business idealistically. Business is a continuous challenge, and you must allow for unforeseen costs. To be successful, you must be intuitive, and think and plan ahead. If you don't enjoy it, there's no point in it. You must be good at what you do, believe in what you do and enjoy what you do, and you will be successful.

Trend forecasts Spring/Summer 2016

Jaana Jätyri -
Founder and CEO of the Trend Forecasting Agency Trendstop and Publisher of fashion TrendTracker app.

Jaana Jätyri is Founder and CEO of the specialist trend forecasting agency Trendstop. com, a leading global fashion and creative lifestyle agency founded in 2002. The Agency offers a range of products and services to its clients. These range from trend analysis and reports, live briefings, trend presentations, inspirational workshops to hands-on trend consultancy which focuses on increasing the sales of fashion collections to specific target audiences. Her clients include Ralph Lauren, Hugo Boss, L'Oréal, Diesel, Asos, H&M, Topshop, Next, Peek & Cloppenburg and many other leading retailers, brands and suppliers.

Jaana is highly focused in her work, providing directional information on colour, branding and future trends to the industry. Her company Trendstop.com specialises in fashion trend forecasting and trend translation, womenswear, menswear, kidswear, colour, print and graphics, accessories, footwear, knitwear, lingerie, denim, home, stationery, early consumer inspiration for marketing and communications, and trend buying direction.   Jaana is also the publisher of the fashion TrendTracker™ ap. developed for mobile phones and tablets, which she developed for all fashionistas; fashion bloggers, designers, buyers, journalists, retailers and creative industry professionals, to read and learn about new international trends with runway photos and video galleries. For further details of Trendstop; TrendTracker and Jaana's work see Twitter and Pinterest: @jaanajatyri   @trendstop   Instagram: @jaana_trendforecaster

An Interview with Jaana Jätyri, CEO Trendstop.com

WOMENSWEAR INSIGHTS
S/S 2016

trendstop
Trend forecasts you can trust.

ANGULAR

SHARP & SCULPTED

TONAL STYLING

You are the founder and CEO of trend forecasting agency Trendstop, what inspired you to establish your own trend forecasting agency?

I moved to London from my native Finland when I was 19 years old. I always wanted to work as a fashion creative. I graduated from Central Saint Martins with a first class honours degree in Fashion Design with Marketing, and fell in love with digital fashion, which was very new then in the 90s. I set up a digital design consultancy creating fashion CAD libraries for the industry. My first clients were Marks & Spencer and River Island. As my clients began asking for advice on next season's styles, I started developing runway based CAD libraries, and more in-depth research into fashion trend influences. Trendstop was launched in 2002.

Did you have a specific vision for the business?

My vision is to show companies how through a thorough understanding of the trend consumer, combined with the appropriate trend translation for the target audience, companies can increase their sell-through and full price sales. You can read more about this in my book Translating Trends into Profits (Oct 2015). I also love to inspire people, and show how inspiration and sellability can co-exist.

What is your greatest career challenge to date?

There can be certain challenges in getting the creative and commercial departments in companies to understand trends on the same level. We in fact offer trend training courses to educate retail staff on how the trend cycles and trend timing work.

Another issue is the current over-saturation of 'trends' in the market. – As anyone can set themselves up as a commentator. Various magazines, blogs and sites have flooded the industry with unreliable trends lacking in validation, which can lead to confusion in the trend decision making process in businesses.

As founder of Trendstop, how do you balance the creative and commercial side of the business?

We take a lot of pride in our creative vision, but considering the commercial reality is the cornerstone of our work. Once we have analysed and creatively explained the most relevant trends coming through for a season, we then track each of those trends to ensure our predictions are spot-on for our clients, following development from initial conception all the way to the retail floor.

Why is trend forecasting important and how can it help in building a successful fashion/textile business?

If a business lacks knowledge on what their target consumer will want to buy e.g. 18 months from now, and how to deliver it to them, there will be waste somewhere in the business, in terms of time, money, resources and retail sell-through. As the consumer is becoming increasingly trend aware, and even trend driven; fashion retail is becoming more and more competitive and fast paced, it is therefore vital for companies to have the right trend information so they are aware of future trends ahead of time, and have the right tools to turn trend concepts into business returns.

Is there anything about your role as a trend watcher and translator of trends that has surprised you?

In my travels around the world, I often come across new developments in fashion that are unexpected and inspiring – that's the beauty of working in trends, as we're always looking to the future. In business terms, it is still surprising how little trends are sometimes understood in the industry.

What do you attribute to your success?

I have a vision for trend, throughout my life and career I have been able to hone my skills as a trend forecaster. I have a wonderful team of seasoned industry experts and trend spotters around the globe to help realise that vision, and we have amazing clients and partners who are truly a pleasure to work with. As with everything in business, nothing comes without hard work and a bit of good luck along the way.

What advice would you give to someone who is considering setting up their own business in the Fashion and Textile industry today?

If you believe in something and you are truly good at it, aim to be the best and don't give up. With a positive attitude and a good effort you will get there. If you are not able to do everything yourself, why not look for partners or collaborators who can help you and benefit from what you offer.

Bora Aksu

Bora Aksu, the London based Turkish designer graduated from Central St Martins MA in 2002, and was hailed as 'the star of the show' by The Daily Telegraph, the Guardian and The Independent. Success continued, and in 2003 he was awarded sponsorship from the ARG Group allowing him to make his debut off-schedule show at London Fashion Week. Due to the success of this show he received a New Generation Award (NEWGEN) from the British Fashion Council, which placed him on the official London Fashion Week schedule for the next season, and due to his continued success he remains on the official London Fashion Week schedule up to this day.

Bora rarely gives interviews, concentrating on his work as a designer. He is renowned and well respected in the industry for his commitment and dedication to fashion, as illustrated in 2012, when he was presented with Designer of the Year at the Flle Style Awards, Turkey, and he was also Invited to join the judging panel of the WGSN Global Fashion Awards. Bora has gained international recognition for his work with his collections selling around the globe, with stockists in Bahrain, China, Hong Kong, Istanbul, Italy, Japan, Kuwait, Lebanon, Rome, Saudi Arabia, Singapore and Taiwan. To view Bora's latest collections visit the Bora Aksu website: www.boraaksu.com

Bora Aksu collection 'A Dancer with Wings',
Spring/Summer 2015

Bora Aksu collection Spring/Summer 2015

An Interview with Bora Aksu

You have been incredibly successful in your work, what do you attribute to your success?

I think being able to do what I love is the most crucial thing; I never thought that I would do something that I would love and be successful. Since a young age I have always had a secret admiration for fashion, and as a child my starting point was my raw drawing ability, and through my illustrations, I found doors opened to my imaginary world. I think my initial fashion ideas came from people around me; my mum, my family and observing their attitudes and the way they dressed, and I wanted to almost capture this. It was the time when I realised that fashion was much more to me than just drawings or fabrics or clothes, and I discovered the amazing link between 2D drawings to 3D garments. This transformed my thinking, which I found almost magical in a good way. Once I made the decision to study fashion, I moved to London to study at Central Saint Martins (CSM) on the BA and MA. Once you have a direction in life, everything falls into place really quickly.

What's the concept behind the Bora Aksu label?

I am an incurable romantic and my aim as a designer is to seek and define beauty in my own terms. Fashion design for me is a visual language that enables me to communicate with the outside world. Being a good designer you need to learn the subject from A to Z to understand the whole process of pattern cutting, and also how to use fabrics, but this involves more than just technical training. The way you execute an idea is the most important part and this can't be resolved with just paper and pencil, it needs a hands on approach.

My design language is brought to life through experimentation and imagination through the ability to cut the cloth to produce abstract and complex shapes. The fabric choice in the drape, texture and colour ultimately influences my designs, helping to translate ideas into actual garments. Each fabric works differently under the needle, each pleat or ruffle falls a certain way depending on how you drape it on the dress form. My ideas are moulded, altered and manipulated into designs. This is an important process that takes personal consideration and can make or break a garment, and being a perfectionist requires tireless effort to improve a design. At times I have draped directly onto a person and this has resulted in accidental design ideas, which has been at the heart of some of my most important work.

What are the main influences when designing and where do you get your inspiration from?

Anything or anyone can be an inspiration, I don't have any boundaries. Even though at times I had no money I was surrounded by inspiration - you need to be able to make something beautiful out of nothing. With fluid materials, I create three-dimensional structures that define my creativity. Whether it's the past or the present, all my ideas come from what's going on around me: the city where I live and also the city I came from has a huge impact on my creativity. Where you live and what you see on a daily basis is necessary for inspirational reference, which I try to use as a 'tool' instead of a 'crutch'. As soon as an idea comes to mind I I sketch it out. When you mix ideas there is this ethnic quality, mixed with a spiritual vibe. I think it's very inspiring to work with people from different creative fields, as this can give a totally fresh approach in the development of great ideas.

Bora Aksu collection on the catwalk, Autumn/ Winter 2015. Photo credit: catwalking.com

What support did you have, and did you seek any advice in setting up the business?

London Fashion Week and London Fashion are known for new and exciting talent. The fashion colleges play an important part in this process and Central St Martins (CSM) is a powerful force. Studying on the MA at CSM, under the Louise Wilson umbrella gave me total realisation of "what you are all about" concept. This was a time to find my true self and express my design identity. After the graduation show, which I believe was a turning point in my life, I received a sponsorship award. This helped finance my first off schedule show, and I was then presented with the New Generation Award, which I received four consecutive times, presented by the British Fashion Council. The BFC has been a great supporter, and for this I am truly thankful, and it has totally helped me to be securely rooted in the fashion industry.

What was the most difficult part in establishing your own fashion label?

The sponsorship award I received supported the financial aspect of starting my fashion label, but on the other hand, I was not prepared or sufficiently equipped to set-up my own label in a business sense. After my first fashion show; I received orders from Japan; Hong Kong and London, and I actually had no idea how to produce them. This was a hard time for me, I had to either carry on or find a way to complete the orders or give up totally. Even though it was hard I managed to produce the orders with help from friends. It was almost like learning how to swim in the ocean. I wouldn't recommend it to anyone.

What is your proudest achievement in your work to date?

I find receiving awards a humbling experience. In 2010 I was invited to Buckingham Palace to meet the Queen, and receive thanks for my contributions to the British fashion industry; this was a big highlight in my career. In 2012, I met the Queen again when I designed and exhibited a special dress for the Queen's Jubilee celebration. These are all very priceless experiences, but most importantly is my design ability and the privilege of nurturing this gift. I think we are all born with different gifts, but I guess it is up to us whether we nurture these gifts, keep them or abandon them. When your gift becomes a passion you don't even think of it because you can't help doing it. I guess that was the case for my fashion design path. I love it so much that I don't know how I would feel without it. For me this is the biggest achievement. I think it's a blessing in life to be able to do what you love and I wouldn't change it for anything.

How many collections do you produce a year, and where do you show?

Right now we produce four main collections presented through catwalk shows at London Fashion Week twice a year, and then we present pre and resort collections in a showroom.

What is the future vision of your work?

My design world is my own cocoon, so it's always very personal. For me opening my own store is the ideal way to present this personal world, so that is my ultimate future plan.

What advice would you give to someone who is considering setting up their own fashion label?

There is a lot to say, but most importantly knowing the fact that fashion design is not a job that you can do during working hours; it is a life-long commitment that runs in a designer's blood. Understanding this commitment is one of the reasons why you need to love what you do, otherwise it's impossible not to burnout.

Wayne Hemingway (MBE)

Wayne and Gerardine Hemingway at home   *Red or Dead, Autumn/Winter collection 1994*

Wayne Hemingway (MBE) is a multi-talented, award winning designer of fashion, interiors, graphics and products, a writer, columnist, educator and entrepreneur, public speaker and lifestylist. He launched his first business in the early 80s, selling clothes on Camden Market, with his then girlfriend, now wife Gerardine. This formed the foundations of the fashion label Red or Dead. The success of the label was recognised, receiving such accolades as Street Style Designer of the Year Award, for three consecutive years 1996, 1997 and 1998, presented by the British Fashion Council. They also showed at London Fashion Week for over 20 years, and had 23 shops worldwide achieving international acclaim.

In 1981, Wayne and Gerardine established HemingwayDesign, an award winning, multi-disciplinary design agency, specialising in affordable and social design. They work on projects from founding and organising public festivals, regeneration and housing to their ventures involving fashion, graphics, interiors and products for the home, such as the surface view murals and canvasses, Hemingway haberdashery to 'stuff for your bathroom', and to museum design. The company is now led by two generations of the Hemingway family and a wider team of talented designers. Renowned for their entrepreneurship, they have built brands from Red or Dead to the Vintage Festival; the Classic Car Boot Sale; The Festival of Thrift; Hemingway Digital; Land of Lost Content and ShackUp; KiosKiosk.

After successfully selling their iconic brand Red or Dead in the late 1990s, HemingwayDesign has embarked on an extraordinary journey working on urban design projects with housing providers. They have worked designing and developing affordable and socially responsible housing. Acknowledgment for both Wayne and Gerardine's commitment to design as creative visionaries and educators has been recognised through numerous awards and honours. These have included the receipt of Honorary Senior Fellowships from Regent's University London, and MBE's for services to design. In 2014 Wayne was awarded the UCL Entrepreneurial Alumnus of the Year Award for the impact he has made using his business skills in the development of Red or Dead, Vintage and HemingwayDesign, and the impact that HemingwayDesign has made on the wider society.

Wayne has made an exceptional contribution as a visionary, a designer, a business man and social entrepreneur. He is a board member on Creative Lancashire, the Design Council Trustee Board and the Design Council CABE Committee. He is someone who wants to develop and improve things, and who is aspirational in his work striving to enrich the quality of life. For further information of the work of HemingwayDesign visit their website: www.hemingwaydesign.co.uk

The Staiths South Bank on the banks of River Tyne, Gateshead

An Interview with Wayne Hemingway

You have been incredibly successful in all business, what do you attribute to your success?

Two people getting together, working together, having a vision and enjoying ourselves in our work. Gerardine is inspirational to work with and is always buoyant. We are both very hardworking and we love a challenge. Gerardine and I couldn't have done it without each other.

When you first started out in business did you have a specific vision for the business and Red or Dead?

We wanted to stay true to our roots, to stay affordable, improve on what's has been before, and just enjoy it.

On reflection would you have done anything differently at the onset of your business?

No, we have had lots of fun; we always have lots of ideas, and have always enjoyed working together as a team.

What are the most important attributes of people you work with?

In our work we have always surrounded ourselves with good people who care about getting a job done and have pride in what they do.

What kind of culture exists at HemingwayDesign?

HemingwayDesign has a culture that is decent, the business is not just about making money, but thinking and understanding the end user. Everyone is encouraged to take a lead and allowed to question ideas.

With the business continually growing and developing, how do you stop yourself becoming too distant from the creativity which appears central to HemingwayDesigns?

It is important that we make sure any partners we work with, such as manufacturers are excellent, allowing us to concentrate and get on with our work.

You have worked in design from fashion with Red or Dead, to vintage festivals and to urban housing developments, what is your most enjoyable project to date?

We have enjoyed it all, but our work involving urban housing has been very exciting. The development at Staiths South Bank involved the design and development of approximately 760 homes, which were built by George Wimpey City on the banks of River Tyne, Gateshead. This collaboration involved lots of research, discussion, planning and persuasion, working with architects and builders. Feedback from the residents has been a great accolade to the success of the project.

On a final note, what advice would you give to someone who is setting up in business today?

Be brave, follow your instinct, and never be afraid to ask for advice, make friends along the way, and always keep evolving.

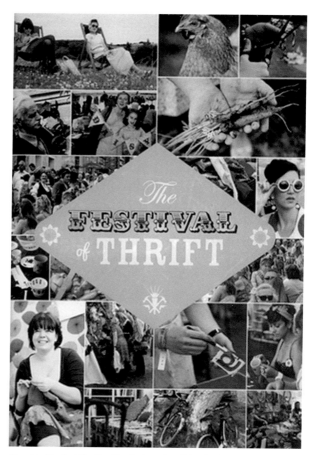

The Festival of Thrift – the first national festival celebrating everyday living with upcycling, recycling and sustainable living, founded by HemingwayDesign

The Land of Lost Content is the world's largest archive of 20th century popular culture, founded by HemingwayDesign

Useful Websites and Resources

Agency Workers and Employment Agencies
Website: www.nidirect.gov.uk/index/information-and-services/employment/
understanding-your-work-status/agency-workers-and-employment-agencies

Apprenticeships
www.apprenticeships.gov.uk

Arts and Business
Website: http://artsandbusiness.bitc.org.uk

British Chambers of Commerce (BCC)
Website: www.britishchambers.org.uk

Business Growth Service
Website: www.gov.uk/business-growth-service

Creative Choices
http://ccskills.org.uk

Find Invest Grow (FIG)
Website: www.findinvestgrow.com

Growth Voucher Programme
Website: www.gov.uk/apply-growth-vouchers

Homeworking Guidance for Employers
Website: www.hse.gov.uk

Investors in People (IIP)
Website: www.investorsinpeople.co.uk

National Apprenticeship Service
Website: www.apprenticeships.gov.uk

The National Council for Work Experience (NCWE)
Website: www.work-experience.org

The Recruitment and Employment Confederation (REC)
Website: www.rec.uk.com

The UK Association of Virtual Assistants
Website: www.ukava.co.uk

UK Business Angels Association
Website: www.ukbusinessangelsassociation.org.uk

UK Trade and Investment
Website: www.gov.uk/government/organisations/uk-trade-investment

Further Reading

Aldridge, Jacqueline & Derrington, A, M, *The Research Funding Toolkit: How to Plan and Write Successful Grant Applications.* SAGE Publications Ltd, 2012

Buckingham, *Christopher, Crowdfunding Intelligence: The Ultimate Guide to Raising Investment Funds on the Internet.* London: LID Publishing, 2015

Mullen, M & Petrie, D, *The Business Finance Guide for Business Growth: A Journey from Start-up to Growth.* British Business Bank and ICAEW, 2014

Traynor, Tom, *The Directory of Grant Making Trusts.* Directory of Social Change, 2014 (23rd Revised edition)

Fashion and Textile Information Directory

Behrens & Sons, Manchester shippers' ticket. Manchester textile merchants used pictorial trademarks for their export products. These trademarks relied on pictures more than words so that they would be recognisable regardless of language or literacy. Courtesy of the Museum of Science and Industry.

Fashion and Textile Information Directory

Welcome to the **Fashion and Textile Information Directory,** which provides an excellent resource listing over 1000 references offering contacts for support, services and opportunities. Whether you are a new business start-up that wants to expand, a student, a graduate, lecturer or just have a love of fashion and textiles, you will find many interesting and relevant resources in this section.

Content

Business Advisory and Support Services

Exhibition Organisers

Fashion, Textiles and Associated Exhibitions and Trade Fairs - UK

Grants, Awards, Finance and Funding Opportunities

Legal Support

Museums, Research Centres, Collections and Galleries

Organisations, Guilds, Networks and Associations

Recruitment Agencies and Services

Trend Forecasting Services and Consultancies

V&A Fashion Gallery (c) Victoria and Albert Museum, London.
Courtesy of the Victoria and Albert Museum, London

Business Advisory and Support Services

The following contacts listed in this section provide a range of useful business advisory and support services from business legislation, to consumer rights and issues, business networks, financial services and much more. Take advantage of the services available, as there is so much information, advice and support to access for new and growing businesses.

ACID (Anti Copying in Design)

ACID is 'a membership trade organisation for designers, to prevent plagiarism in the design and creative industries, supporting members to understand and protect their rights'.
ACID (Anti Copying in Design) Ltd
Email: help@acid.uk.com   Website: www.acid.uk.com

The British Chambers of Commerce (BCC)

The British Chambers of Commerce (BCC) is an independent business network with Chambers across the UK. See the BCC website for details of local Chambers, business services, networking opportunities, events and news.
The British Chambers of Commerce. (London Office). 65 Petty France, London, SW1H 9EU
Website: www.britishchambers.org.uk

British Council

The British Council is the UK's international organisation for cultural relations and educational opportunities. The Council has a superb website that provides details of the Council's work in the Arts (Department of Architecture, Design, Fashion (ADF); the Creative Economy; Cultural Skills and Visual Arts); UK and International projets; residencies; resources; funding opportunities; global connections and much more.
British Council.
Tel: 0161 957 7755
Email: general.enquiries@britishcouncil.org   Website: www.britishcouncil.org/arts

British Exports Association (BExA)

The British Exporters Association (BExA) is an independent national trade association representing the interests of the export community. Visit BExA website for further details.
British Exports Association (BExA)
Website: www.bexa.co.uk

British Fashion Council (BFC)

The British Fashion Council (BFC) is committed to 'developing excellence and growth in a sector that is a significant contributor to the British economy'. They have a comprehensive website providing details of the Council's services, along with the BFC Directory of contacts, and info on Designer Business Support, NewGen, NewGen Men, the Fashion Trust, the BFC Education Foundation and education support. Other information includes the latest in Fashion business news, a fashion calendar and much more providing the very latest facts and reportage relating to British Fashion.
British Fashion Council (BFC)
Website: www.britishfashioncouncil.co.uk

Business in the Community

Business in the Community is the 'Prince's Responsible Business Network'. Members work together to tackle issues that are vital to creating a fairer society and a more sustainable future. Visit their website for membership details, services, programmes and resources.
Business in the Community. (Head Office). 137 Shepherdess Walk, London, N1 7RQ
Tel: 020 7566 8650
Email: info@bitc.org.uk   Website: www.bitc.org.uk

Business Design Centre

The Business Design Centre was 'the UK's first integrated trade, exhibition and conference centre and hosts over 80 exhibitions and 250 conferences every year'. Exhibitions include: New Designers, London

Art Fair, Country Living Fairs and the Gadget Show Live. It also houses over 100 businesses who occupy the offices and showrooms within the Centre.
Business Design Centre. 52 Upper Street, Islington, London, N1 0QH
Tel: 0207 288 6272
Email: benp@bdclondon.co.uk Website: www.businessdesigncentre.co.uk

Business Franchise Association (bfa)
The British Franchise Association (bfa) acts in the interests of the industry as a whole in assessing and accrediting franchising companies. Visit the bfa website for details of the bfa, membership, the Associations guidelines for joining a franchise and franchising your business, and details of forthcoming bfa-accredited franchise exhibitions.
British Franchise Association (bfa). 85f Park Drive, Milton Park, Abingdon, OX14 4RY
Tel: 01235 820470
Website: www.thebfa.org

British Gateway of Scotland
Business Gateway of Scotland is a publicly funded service providing access to support and advice to businesses in Scotland. Visit the Gateway's website for details of local offices, workshops and events, online support, news and services. They also offer a range of excellent Business Guides.
British Gateway of Scotland
Tel: 0845 609 6611
Website: www.business.scotland.gov.uk

British Private Equity and Venture Capital Association (BVCA)
The BVCA is the 'industry body and public policy promoter for the private equity and venture capital industry in the UK'. See the BVCA website for further information on the Associations activities and membership details.
British Private Equity and Venture Capital Association (BVCA)
Email: bvca@bvca.co.uk Website: www.bvca.co.uk

British Standards Institute (BSI)
The BSI is the business standards company whose main activities involve the production of standards and the supply of standards-related services. See the BSI website for details of developing standards, training, certification and verification, supply chain solutions, events and international projects.
British Standards Institute
Email: cservices@bsigroup.com Website: www.bsigroup.co.uk

The British Library Business and IP Centre
Founded in 2006, the Business and IP Centre at the British Library supports businesses, entrepreneurs and inventors develop their organisations working across a range of industry sectors. Services on offer include business advice, support and free business resources. Visit the Centre's website for details of services, resources, workshops, databases, publications, webinars and calendar of future events.
The British Library Business and IP Centre. 96 Euston Road, London, NW1 2DB
Tel: 020 7412 7901
Website: www.bl.uk/bipc

Business is Great
'Support, advice and inspiration for growing your business', Business is Great offers an excellent website offering lots of useful information for new start-ups including ideas for businesses, new markets, finance, regulations and legislation.
Business is Great
Website: www.greatbusiness.gov.ukl

Centre for Fashion Enterprise (CFE)
The Centre for Fashion Enterprise (CFE) is a Fashion business incubator based at the London College of Fashion. See the Centre's website for further details of services and activities.
Centre for Fashion Enterprise (CFE)
Website: www.fashion-enterprise.com

Chartered Institute of Marketing (CIM)

The Chartered Institute for Marketing (CIM) is a leading international professional marketing body that 'exists to develop the marketing profession, maintain the professional standards and improve the skills of marketing practitioners'. Visit the CIM website for details of services and membership, marketing expertise and resources, the CIM weekly news bulletin, awards, training and mentoring network, webinars and the CIM's marketing information hotline.

The Chartered Institute of Marketing (CIM)
Tel: 01628 427120
Website: www.cim.co.uk

Chartered Institute of Patent Agents (CIPA)

The Chartered Institute of Patents Agents (CIPA) is the 'professional and examining body for patent attorneys in the UK'. The CIPA website provides information relating to patents, trademarks, designs and copyright. Listed is a useful Directory of Patent Attorneys, IP advice clinics and other IP rights, professional development and membership details.

Chartered Institute of Patent Agents (CIPA). 95 Chancery Lane, London, WC2A 1DT
Tel: 020 7405 9450
Email: mail@cipa.org.uk   Website: www.cipa.org.uk

Cockpit Arts

Cockpit Arts is an award winning social enterprise and a creative-business incubator. See the website for further details of their consultancy service including assistance with product development, range planning and much more.

Cockpit Arts. Cockpit Yard, Northington Street, London, WC1N 2NP
Tel: 020 7419 1959
Email: info@cockpitarts.com Website: www.cockpitarts.com

Community Development Finance Association (CDFA)

The CDFA is a membership body for providers of fair and affordable loans, and operates across the UK. Their members are 'non-profit organisations that lend to people and businesses unable to get finance from traditional sources'.

Community Development Finance Association (CDFA)
Tel: 020 7430 0222
Email: info@cdfa.org.uk   Website: www.findingfinance.org.uk

Companies House – Gov. UK

Companies House is an executive agency of the Department for Business, Innovation and Skills (BIS), and the United Kingdom's registrar of companies, and all limited companies in England, Wales, Northern Ireland and Scotland. Companies House website includes a wide range of information for anyone setting up a business, including advice about company returns, finance and services relating to finding information on companies, filing information and data products.

Companies House
Website: www.companieshouse.gov.uk

Creative Industry Finance

Creative Industry Finance is a programme designed to assist creative and cultural enterprises in securing the finance and investment they need to successfully develop and grow into sustainable businesses. The programme offers tailored advice with a focus on supporting businesses through the process of applying to one of their leading partners for a business development loan.

Creative Industry Finance. Somerset House, Strand, London, WC2R 1LA
Tel: 0207 759 1114
Email: info@creativeindustryfinance.org.uk   Website: www.crativeindustryfinance.org.uk

Creative Skillset

Creative Skillset is the industry skills body for the creative industries, including fashion and textiles. Led by research into the skill needs of the industries, they devise solutions that increase productivity and foster growth. One such solution for the fashion and textile industry has been the development of a broad range of apprenticeships, which enable smaller companies to scale-up and mould skills to fit their own business needs. They offer consultation for accessing funding and training and offer industry accreditation for HE and apprenticeship courses to help businesses identify the best quality graduates and talent. You can find this talent on Hiive.co.uk (Connect, Collaborate, Grow).

Creative Skillset. Focus Point, 21 Calendonian Road, London, N1 9GB

Tel: 020 7713 9800

Email: Info@creativeskillset.org   Website: http://creativeskillset.org

Cultural Enterprise Office (CEO)

The Cultural Enterprise Office (CEO) supports Scotland's creative businesses. Services include helping creative micro-businesses and individuals build the skills and knowledge they need to succeed. See the CEO website for further details.

Cultural Enterprise Office.

Studio 114, First Floor, South Block, 60-64 Osborne Street, Glasgow, G312UF

Tel: 0333 999 7989

Email: info@culturalenterpriseoffice.co.uk   Website: www.culturalenterpriseoffice.co.uk

Design and Artists Copyright Society (DACS)

DACS is a not-for-profit visual artists' rights management organisation that campaigns for artists' rights, championing their sustained contribution to the creative economy. They collect and distribute royalties to visual artists and their estates. See the Society's website for details of their work and services.

Design and Artists Copyright Society (DACS). 33 Old Bethnal Green Road, London, E2 6AA

Tel: 020 7336 8811

Email: info@dacs.org.uk   Website: www.dacs.org.uk

Department for Business Innovation & Skills (BIS)

The Department for Business, Innovation & Skills (BIS) is the department for economic growth, which 'invests in skills and education to promote trade, boost innovation and help people to start and grow a business'. BIS has an informative website, and gives details of business and enterprise, consumer rights and issues, UK economy, financial services, trade and investment, science and innovation, further education and skills, and higher education, and lists all offices throughout the UK.

Department for Business, Innovation and Skills (BIS)

Email: enquiries@bis.gsi.gov.uk

Website: www.gov.uk/government/organisations/department-for-business-innovation-skills

Design Council

The Design Council is 'a centre of new thinking and insight into new ways to do business, and offers events, practical demonstrations and support programmes for private industry and the public sector, investing in the future of UK design'. The Council has an informative website providing the history of the Council, details of the Council's services, projects, knowledge, resources, a calendar of events, case studies and news, and features many very useful links.

Design Council. Angel Building, 407 St John Street, London, EC1V 4AB

Tel: 020 7420 5200

Email: info@designcouncil.org.uk   Website: www.designcouncil.org.uk

Disabled Entrepreneurs Network

The Disabled Entrepreneurs Network was established to inspire, encourage and support disabled people to start up a profitable business. Their website features networking opportunities, inspirational stories, information, special discounts on business services and provides up-to-date news and more.

Disabled Entrepreneurs Network

Tel: 020 8123 4948/07851 830908

Website: www.disabledentrepreneurs.co.uk

East Midlands Incubation Unit (EMIN)

East Midlands Incubation Unit (EMIN) is a support network founded by a collaboration of universities over eleven years ago. EMIN provides business incubation services to member centres and start-up businesses through its range of online support including access to a range of specialist services; helping businesses start-up and grow.

East Midlands Incubation Unit. 28 Friar Gate, Derby, DE1 1BX

Tel: 01332231875

Email: info@emincubation.co.uk   Website: www.emincubation.co.uk

Enterprise Europe Network
Launched in 2008, the Enterprise Europe Network helps small and medium-sized enterprises (SMEs) make the most of business opportunities in the EU and beyond'. Visit the Enterprise Europe Network website for further details about services, news and media, events calendar, sector groups and for details of location of your nearest Enterprise Europe Network branch.
Enterprise Europe Network
Website: http://een.ec.europa.eu

Enterprise Northern Ireland (ENI)
Established in 2000, Enterprise Northern Ireland represents the Local Enterprise Agencies, Enterprise Northern Ireland (ENI) and works with entrepreneurs helping them set up and establish business in Northern Ireland. See the ENI website for details of services and programmes such as the Regional Start Initiative, Business Boot Camp, Exploring Enterprise 2, networking opportunities and loan funding.
Enterprise Northern Ireland (ENI)
Website: www.enterpriseni.com

European Business & Innovation Centres Network (EBN)
The EBN is a network of around 150 quality-certified EU business and innovation centres and organisations that support the development and growth of innovative entrepreneurs, start-ups and SMEs. See website for further details.
European Business & Innovation Centres Network (EBN)
Email: info@ebn.euWebsite: http://ebn.be

The European Patents Office (EPO)
The EPO for Europe supports innovation, competitiveness and economic growth across Europe. See the EPO website for details of services including searching and applying for patents, law and practice, conferences and events, resources and latest news.
The European Patents Office
Tel: 00 800 80 20 20 20   (Customer Services)
Website: www.epo.org

European Trade Mark and Design Network (ETMDN)
The European Trade Mark and Design Network (ETMDN) is the hub that connects National and Regional Intellectual Property Offices, user associations and other IP organisations that 'work together towards attaining a true trade mark and design system in Europe'.
European Trade Mark and Design Network (ETMDN)
Website: www.tmdn.org

Fashion Capital
FashionCapital.co.uk offers a 'one-stop online resource' providing insight into the world of fashion, manufacturing and business. The online resource FashionCapital.co.uk provides a wealth of information comprising of eight key sections: Industry; Learning; Apprenticeships; Jobs and Forums; Events; Services and a Membership Forum.
Fashion Capital (Head Office).
Unit 14, Crusader Industrial estate, 167 Hermitage Road, London, N4 1LZ
Website: www.fashioncapital.co.uk

Fashion Enter
Fashion Enter is a not for profit which strives to be a centre of excellence for sampling, grading, production and for learning and development of skills within the fashion and textiles industry. Business mentoring and workshops are available. See website for further details of services and activities.
Fashion Enter Ltd. Unit 14, Crusader Estate, 167 Hermitage Road, London N4 1LZ
Tel: 0208 8093311
Email: info@fashion-enter.com   Website: fashioncapital.co.uk

The Fashion Network
Based in Manchester and London, The Fashion Network operates as a social platform for fashion industry professionals across the UK, providing help for businesses and individuals with talent, business and professional development, and with support for recruitment and marketing.
The Fashion Network. 20 Dale St, Manchester, M1 1EZ
Tel: 0161 819 2145
Email: hello@thefashionnetwork.co.uk   Website: www.thefashionnetwork.co.uk

Federation of Small Businesses (FSB)
The Federation of Small Businesses (FSB) is the UK's largest campaigning group promoting and protecting the interests of the self-employed and owners of small businesses within the UK. Visit the FSB website for details of services.
Federation of Small Businesses. Sir Frank Whittle Way, Blackpool, Lancashire, FY4 2FE
Tel: 0808 20 20 888
Website: www.fsb.org.uk

Highlands and Islands Enterprise (HIE)
Highlands and Islands Enterprise (HIE) is the Scottish Government's economic and community development agency for the north and west of Scotland.
Highlands and Islands Enterprise (HIE). Fraser House, Friar's Lane, Inverness, IV1 1BA, Scotland
Tel: 01463 234 171
Email: info@hient.co.uk   Website: www.hie.co.uk

HM Revenue and Customs (HMRC)
HMRC is the UK's tax authority. The HMRC website provides online services including facts on Tax Guidance for Employers, Guidance for Tax Advisors and Agents, and lots of information for new and existing businesses. This includes registering for VAT, starting a business, import and export, pension schemes, partnerships, Capital Gains Tax, Self-Assessment Tax and much more. They also offer an Events Finder to search for local business related training, workshops, networking events and seminars in the UK, promoting many useful free courses.
HM Revenue and Customs (HMRC)
Website: www.hmrc.gov.uk

The Institute of Directors (IoD)
The Institute of Directors (IoD) is an independent association of business leaders. See the IoD website for details of membership, their Business Information Service, the Business Library and professional development including CPD workshops, and details of regional and international centres.
The Institute of Directors (IoD). 116 Pall Mall, St. James's, London SW1Y 5ED
Tel: 020 7766 8888
Website: www.iod.com

The Institute of Enterprise and Entrepreneurs (IOEE)
The Institute of Enterprise and Entrepreneurs (IOEE) offers professional recognition to entrepreneurs, intrapreneurs, enterprise support professionals and enterprise educators. The IOEE learning and development programmes are promoted and delivered through a network of centres of excellence and academies that share the IOEE's 'passion for enterprise' and have demonstrated their commitment to skills development.
The Institute of Enterprise and Entrepreneurs (IOEE)
Website: https://ioee.uk

The Institute for Small Businesses and Entrepreneurship (ISBE)
The Institute for Small Business and Entrepreneurship (ISBE) is a network for 'people and organisations involved in small business and entrepreneurship, research, policy, education, support and advice'. For further details of the Institute's activities, news, and regional and national workshops and events, visit the ISBE website.
Institute for Small Business and Entrepreneurship (ISBE).
Ground Floor, 137 Euston Road, London, NW1 2AA
Email ISBE: info@isbe.org.uk   Website: www.isbe.org.uk

Intellectual Property Office (IPO)
The Intellectual Property Office (IPO) is the official government body responsible for granting Intellectual Property (IP) rights in the UK. The four main types of IP rights are patents, trademarks, designs and copyright. See the IPO website for further information.
Intellectual Property Office
Email: information@ipo.gov.uk   Website: www.ipo.gov.uk

Introbiz

Introbiz is considered to be 'Wales leading business network'. There are over 250 members within the Introbiz network and between 60-100 of these businesses attend their weekly events. They pride themselves on being able to connect with their target audience; after all 'it's not what you know, but who you know'. Introbiz are the organisers of both national and international business networking events including Wales' biggest business exhibition - Introbiz Business Expo.
Introbiz
Tel: 02920 291002
Email: info@intobiz.co.uk   Website: introbiz.co.uk

Knowledge Transfer Partnerships (KTP)

Knowledge Transfer Partnerships (KTP) supports UK businesses wanting to 'improve their competitiveness, productivity and performance by accessing the knowledge and expertise available within UK Universities and Colleges'. They offer access to funding, innovative ideas and academic expertise. See website for details of forthcoming events, case studies and the Knowledge Transfer Network (KTN).
Knowledge Transfer Partnerships (KTP).
Technology Strategy Board, North Star House, North Star Avenue, Swindon, SN2 1UE
Tel: 0300 321 4357
Website: www.ktponline.org.uk

Mintel Group Ltd.

Mintel Group Ltd is a 'world leading market intelligence agency', providing expertise relating to market research and analysis, consumer research, competitive analysis, and data relating to products, services and product innovation.
Mintel: Mintel Group Ltd. 11 Pilgrim Street, London, EC4V 6RN, UK
Tel: 020 7606 4533
Website: www.mintel.com

National Asian Business Development Network (NABA)

The National Asian Business Development Network (NABA) was founded to unite regional Asian business associations from across the country, and to represent them on issues of national importance such as legislation and government relations.
National Asian Business Development Network (NABA)
Email: info@nabauk.org   Website: www.nabauk.org

The National Enterprise Network

National Enterprise Network is a membership body 'representing those working in the enterprise support sector across England'. They represent a variety of enterprise support organisations, including enterprise agencies, local authorities and other specialist providers.
The National Enterprise Network
Email: enquiries@nationalenterprisenetwork.org   Website: www.nationalenterprisenetwork.org

Prime (The Prince's Initiative for Mature Enterprise)

The Prince's Initiative for Mature Enterprise (PRIME) was established by HRH The Prince of Wales. Since 1999, PRIME has helped more than 28,000 over 50s who are unemployed or facing redundancy, to explore self-employment. They offer support through free training courses, mentoring support, online resources, and business and networking events.
Prime. 137 Shepherdess Walk, London N1 7RQ
Email: info@prime.org.uk Website: www.prime.org.uk

Prime Cymru

The Prince's Initiative for Mature Enterprise in Wales
Prime Cymru
Tel: 0800 587 4085
Email: enquiries@prime-cymru.co.uk   Website: www.prime-cymru.co.uk

Prince's Trust

The Prince's Youth Trust is an organisation that offers a range of training programmes providing practical and financial support to young people to 'encourage and develop skills, confidence and the motivation to move into work, education or training'. Visit the Trust's website for further details of support, training and the Trust's Enterprise Fellowship.

Prince's Trust
Tel: 0800 842 842
Email: info@princes-trust.org.uk   Website: www.princes-trust.org.uk

Scottish Enterprises

Scottish Enterprises work and support Scotland's economic growth. See their website for details of services, industry support, knowledge hub, events and locations of all Enterprise offices.

Scottish Enterprises
Tel: 0845 607 8787
Email: enquiries@scotent.co.uk   Website: www.scottish-enterprise.com

Shell LiveWIRE UK

The Shell LiveWIRE programme offers free online business advice and funding to young entrepreneurs aged 16-30 in the UK. View the Shell LiveWIRE website for details of the Smarter Future Programme, and start-up support, funding opportunities, events, and news.

Shell LiveWIRE UK. Design Works, William Street, Felling, Gateshead, NE10 0JP
Tel: 0191 423 6229
Email: enquiries@shell-livewire.org   Website: www.shell-livewire.org

Small Firms Enterprise Development Initiaitvie (SFEDI)

SFEDI is the Government recognised UK standards setting organisation for business support and business enterprise.

Small Firms Enterprise Development Initiative (SFEDI). Enterprise House, 18 Parsons Court, Welbury Way, Aycliffe Business Park, County Durham, DL5 6ZE
Tel: 0845 467 3218
Website: www.sfedi.co.uk

Start-Up Britain

Start-Up Britain was founded in 2011 by 'entrepreneurs for entrepreneurs, to celebrate, inspire and support enterprise in the UK'. Visit the Start-Up Britain website for details of events and activities, and to view their excellent business resources on starting and growing a business.

Start-Up Britain
Website: www.startupbritain.org

Trading Standards Institute (TSI)

The Trading Standards Institute (TSI) 'promotes and protects the success of a modern economy. It aims to safeguard the health, safety and wellbeing of citizens'. See the TSI website Business Companion, a site sponsored by Department for Business, Innovation and Skills offering free guidance for businesses about trading standards law.

Trading Standards Institute
Tel: 03454 040506
Website: www.tradingstandards.gov.uk

UK Business Angels Association

The UK Business Angels Association is the national trade association representing Angels and early stage investment in the UK. The Association's website provides information including an excellent introduction to Angel Investing, the investment process and accessing Angel finance. It also offers resources and links, and includes a Member's Directory.

UK Business Angels Association. 5th Floor East, Chancery House, 53-64 Chancery Lane, London, WC2A 1QS
Tel: 0207 492 0490
Email: info@ukbusinessangelsassociation.org.uk   Website: www.ukbusinessangelsassociation.org.uk

UK Creative Industries
UK Creative Industries are a partnership of government and industry promoting the UK's creative industries to trade audiences worldwide. The UK's Creative Industries website provides statistics, case studies, news, commentary, event details and other resources associated with the creative sectors.
UK Creative Industries
Tel: 0207 235 7020
Email: info@creativeindustries.co.uk   Website: www.thecreativeindustries.co.uk

UK Trade and Investment (UKTI)
UKTI works with UK based businesses to ensure their success in international markets through exports, and also encouraging and supporting overseas companies to look at the UK as the best place to set up or expand their business.
UK Trade and Investment (UKTI)
Tel: 020 7215 5000
Email: enquiries@ukti.gsi.gov.uk
Website: www.gov.uk/government/organisations/uk-trade-investment

Women in Rural Enterprise (WiRE)
Women in Rural Enterprise (WiRE) is an organisation offering support to businesswomen in rural areas. WIRE local network groups meet regularly throughout the UK. They offer support, business advice and training courses, and an online community. Membership details are available on the WIRE website.
WiRE
Email: info@wireuk.org   Website: www.wireuk.org

Young Creative Entrepreneur (YCE)
The Young Creative Entrepreneur (YCE) programme supports and connects innovative and entrepreneurial leaders in creative and cultural industries around the world.
Young Creative Entrepreneur Programme.
(Postal Address) British Council Customer Service UK, Bridgewater House, 58 Whitworth Street, Manchester, M1 6BB
Tel: 0161 957 7755
Email: general.enquiries@britishcouncil.org
Website: http://creativeconomy.britishcouncil.org/projects/young-creative-entrepreneur-programme

An image from the 19th century series of engravings "Progress of Cotton", showing the spinning process

Jacquard Loom - Butterworth & Dickinson Ltd, Burnley, Lancashire

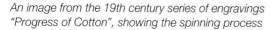

Above images - courtesy of the Museum of Science and Industry

Exhibition Organisers

The Beadworkers Guild

The Beadworkers Guild organise many events and exhibitions including The Great British Bead Show and the Beading Festival. See the Guild's website for details of membership, events and activities.
The Beadworkers Guild
Website: www.beadworkersguild.org.uk

British Fashion Council (BFC)

Formed in 1983, the British Fashion Council (BFC) is a not-for-profit organisation that aims to 'further the interests of the British fashion industry and its designer businesses by using and sharing collective knowledge, experience and resources of the sector'. Key events include London Fashion Week; London Collections Men; British Fashion Awards; London Show Rooms; London Fashion Weekend and Fashion Forum. Visit the BFC's excellent website for further details of the Council's work and strategy, key events, business support, news, calendar, the BFC Education Foundation, and much more.
British Fashion Council (BFC)
Website: www.britishfashioncouncil.co.uk

Designersblock

Since 1998, Designersblock have been producing major annual international design shows. They curate and produce exhibitions, events and experiences in the UK and internationally working with a network of independent designers, creative partners, commercial clients and brands to bring innovative ideas to the widest possible audience. Designersblock have produced over 100 multi-disciplinary events in 10 countries, providing a platform for more than three thousand individuals and companies from 30 nationalities. Their exhibitions and projects feature fashion, textiles, jewellery, furniture, lighting, product and architecture.
Designersblock. 32 Cremer Street, London, E2 8HD
Tel: 07815 87 1472
Email: info@designersblock.org.uk   Website: www.verydesignersblock.com

Great Northern Events (NW) Ltd

Great Northern Events (NW) Ltd are the organisers of the Great Northern Contemporary Craft Fair (GNCCF), which is an award winning, high profile fair that celebrates the best in contemporary craft, and is regarded as one of the leading selling events in the North of England. Over 150 designers and makers are selected by an independent panel to showcase and sell their work.
Great Northern Events (NW) Ltd. 23 Bellfield Road, Didsbury, Manchester M20 6BJ
Tel: 07973574735
Email: enquiries@greatnorthernevents.co.uk   Website: www.greatnorthernevents.co.uk

Grosvenor Shows Ltd

Grosvenor Shows Ltd organise events throughout the UK, including a number of Quilt Shows around the UK and the Great Northern Needlecraft Show in Harrogate.
Grosvenor Shows Ltd. 282 High Road, Whaplode, Spalding, Lincolnshire, PE12 6TG
Tel: 01406 372600 / 01406 372601
Email: grosvenorshows@btconnect.com   Website: www.grosvenorshows.co.uk

Harvey Management Services Ltd

Harvey Management Services Ltd are the organisers of the Decorative Antiques and Textiles Fair, held annually in January, April and September/October at Battersea Evolution, Battersea Park, London SW11. More than 140 exhibitors from the UK and Europe offer antiques and 20th century design for interior decoration. Textile dealers sell antique and vintage ikats, suzanis, embroideries, printed and hand-painted fabrics, quilts, passementerie and draper's trimmings, rugs and runners, kelims, tribal, textiles and much more.
Harvey Management Services Ltd. 4 Church Street, London NW8 8ED
Tel: 020 7616 9327
Email: fairs@decorativefair.com   Website: www.decorativefair.com

ICHF Ltd

ICHF Ltd (International Craft and Hobby Fair Ltd) established in 1976 are the organisers of the following shows: Craft Hobby and Stitch International (CHSI); Art Materials Live; Sewing for Pleasure and Fashion,

Embroidery and Stitch.
ICHF Ltd. Dominic House, Seaton Road, Highcliffe, Dorset BH23 5HW
Email: info@ichf.co.uk (General enquiries)   Website: www.ichfevents.co.uk

IDEX Exhibitions Ltd

IDEX is a leading UK-based producer of exhibitions, business information, seminars, conferences, and publications. IDEX exhibitions organises Fashion SVP, which is a unique fashion manufacturing event held at Olympia, London. IDEX also organises the Off-Price Show specialising in discounted fashion wholesale.
IDEX Exhibitions Ltd. 25-27 Westow Street, Foresters Hall, London, SE19 3RY
Tel: 0208 771 3555
Email: b.carter@idexmedia.com
Website: www.fashionsvp.com www.offpriceshow.co.uk www.idexmedia.com

London Antiques Rug and Textile Art Fair (LARTA)

London Antiques Rug and Textile Art Fair (LARTA) is the UK's most important event for fine antique rugs and textiles, where collectors and aficionados know they will see a wide and excellent selection of rare and beautiful antique and vintage rugs, carpets and textiles available on the UK market. Designers, decorators and the international trade also visit to source items originating from Anatolia and Turkey, the Caucasus, Persia, Central Asia, India and China, as well as Europe and Africa. Works are of all periods up to the early 20th century. This event is usually held in London in April but dates can vary year to year. See website for further details.
London Antiques Rug and Textile Art Fair (LARTA). Aaron Nejad Antique Carpets, Block A, 105 Eade Road, London N4 1TJ
Tel: 020 86178670
Email: anejad@talktalk.net   Website: www.larta.net

Maltings Craft

Maltings Craft are organisers of Unravel: A Festival of Knitting; Thread: the Festival of Textiles; The Festival of Crafts, and much more. For further details see the Maltings Craft website.
Maltings Craft
Website: http://craft.farnhammaltings.com

Media 10 Limited

Media 10 Limited is an events, publishing and digital media company. Their portfolio includes events such as 100% Design; Britain and Ireland's Next Top Model Live; Clerkenwell Design Week; The London Design Trail and Grand Designs Live.
Media 10 Ltd. Crown House, 151 High Road, Loughton, IG10 4LF
Tel: 020 3225 5200 (General enquiries)
Email: info@media-ten.com Web: www.media-ten.com

Ocean Media Group (OMG)

Ocean Media Group (OMG) is an events company who organise consumer and trade events. They have a strong wedding portfolio that includes The London Bridal Show; The Harrogate Bridal Show; The National Wedding Show and the White Gallery London - the premium international trade event showcasing bridal collections from some of finest UK and international designers.
Ocean Media Group (OMG)
Website: www.oceanmedia.co.uk

P & A Antiques Ltd

P & A Antiques Ltd., are organisers of specialist fairs and events including The London Vintage Fashion Fair and The London Antique Textiles, Vintage Costumes, Tribal Art and Antiques Fair, which gathers specialist dealers.
P & A Antiques Ltd
Tel: 020 8543 3028
Email: info@pa-antiques.co.uk Website: www.pa-antiques.co.uk

The Platinum Group of Companies

The Platinum Group are organisers of the National Asian Wedding Show and India Fashion Week,

London showcasing some of India's leading designers in the UK. See website for further details of services and events.
The Platinum Group
Email: info@platinum-group.com   Website: www.platinum-group.com

The Prysm Group
The Prysm Group are trade exhibition organisers. Their portfolio of events includes The Business Show, an event held over two days and is now the UK's largest business event, attracting more than 25,000 businesses. See the Group's website for details of forthcoming events.
The Prysm Group (Postal address) Prysm Media Group, Suite 6c, Whitefriars, Bristol, BS1 2NT
Email: reception@prysmgroup.co.uk
Website: www.prysmgroup.co.uk   Website: www.greatbritishbusinessshow.co.uk

Textile Events
Textile Events was established in 2007 by John Kelley at a private members club in Marylebone. At the first fair they had 25 exhibitors set out in two rooms with just tables, chairs, signs and rails. The style and concept has been so successful that it continues today with over 360 exhibitors showing at the January 2015 exhibition. Organisers of the London Textile Fair; The London Print Design Fair; Texfusion – The London Asia Textile Fair.
Textile Events. 8 Gisburn Road, London, N8 7BS
Tel: 020 8347 8145
Websites: www.thelondontextilefair.co.uk www.thelondonprintdesignfair.co.uk
www.londonasiatextilefair.co.uk

The Textile Institute
The Textile Institute is a worldwide professional membership organisation for textile professionals spanning every sector and occupation relating to fibres and their uses. Activities include professional qualifications; medals; scholarships; bursaries; publications; business information and events including Techtextil, the leading international trade fair for technical textiles and nonwovens. The Textile Institute sponsors and co-sponsors many international events. Visit the website for further details of forthcoming events, activities and services.
The Textile Institute. (International Headquarters and National Offices),
1st Floor, St. James's Buildings, Oxford Street, Manchester, M1 6FQ, UK
Tel: +44(0)161 237 1188
Email: tiihq@textileinst.org.uk Website: www.textileinstitute.org

Trident Exhibitions Ltd
Organisers of national exhibitions and conferences including The Creative Crafts Shows
Trident Exhibitions Ltd
Email: info@trident-exhibitions.co.uk   Web: www.tridentexhibitions.co.uk

Tutton and Young Ltd
Tutton and Young Ltd are curators of three annual contemporary art, craft and design fairs - Brighton Art Fair, Made London; Made Brighton and The Design Craft Fairs.
Tutton and Young Ltd. PO Box 4729, Worthing, BN11 9LD
Tel: 01903 608757
Email: info@tuttonandyoung.co.uk   Website: www.tuttonandyoung.co.uk

The Wool Clip
The Wool Clip is a Cumbrian cooperative and also organisers of the Woolfest, an event founded in 2004, celebrating natural fibres and the promotion of wool, spinning, knitting and associated textiles. For further details visit the Wool Clip website or contact the Wool Clip Shop.
Wool Clip Shop. Priest's Mill, Caldbeck, Cumbria CA7 8DR
Tel: 016974 78707
Website: www.woolfest.co.uk

Upper Street Events Ltd
Upper Street Events Ltd. is a leading UK-based consumer-focused events company, and organisers of exhibitions including New Designers, The Knitting and Stitching Show, The Festival of Quilts and the London Art Fair.
Upper Street Events Ltd
Website: www.upperstreetevents.net

Fashion, Textiles and Associated Exhibitions and Trade Fairs - UK

This section of the Directory details the major UK Fashion and Textile trade fairs from Graduate Fashion Week, London Fashion Week, New Designers to events covering all aspects of the industry. Whether setting up in business, launching your first collection or expanding your business, there is something in this section for everyone. Details of events are listed, however, the dates and frequency of events have been omitted due to the changing nature of event programmes. Full details are generally available on the event website, in addition to specifics listing exhibitors, awards, entry costs and methods of booking.

African Fashion Week, London
African Fashion Week celebrates London's unique and diverse cultural heritage, showing the colourful and exciting mix of Western and African culture, and at the same time promoting Africa's culture and interpreting it into contemporary designs.
African Fashion Week
Tel: 0203 217 0822
Email: info@africafashionweeklondonuk.com   Website: http://africafashionweeklondon.com

The Asiana Bridal Show
The Asiana Bridal Show is an event to meet UK top wedding service suppliers all under one roof including bridal fashion designers, hair, make-up and mehndi artists, photographers, venues, caterers, décor companies, florists and a whole lot more.
The Asiana Bridal Show. i and i Media Ltd. 46-48 East Smithfield, London E1W 1AW, UK
Tel: 020 7709 2021
Email: advertise@asiana.tv   Website: www.asianabridalshow.com

Asian Wedding Exhibition, London
The Asian Wedding Exhibition provides a showcase for designer collections from India, Pakistan and UK.
Asian Wedding Exhibition, London
Tel: 0208 123 6610
Email: info@nationalasianweddingshow.co.uk   Website: www.nationalasianweddingshow.co.uk

British Craft Trade Fair (BCTF)
The British Craft Trade Fair (BCTF) is organised by PSM Ltd. The Fair is strictly trade-only and showcases work from British and Irish makers. The BCTF differs from other trade fairs in that no mass-manufactured products or products made overseas are allowed. See website for further details.
The British Craft Trade Fair. PSM Ltd. Hammonds Barn, London Road, Burgess Hill
West Sussex, RH15 9QJ
Tel: 01444 246446
Email: info@bctf.co.uk   Website: www.bctf.co.uk

British Wool Weekend
The aim of British Wool Weekend is to 'raise the profile of British Wool and the many related products produced from British wool'. Exhibitors include specialists in spinning, weaving, knitting, crochet, cross stitch, embroidery, hand dyeing, felting and many other textile processes.
British Wool Weekend
Email: info@britishwool.net   Website: www.britishwool.net

Bubble – Kids Trade Show, London
The UK's children's trade event, Bubble London runs for two days every summer and winter. Each edition sees over 280 exhibitors from across the childrenswear industry gather at Islington's Business Design Centre, where they showcase the latest in kid's fashion, accessories, gifts and homeware.
ITE MODA LTD. Old Town Hall, Lewisham Road, Slaithwaite, Huddersfield, HD7 5AL
Tel: 01484846069
Email: Bubble.Marketing@ite-exhibitions.com   Website: www.bubblelondon.com

Clothes Show Live

The Clothes Show Live is a popular event that takes place at the NEC Birmingham. The Show is divided into four shopping areas: Boutique, Cheap and Chic, Vintage/New Designers/Brands and Hair and Beauty. Event highlights include designer and image catwalks, fashion seminars, fashion theatre, workshops and creative awards, model scouting and model master classes. The Show also offers a university and college forum, educational roadshows and careers information.

Clothes Show Live
Website: www.clothesshowlive.com

Collect

Collect: the International Art Fair for Contemporary Objects is the Crafts Council's flagship selling event that 'brings together the world's finest galleries representing exceptional work of museum-quality from their portfolio of artists'.

Collect. Crafts Council. 44a Pentonville Road Islington London N1 9BY
Tel: + 44 (0) 20 7278 7700
Email: events@craftscouncil.org.uk   Website: www.craftscouncil.org.uk/what-we-do/collect

Country Living

Fashion and accessories, home and interiors and crafts, garden and outdoor living are all exhibited at the Country Living Exhibitions – Christmas Fairs (London, Glasgow and Harrogate) and the London Spring Fair. See website for further details of dates and venues.

Country Living. Upper Street Events Ltd, 58 White Lion Street, Islington, London, N1 9PP
Website. www.countrylivingfair.com

Craft, Hobby and Stitch International

Craft Hobby and Stitch International is Europe's largest dedicated trade show for the art, craft, needlecraft, fabric, and hobby industries.

International Craft and Hobby Fair Ltd. Dominic House, Seaton Road, Highcliffe, Dorset, BH23 5HW
Tel: 01425 272711   (Exhibitors and General Enquiries)
Email: info@chsi.co.uk Website: www.chsi.co.uk

The Decorative Fair of Antiques and Textiles

The Decorative Fair of Antiques and Textiles organised by Harvey (Management Services) Ltd is held annually in January, April and September/October at Battersea Park, London SW11. More than 140 exhibitors from the UK and Europe offer antiques and 20th century design for interior decoration. Textile dealers sell antique and vintage ikats, suzanis, embroideries, printed and hand-painted fabrics, quilts, passementerie and draper's trimmings, rugs, kelims, tribal, textiles and much more.

The Decorative Fair of Antiques and Textiles.
Harvey (Management Services) Ltd., 4 Church Street, London, NW8 8ED
Tel: 020 7616 9327
Email: fairs@decorativefair.com   Website: www.decorativefair.com

Decorex International

Decorex International is an interior design trade show in London with over 300 exhibitors and has a seminar programme, workshops and Future Heritage section exhibiting the work of designer/makers working in ceramic, metal, textile, wood and plastic.

Decorex International. Syon Park, West London, TW8 8JF
Tel: +44 (0)207 921 8406 (General and sales enquiries)
Email: gemma.mckay@ubm.com Website: www.decorex.com

Fashion, Embroidery and Stitch

Fashion, Embroidery and Stitch showcases a wide range of textile arts, and a vast range of fabric and embellishment supplies.

Fashion, Embroidery and Stitch.
International Craft & Hobby Fair Ltd., Dominic House, Seaton Road, Highcliffe, Dorset, BH23 5HW
Tel: 01425 272711 (General Enquiries)
Email: info@ichf.co.uk   Website: www.fashionembroidery.co.uk

Fashion Fringe

Fashion Fringe is an annual award platform founded by Colin McDowell in 2003 in conjunction with IMG Fashion. It offers talented and emerging designers the chance to launch their label in London through a combined programme of mentoring, studio space, financial support and a catwalk show at London Fashion Week.

Fashion Fringe. The Network Building, 97 Tottenham Court Road, London, W1T 4TP
Tel: 0207 665 5524
Email: fashionfringe@imgworld.com   Website: www.fashionfringe.co.uk

Fashion Scout

Fashion Scout is a fashion showcase for emerging and established design talent.
Fashion Scout
Enquiries: enquiries@fashionscountevents.com
Website: www.fashion-scout.co.uk

Fashion SVP

Fashion SVP is an event designed for those who buy direct from factories. The show provides an opportunity to meet suppliers Europe, Eastern Europe and the Mediterranean providing 'near-shore' manufacturing services. Services on display include: high quality CMT (Cut, Make and Trim), specialist processes, fabric ranges, complex garments, and in-house services including design and garment testing, technical services and quality control. The Seminar programme offers valuable insight and advice by speakers from the retail industry, retail trend consultancies and manufacturers. It provides up-to-date information on the latest developments in the UK and further afield, for example, Far East, costing and negotiation, ethical and sustainable sourcing, new technology and regulatory issues.

Fashion SVP. IDEX Exhibitions Ltd., Foresters Hall, 25-27 Westow Street, London, SE19 3RY
Tel: +44 (0) 208 771 3555
Email: info@fashionsvp.com   Website: www.fashionsvp.com

Festival of Quilts

The Festival of Quilting is a celebration of quilting with over 300 exhibitors offering essential supplies, galleries from international artists, an Academy Programme, lectures, and a magnificent display of over 1,000 competition quilts. The event is described as the 'ultimate quilting experience'.

Festival of Quilts. Upper Street Events Ltd, 58 White Lion Street, Islington, London, N1 9PP
Tel: 020 7688 6830 (General Enquiries)
Website: www.thefestivalofquilts.co.uk

Festival of Thrift

The Festival of Thrift is a 'British celebration of scrimping with style', celebrating everyday living with upcycling, recycling and sustainable living. The Festival aims to 'show you how reusing, recycling and upcycling can be fun, save you money and benefit the environment at the same time'. Awarded the 2015 Observer Ethical Award for Arts and Culture.

The Festival of Thrift
Website: www.festivalofthrift.co.uk

Fibre East

Fibre East is an event that celebrates and supports British fibre and craft, including the crafts of hand spinning, knitting, dyeing, weaving and crochet to name but a few.

Fibre East
Email: info@fibre-east.co.uk   Website: www.fibre-east.co.uk

FreeRange

Free Range is an Old Truman Brewery project set up by Tamsin O'Hanlon to provide new creative graduates with the opportunity to showcase their work on an international level to the public and industry. The annual Free Range exhibitions present the work of art and design students in categories including: fashion, art, graphics, photography and interior design.

Freerange. The Old Truman Main Reception. 91-95 Brick Lane, London, E1 6QL
Email: info@free-range.org.uk   Website:www.free-range.org.uk

Frock Me Vintage Fashion Fair

Frock Me is a London vintage fashion fair with a huge cult following and is held at Chelsea Old Town Hall throughout the year. First established in the 1990s, the Fair brings together many stalls of the finest vintage clothing, textiles, accessories and haberdashery in the capital with regular traders at each fair. Great for vintage lovers to spend hours browsing through rail after rail of amazing one-off finds.
Frock Me Vintage Fashion Fair
Tel: 020 7503 9171
Email: info@frockmevintagefashion.com　Website: www.frockmevintagefashion.com

Graduate Fashion Week (GFW)

Graduate Fashion Week (GFW) founded in 1991 by Jeff Banks CBE, Vanessa Denza MBE and John Walford celebrates the creativity and innovation of students and graduates within fashion. It is recognised as one of the world's leading event for fashion graduates, showcasing the work of over 1,000 graduates from the most influential and inspiring UK and international universities. Each June, the event is held attracting over 20,000 guests, and features 22 catwalk shows, exhibitions from over 60 universities and a Gala Award Show, alongside exhibitions, talks and workshops. Visit the GFW website for details of exhibiting universities and colleges, previous award winners, details of sponsors, the GFW Careers Guide including pre-university tips and business start-up advice.
Graduate Fashion Week. FSI Events Vents Ltd. Studio 9, Zeus House,16-30 Provost Street, London, N1 7NG
Tel: 020 7251 9315
Email: enquiries@gfw.org.uk　Website: www.gfw.org.uk

Great British Bead Show

The Great British Bead Show is the largest beadwork event in the UK and is organised by the Beadworkers Guild, along with the Beading Festival.
The Beadworkers Guild (Mail). 4 Honor Oak Road, London, SE23 3SF
Tel: 07837 649712
Email: enquiries@beadworkersguild.org.uk Website: www.beadworkersguild.org.uk

Great Northern Contemporary Craft Fair (GNCCF)

Great Northern Contemporary Craft Fair (GNCCF) is organised by Great Northern Events NW Ltd., and is an award winning, high profile fair that celebrates the best in contemporary craft in fashion and textiles, print-making, jewellery, interiors, ceramics, glass, wood, paper, silver, metal, product design and more. The event is regarded as one of the leading selling events in the North of England.
Great Northern Contemporary Craft Fair (GNCCF). Great Northern Events NW Ltd. 23 Bellfield Road, Didsbury, Manchester M20 6BJ
Tel: 07973574735
Email: enquiries@greatnorthernevents.co.uk　Website: www.greatnorthernevents.co.uk

The Great Northern Quilt and Needlecraft Show

Organised by Grosvenor Shows Ltd., The Great Northern Quilt and Needlecraft Show presents displays of quilts with entries invited from all over the world, including feature displays, a wide range of trade stands and workshops.
Grosvenor Shows Ltd. 282 High Road, Whaplode, Spalding, Lincolnshire, PE12 6TG
Tel: 01406 372600/01406 372601
Email: grosvenorshows@btconnect.com　Website: www.grosvenorshows.co.uk

Hammersmith Vintage Fashion Fair

Since 1999, The Hammersmith Vintage Fashion Fair is an inspiration to 'Fashionistas' and is an excellent source of one off bargains. This is a monthly event. Organised by P & Antiques Ltd. See their website for further information and dates of fairs.
Hammersmith Vintage Fashion Fair. Hammersmith Town Hall, London, W6 9JU
Tel: 020 8543 3028
Email: info@pa-antiques.co.uk　Website: www.pa-antiques.co.uk

Handmade Living Show

The Handmade Living Show is an event which showcases products such as fashion accessories, textiles, jewellery, gifts and handicrafts, along with a range of inspirational workshops, presentations and talks

throughout the event.
Handmade Living Show
Email: info@handmadelivingshow.co.uk   Website: http://handmadelivingshow.co.uk

Harrogate Bridal Fair/Exhibition
Harrogate Bridal Fair is organised by the Ocean Media Group Ltd., who are also organisers of The London Bridal Show and White Gallery London, and The National Wedding Show. Ocean Media Group also publishes Bridal Buyer Magazine reporting on bridal industry news in the UK.
Ocean Media Group
Tel: 01423 770 120
Email: wendy@bridal-uk.com   Website: www.theharrogatebridalshow.co.uk

India Fashion Week London
India Fashion Week showcases some of India's leading designers in the UK.
India Fashion Week London. The Platinum Group. Suite 28, Quadrangle House, Stratford,
Email: info@platinum-group.com   Website: www.platinum-group.com

The IMC Menswear Show
The IMC Menswear Show is organised by the IMC Buying Group who invite 40-50 manufacturers to show their ranges. See the IMC website for details and dates of events.
The IMC Menswear Show
Website: www.imcmenswear.co.uk

Knitting and Stitches Show (London, Harrogate, Ireland)
Organised by Creative Exhibitions Ltd., the highly popular Knitting and Stitches Show offers supplies for 'everything that you would possible need for your sewing, knitting or craft projects'. There are workshops, the Gallery of Textile Artists, 'Prima Make' and contemporary quilt displays.
Creative Exhibitions Ltd. Exhibition House, 8 Greenwich Quay, London, SE8 3EY
Email: email@twistedthread.com   Website: www.twistedthread.com

London Antiques Rug and Textile Art Fair (LARTA)
London Antiques Rug and Textile Art Fair (LARTA) is one of the UK's most important event for fine antique rugs and textiles, where collectors and aficionados know they will see a wide and excellent selection of rare and beautiful antique and vintage rugs, carpets and textiles available on the UK market. Designers, decorators and the international trade also visit to source items originating from Anatolia and Turkey, the Caucasus, Persia, Central Asia, India and China as well as Europe and Africa. Works are of all periods up to the early 20th century. This event is usually held in London in April but dates can vary year to year. See the LARTA website for further details.
London Antiques Rug and Textile Art Fair (LARTA).
Aaron Nejad Antique Carpets, Block A, 105 Eade Road, London N4 1TJ
Tel: 020 86178670
Email: anejad@talktalk.net   Website: www.larta.net

London Antique Textiles and Tribal Art Fair
Established in 2000, the London Antique Textiles and Tribal Art Fair gathers specialist dealers in antique textiles, vintage costumes and tribal art.
P & A Antiques Ltd
Tel: 0208 543 3028
Email: info@pa-antiques.co.uk   Website: www.pa-antiques.co.uk

London Design Festival
First staged in 2003, the London Design Festival is an annual design event supported by the Arts Council, England, and comprises of over 300 events and exhibitions staged by hundreds of partner organisations across the design spectrum and from around the world. See the website for details of attending and taking part, projects, gallery and sponsors.
London Design Festival. 33 John Street, London, WC1N 2AT
Tel: 020 7242 6022
Email: hello@londondesignfestival.com   Website: www.londondesignfestival.com

London Edge Reloaded

London Edge Reloaded is the new look London Edge. 'As the lines blur between music, fashion and the subcultures they create, the alternative landscape is shifting. With this is mind, LondonEdge has become 'Reloaded'. It has been redesigned presenting new cutting-edge designers and brands, emerging fashion trends and alternative fashion'.

LondonEdge Ltd
Tel: 0116 289 8249
Email: info@londonedge.com   Website: www.londonedge.com

London Fashion Week (LFW)

Founded in 1984, London Fashion Week (LFW) organised by the British Fashion Council is a Fashion trade show held in London twice each year in February and September, and ranks alongside New York, Paris and Milan. It provides a superb platform for catwalk shows, designer showrooms for UK and International designers to engage with buyers and press.

London Fashion Week (LFW).
British Fashion Council. Somerset House, South Wing, Strand, London, WC2R 1LA
Tel: +44 (0) 870 112 9088 (Tickets and information hotline)
Website: www.londonfashionweek.co.uk

London Fashion Weekend

Somerset House plays host to Britain's biannual consumer fashion showcase - London Fashion Weekend, providing first-hand insider knowledge and style advice from London Fashion Week's most famous British brands. There is designer shopping, a programme of catwalk shows, pop-up shops, hair and beauty and educational panels from leading industry experts.

London Fashion Weekend
Email: info@londonfashionweekend.co.uk   Website: www.londonfashionweekend.co.uk

The London Print Design Fair (TLPDF)

A print-focused trade show launched by John Kelley, organiser of The London Textile Fair, and Texfusion – the London Asia Textile Fair to meet industry demand. The London Print Design Fair (TLPDF) is a prestigious print design and vintage clothes fair. The event showcases a unique offer of print design, embroidery, knit and vintage design with many national and international studios presenting their latest collections under one roof, attracting influential buyers and designers on the UK fashion scene.

The London Print Design Fair (TLPDF). Textile Events. 8 Gisburn Road, London, N8 7BS
Tel: 020 8347 8145
Email: genny@textileevents.co.uk   Websites: www.thelondonprintdesignfair.co.uk

The London Textile Fair (TLTF)

The London Textile Fair (TLTF) is one of the UK's premier platforms for European fashion fabrics, clothing and accessories. TLTF attracts the prestigious European mills and provides manufacturers and their agents with the opportunity to showcase their latest collections to the most influential buyers and designers in the UK fashion scene.

London Textile Fair. Textile Events, 8 Gisburn Road, London, N8 7BS
Tel: 020 8347 8145
Email: genny@textileevents.co.uk   Websites: www.thelondontextilefair.co.uk

London Print Design Fair

Made by Hand

Made by Hand is the showcase of a selective group of 135 makers and artists. The event also offers a programme of children's and adult workshops, demonstrations and talks about contemporary craft and art by leading makers, historians and curators.

Made by Hand
Email: hello@madebyhand-wales.co.uk
Website: http://madebyhand-wales.co.uk

Manchester Antique Textile Fair

Manchester Antique Textile Fair is organised by the Textile Society, and is a 'firm favourite for enthusiasts interested in buying antique and vintage costumes and textiles to collect, wear or discover'. The selection is vast with stands selling Oriental and Eastern European costumes and textiles, English costumes and textiles, fans, lace and linens as well as plenty of vintage clothes and textiles. See website for further details.

Manchester Antique Textile Fair
Website: www.textilesociety.org.uk/events/event-details

Margin, London

Founded in 2002, Margin is an independent fashion trade event in London renowned for providing a successful launch pad for exciting, directional new designers, alongside credible established brands.

Margin, London
Website: http://margin.tv

ITE MODA Ltd

As one of the UK's leading fashion trade event Moda is an essential destination for buyers looking to explore new brands. Moda's B2B fashion exhibition incorporates five shows in specialist sectors including womenswear, menswear, footwear, lingerie & swimwear and accessories, meaning there's something to suit everybody's buying needs. Catwalk shows, seminar programmes offer the latest updates from the industry.

ITE MODA Ltd. The Old Town Hall, Lewisham Road, Huddersfield, HD7 5AL
Tel: 01484 846069
Website: www.moda-uk.co.uk

National Asian Wedding Show

The National Asian Wedding Show takes place across the UK, with their flagship show held at ExCel, London.

India Fashion Week London. The Platinum Group. Suite 28, Quadrangle House, Stratford,
Email: info@platinum-group.com   Website: www.platinum-group.com

National Wedding Show

Organised by Ocean Media Group, the National Wedding Show has been running for over 20 years and attracts over 4,500 visitors to The North East Wedding Show and over 5,000 visitors to The London ExCeL Wedding Show. The events are attended by over 300 wedding specialists exhibiting their designs and services, along with a catwalk event.

National Wedding Show.
Ocean Media Group Ltd. One Canada Square, 19th Floor Canary Wharf, London, E14 5AP
Website: www.nationalweddingshow.co.uk

New Designers

Founded 30 years ago, New Designers is an exhibition that has launched the careers of thousands of the UK's design graduates from many of the UK's highly regarded design courses at universities and colleges. The two week annual event in June/July brings together education, private and public enterprises and the media, and is an important and exciting show for all involved in design. Features include talks, presentations, the Design Council Future Pioneer programme, workshops and awards. Exhibitors comprise of graduate stands, One Year On, and also additional stands which have included the British Arts Council, the Intellectual Property Office, the Society of Designer Craftsmen, the Society of Artists Agents, Handmade in Britain and Ideas Tap.

New Designers
Tel: 020 7288 6738
Email: nd@upperstreetevents.co.uk   Website: www.newdesigners.com

One Year On

One Year On is a destination feature within New Designers that presents young, entrepreneurial designers who are in their first year of business, and is the place to go to buy directly from selected designers. It runs across both weeks of the New Designers show and covers all disciplines.

One Year On.
New Designers
Tel: 020 7288 6738
Email: nd@upperstreetevents.co.uk　Website: www.newdesigners.com

Pulse

Pulse is a 'one-stop shop' for new products across fashion, accessories, home and gifts attracting and serving the needs of retailers' year on year. It provides an excellent opportunity to source new products from a mix of established brands and up-and-coming designer makers.

Pulse
Tel: 020 7384 7743
Website: www.pulse-london.com

Pure London

Pure London, UK is an important fashion trade event in the fashion calendar, with over 9000 brands of contemporary and directional womenswear, young fashion, accessories and footwear. Pure, London offer an excellent programme of trend presentations and catwalk shows. They also offer business seminars providing updates on the UK Fashion Industry, UK Trade and Investment and Fashion Retail from industry experts.

Pure, London
Tel: 0203 033 2500 (Visitor Enquiries)　Tel: 0203 033 2397 (Exhibitor Enquiries)
Email: visitor.help@i2iassist.com (Visitor Enquiries)　Email: Exhibitor.help@i2iassist.com
Website: www.purelondon.com

Scoop

Scoop is a premium women's apparel and accessories trade show held at the iconic Saatchi Gallery, London. Their exhibitors are leaders in the industry – directional, talented, successful and unique. Launched in February 2011, by Karen Radley, Scoop has fast become a key destination for showcasing international contemporary collections including De'Hart, Pyrus, Paul and Joe Sister, Goat, Agnelle, Duffy, Mercantia, Vivienne Westwood and many more.

Scoop London. The Saatchi Gallery, Duke of York's HQ, Kings Road, London SW3 4RY
Email: maria@scoop-international.com　Website: www.scoop-international.com

Scoop London

Launched in September 2015, Scoop London is a bi-annual show featuring international designers and collections from premium and emerging international talent.

Scoop London. The Saatchi Gallery, Duke of York's HQ, Kings Road, London SW3 4RY
Email: maria@scoop-international.com　Website: www.scoop-international.com

Scoop International

Launched in February 2011, Scoop is a boutique womenswear tradeshow, showcasing emerging and established directional fashion designers across two London venues featuring more than 400 collections to represent the best in contemporary and premium women swear, accessories, footwear and lifestyle products.

Scoop International
T. 020 7289 9399
Email: karen@karenradley.co.uk　Website: www.scoop-international.com

Sewing for Pleasure

Sewing for Pleasure is an event open to the general public offering supplies, ideas and innovations in the stitching world including dressmaking and home styling ideas, kits, patterns, fabrics and threads, along with a programme of talks, presentations and demonstrations.

International Craft and Hobby Fair Ltd. Dominic House, Seaton Road, Highcliffe, Dorset, BH23 5HW
Tel: 01425 272711 (General enquiries)
Email: info@ichf.co.uk　Website: www.sewingshow.co.uk

Showcase Ireland

Showcase is Ireland's Creative Expo, which is now in its 38th year, offers a showcase for over 435 exhibitors presenting unique, design-led products in fashion, knitwear, crafts, gifts and home. Other features of the event include the Enterprise Zone, runway shows and a special curated exhibition area, presentations and a seminar programme.

Showcase Ireland Events Ltd
Tel: +353 1 2958185   (General Enquiries)
Email: info@showcaseireland.com   Website: www.showcaseireland.com

Texfusion - The London Asia Textile Fair

Texfusion is the first trade UK fair catering exclusively for manufacturers from the Asian market. The fair presents a carefully selected group of high quality Asian companies with a wide range of 100% made-in-Asia textile and accessories. The Fair offers visitors the opportunity to source from manufacturers in China, Thailand, Vietnam, Bangladesh, India and Korea.

Texfusion - The London Asia Textile Fair. Textile Events. 8 Gisburn Road, London, N8 7BS
Tel: 020 8347 8145
Email: genny@textileevents.co.uk   Websites: www.londonasiatextilefair.co.uk

Textile Forum

Textile Forum is the luxury fashion fabric exhibition aimed at designers, manufacturers and retail fabric specialists. Exhibitors are mainly from the UK and the Continent, and can supply small minimums and stock lines in addition to handling volume orders.

Textile Forum. c/o Organiser, Linda Laderman PR Ltd, 11-13 Bayley Street, London, WC1B 3HD
Tel: 07802 501913
Email: linda.laderman@textileforum.org.uk   Website: textileforum.co.uk

Top Drawer

Top Drawer, London presents an inspirational showcase of over 800 selected British and international suppliers and designer-makers. Top Drawer takes place twice a year in January and September at the 'start of prime buying seasons, giving retailers the opportunity to stay ahead of the latest trends and launches, restock and refresh their stores'.

Top Drawer
Website: www.topdrawer.co.uk

100% Design

100% Design is officially the UK's largest design trade event with over 27,000 visitors including architects, interior designers, retailers and designers. The event is held in September and is the biggest event during the London Design Festival.

100% Design
Website: www.100percentdesign.co.uk

Unravel

Unravel is a festival of Knitting with exhibitors, suppliers, workshops, and 'Best in the Show'.

Unravel. Farnham Maltings, Farnham, Surrey, GU9 7QR0
Tel: 01252 745444
Website: http://craft.farnhammaltings.com

Vintage Fashion Fair

Founded in 2008, the Vintage Fashion Fair features vintage traders spanning the 1920s to the 1990s, a vintage tea party, a vintage hair salon and live acts.

Vintage Fashion Fair
Email: info@vintagefairsuk.co.uk   Website: www.thevintagefair.com

Wonderwool Wales

A festival of Welsh wool and natural fibres, Wonderwool Wales is an annual event founded in 2006 in order to 'promote wool and natural fibre production and its use in Wales'. Wonderwool Wales has exhibitors and trade stands covering all aspects of felting, knitting, weaving, spinning and crochet along with textile art, including raw materials, equipment, books and finished product.

Wonderwool Wales
Email: enquiries@wonderwoolwales.co.uk or bookings@wonderwoolwales.co.uk
Website: www.wonderwoolwales.co.uk

Grants, Awards, Finance and Funding Opportunities

How do you survive, prosper and support yourself as an artist, designer, craftsman, practitioner or new business initiative? Whether you are seeking funding to start a new enterprise, develop and support a business, study for career development, support graduate progression or for academic research, there is usually some support available somewhere.

Listed in this section are details of government and National Lottery funding, links to private investors, funding grants, enterprise bursaries, scholarships and loans to develop and support a range of knowledge and exchange activities and initiatives. Details of specific funds have not all been listed due to changes in the awards but the listed associations, businesses enterprises and councils all offer a fantastic range of information on their websites providing opportunities, profiled projects and much more.

AHRC (Arts and Humanities Research Council)

The AHRC is a 'national funding agency supporting both arts and humanities research'. See the Council's superb website for the latest news and details of events, listing current funding opportunities including Postgraduate Funding, Research Funding, Knowledge Exchange and Partnership, International Research, details of funded projects and much more.
AHRC (Arts and Humanities Research Council)
Emails: enquiries@ahrc.ac.uk Website: www.ahrc.ac.uk

Alternative Business Funding (ABF)

alternativebusinessfunding.co.uk (ABF) portal provides SME's with a way of sourcing non-bank funding. The portal is easy to use, visit alternativebusinessfunding.co.uk to find out which appropriate alternative funder could help your business funding.
Alternative Business Funding (ABF).
Email: mark.johnson@clifton-asset.co.uk Website: htpp://alternativebusinessfunding.co.uk

Angel Investment Network

The Angel Investment Network connects UK entrepreneurs and Angel Investors.
Angel Investment Network
Website: www.angelinvestmentnetwork.co.uk

Arts Council – England

'The Arts Council England champions, develops and invests in artistic and cultural experiences that enrich people's lives'. See the Council's informative website for details of initiatives, funding opportunities plus links to other sources of funding, advice and guidance, news, job opportunities in the arts sector and details of conferences, seminars and training.
Arts Council – England
Website: www.artscouncil.org.uk/funding/grants-arts

Arts Council – Northern Ireland

The Arts Council – Northern Ireland is the 'Funding and Development Agency for the Arts in Northern Ireland'. See the Council's website for details of initiatives, research and development, funding opportunities, advice and guidance, business support, news, job opportunities in the arts sector, and details of conferences, seminars and training.
Arts Council – Northern Ireland
Website: www.artscouncil-ni.org

Arts Council – Scotland

The Scottish Arts Council is the 'lead body for the funding, development and advocacy of the arts in Scotland'. Visit the website for links and resources, events, galleries, workshops, festivals and art fairs, unions, bodies and associations, publications and online resources, community and disability arts, conferences and events. For funding opportunities see Creative Scotland.
Scottish Arts Council
Website: www.scottisharts.org.uk

Arts Council – Wales

Arts Council Wales is 'responsible for funding and developing the arts in Wales'. See the Council's website for details of research publications, funding, sustainable development and much more.
Arts Council – Wales
Website: www.artswales.org.uk

Art Design Media Subject Centre – The Higher Education Academy (ADM-HEA)

The Higher Education Academy (HEA) is the 'national body for enhancing learning and teaching in higher education (HE)'. See website for specifics listing events and conferences, professional development including awards and accreditation, resources, consultancy and services.
Art Design Media Subject Centre – The Higher Education Academy (ADM-HEA)
Website: www.adm.heacademy.ac.uk/awards

The Arts Foundation

'The Arts Foundation supports emerging talent in the Arts' See the Foundation's website providing details on the Foundation's Fellowship Scheme, news and Artists Directory.
The Arts Foundation
Email: info@artsfoundation.co.uk   Website: www.artsfoundation.co.uk

Arts Trust Scotland

The Arts Trust Scotland is an independent Trust that helps working artists in Scotland to develop their skills and ideas. Visit the website for details of grants, eligibility and previous awards.
Arts Trust Scotland
Website: www.artstrustscotland.org.uk

Big Lottery Fund UK

Visit the Big Lottery Fund UK website for details of their mission, values, strategies, funding finder, and funding guidelines.
Big Lottery Fund UK
Email: general.enquiries@biglotteryfund.org.uk   Website: www.biglotteryfund.org.uk

British Academy Research Funding

The British Academy provides a range of grants and fellowships to support research across the humanities and social sciences. Funding opportunities cover UK and international research from the postdoctoral level upwards, supporting the best ideas, individuals and intellectual resources.
British Academy Research Funding
Tel: 020 7969 5200
Website: www.britac.ac.uk

British Business Bank

British Business Bank Investments is the commercial arm of British Business Bank plc. Visit the website for details of the UK Innovation Investment Fund (UKIIF) established to 'support the creation of viable investment funds targeting UK high growth technology-based businesses'.
UK Innovation Investment Fund (UKIIF)
British Business Bank
Website: http://british-business-bank.co.uk/uk-innovation-investment-fund

British Council

The British Council is the UK's international organisation for cultural relations and educational opportunities. The Council has a superb website providing details of the work in the Arts (Department of Architecture Design Fashion (ADF); the Creative Economy; Cultural Skills and Visual Arts) including details of UK and International projets, residencies, resources, funding opportunities and Global connections.
British Council.
Tel: 0161 957 7755
Email: general.enquiries@britishcouncil.org   Website: www.britishcouncil.org/arts

British Fashion Council (BFC)

The British Fashion Council (BFC) was formed in 1983 to 'showcase British designers and to develop London's position as a major player in the international fashion arena'. They have an excellent website providing details of the BFC business support network; designer support; press gallery; the BFC

Colleges Council initiative forming links between industry and fashion graduates from the UK's leading colleges and the BFC Education Foundation. The BFC are the organisers of British Fashion Awards. See the BFC website for details of NEWGEN; NEWGEN MEN; Rock Vault; Fashion Film BFC Contemporary, London Fashion Showcase Funding (LFSF), The BFC/Vogue Designer Fashion Fund; BFC/GQ Designer Menswear Fund and British Fashion Trust.
British Fashion Council (BFC)
Website: www.britishfashioncouncil.co.uk

Business Enterprise Fund (BEF)
Business Enterprise Fund (BEF) is a social enterprise that lends money to both start-ups and existing businesses who are unable to get lending from the banks. See website for further details.
Business Enterprise Fund (BEF).
Email: info@befund.org   Website: www.befund.org

Business Growth Fund (BGF)
The Business Growth Fund (BGF) was established in 2011 to help Britain's growing smaller and medium sized businesses, and is backed by five of the UK's main banking groups – Barclays, HSBC, Lloyds, RBS and Standard Chartered. The mission of the BGF is 'to unlock the potential of fast-growing UK businesses that need long-term capital to drive their future success'. See the Fund's website for specific details.
Business Growth Fund (BGF)
Website: www.businessgrowthfund.co.uk

Buzzbnk
Buzzbnk is a crowdfunding website that enables social entrepreneurs and social ventures to raise funds and build a crowd of supporters.
Buzzbnk.
Website: www.buzzbnk.org

CAPITB Trust
CapitB is an independent charity for the British Clothing and Apparel Industries that offer help to new trainees and small businesses. See website for further details of services.
CAPITB Trust. Access House, Halesfield 17, Telford, TF7 4PW
Tel: 01952 588 533
Website: capitbgrants.com

Community Development Finance Association (CDFA)
The CDFA represent Community Development Finance Institutions (CDFIs), who provide loans and support to people who find it difficult to get finance from commercial banks.
Community Development Finance Association (cdfa).
Email: info@cdfa.org.uk   Website: www.cdfa.org.uk

The Costume Society
The Costume Society aims to 'promote the study and preservation of historic and contemporary dress. Membership is open to anyone with an interest in the subject, whatever the level of interest and enthusiasm'. As a registered charity with educational aims, the Costume Society offers a number of awards and bursaries to students, researchers and trainee museum curators. See the Society's website for details of membership, activities and events, the Yarwood Award, the Patterns of Fashion Award and the Symposium Student Bursary.
The Costume Society
Website: costumesociety.org.uk

Creative Cultural Skills
'Creative and Cultural Skills is a campaigning organisation championing youth employment and fair access'. Visit the Creative Cultural Skills website to view their Mission Statement, Creative Choices programme, research and publications, employer and business advice, tools and resources, training opportunities and much more.
Creative Cultural Skills.
Email: info@ccskills.org.uk   Website: http://ccskills.org.uk

www.creative industries.co.uk

Creative Industries are a partnership of the government and industry promoting the UK's creative industries to trade audiences worldwide. Their website highlights the UK's creative industries by collating statistics, case studies, news, commentary, event details, contacts and other resources related to the creative sector.

Email: info@thecreativeindustries.co.uk   www.creative industries.co.uk

Creative Industry Finance

Creative Industry Finance is a programme designed to assist creative and cultural enterprises in securing the finance and investment they need to successfully develop and grow into sustainable businesses. The programme offers tailored advice with a focus on supporting businesses through the process of applying to one of their leading partners for a business development loan.

Creative Industry Finance. Somerset House, Strand, London, WC2R 1LA

Tel: 0207 759 1114

Email: info@creativeindustryfinance.org.uk Website: info@creativeindustryfinance.org.uk

Creative Scotland

Creative Scotland is the public body that supports the arts, screen and creative industries across all parts of Scotland. Visit the Creative Scotland website for details of funding programmes, funding overview, resources, events, projects and news.

Creative Scotland

Website: www.creativescotland.com

Creative Skillset

Creative Skillset is the industry skills body for the creative industries, including fashion and textiles. Led by research into the skill needs of the industries, they devise solutions that increase productivity and foster growth. One such solution for the Fashion and Textile industry has been the development of a broad range of apprenticeships, which enable smaller companies to scale-up and mould skills to fit their own business needs. They offer consultation for accessing funding and training and offer industry accreditation for HE and apprenticeship courses to help businesses identify the best quality graduates and talent. You can find this talent on Hiive.co.uk (Connect, Collaborate, Grow).

Creative Skillset. Focus Point, 21 Calendonian Road, London, N1 9GB

Tel: 020 7713 9800

Email: Info@creativeskillset.org Website: http://creativeskillset.org

Crowdcube Limited

Crowdcube is an investment crowdfunding platform. See website for details of investment opportunities, investing your money and raising finance.

Crowdcube Limited.

Email: support@crowdcube.com Website: www.crowdcube.com

Crowdfunder.co.uk

Crowdfunding is an alternative means of funding that allows individuals to take their ideas forward and make them a reality with the power of the crowd and change the world around them. 'Everyone has a great idea and at Crowdfunder we want to make as many ideas as possible succeed. Whether you own an existing business, want to launch a new one, are at school, work in the creative industry, need funds for a social enterprise, are a charity, or just an individual with a fantastic idea then we want to help you raise the funds needed for your project'.

Crowdfunder.co.uk. 9-10 Great Sutton Street, London, EC1V 0BX

Website: www.crowdfunder.co.uk

Daiwa Foundation

The Daiwa Foundation is a UK charity, established in 1988 to support closer links between Britain and Japan through a programme of activities and events, scholarships and exchange programmes. The Foundation has an office in Tokyo, Japan, and also has a London-based headquarters that acts as a centre for UK-Japan relations in Britain. For further information visit the Foundation's website.

Daiwa Foundation

Website: www.dajf.org.uk

East Midlands Visual Arts Network (EMVAN)

East Midlands Visual Arts Network (EMVAN) is an open network for all those working in the visual arts, particularly in the East Midlands, with a remit to strengthen the sector. It celebrates and promotes the making and presenting of contemporary visual art and contributes to a flourishing arts habitat in the region. It seeks to broker useful and inter-dependent relationships between artists and organisations; initiate a range of activities designed to meet the needs of the sector; and tackle common issues resulting in new ways of working. Emvan is part of the national contemporary visual arts network and aims to take full advantage of the knowledge, skills and assets of this wider network.

East Midlands Visual Arts Network (EMVAN)
Tel: 0115 914 1320
Email: coordinator@emvan.net   Website: www.emvan.net

East Regional Growth Loan Scheme

The East Regional Growth Loan Scheme supported by the Department for Business, Innovation and Skills is available to 'established incorporated businesses based within the East of England that have a minimum annual turnover of £100k, show strong growth potential and have a medium to long-term funding requirements to deliver that growth'. See website for further details.

East Regional Growth Loan Scheme. Riverside House, 4 Meadows Business Park, Station Approach, Blackwater, Camberley, Surrey, GU17 9AB
Tel: 01276 608510
Email: fundingenquiries@thefsegroup.com   Website: www.thefsegroup.com

East of Scotland Investment Fund (ESIF)

ESIF is a consortium of ten East of Scotland Local Authorities working together to provide loan finance to new and growing small to medium sized enterprises within the east of Scotland.

East of Scotland Investment Fund (ESIF)
Website: www.eastscotinvest.co.uk

EISA: Enterprise Investment Scheme Association

The EIS Association (EISA) is the trade body for the Enterprise Investment Scheme, which helps to provide capital to UK small and medium-sized enterprises (SMEs) through the Enterprise Investment Scheme (EIS) and the Seed Enterprise Investment Scheme (SEIS). For further information visit EISA website.

EISA: Enterprise Investment Scheme Association
Website: www.eisa.org.uk

Enterprise Loans East Midlands (ELEM)

Enterprise Loans East Midlands (ELEM) offer start up loans and business loans. ELEM is provided through First Enterprise Business Agency (FEBA).

Enterprise Loans East Midlands (ELEM). 90 Radford Road, Hyson Green, Nottingham NG7 5FU
Tel: 0845 602 7355 – 01159 423 772

Enterprise Northern Ireland (ENI)

Established in 2000, Enterprise Northern Ireland (ENI) represents the Local Enterprise Agencies working with entrepreneurs to help them in setting up and establishing business in Northern Ireland. See the ENI website for details of services and programmes such as the Regional Start Initiative, Business Boot Camp, Exploring Enterprise 2, networking opportunities and loan funding.

Enterprise Northern Ireland (ENI)
Website: www.enterpriseni.com

Esmée Fairbairn Foundation

Founded in 1961, the Esmée Fairbairn Foundation is one of the largest independent grant-making foundations in the UK. The Foundation funds four main sectors – the Arts, Children and Young People, and Environment and Social Change. Visit the Foundation's website for further details.

Esmée Fairbairn Foundation
Email: info@esmeefairbairn.org.uk   Website: www.esmeefairbairn.org.uk

Fashion Angel

Visit the Fashion Angel website for details of mentoring, networking, events, workshops and business funding for fashion entrepreneurs.

Fashion Angel
Email: info@fashion-angel.co.uk   Website: www.fashion-angel.co.uk

Finance for Enterprise

Finance for Enterprise offers start-up and business loans for South Yorkshire and/or the Sheffield City Region. The Enterprise website provides lots of useful resources from business planning basics to calculating start-up costs, to business law, marketing and social enterprises.
Finance for Enterprise
Website: http://finance-for-enterprise.co.uk

Finding Finance

The Finding Finance website founded by the trade body the Community Development Finance Association (CDFA) for 'providers of fair and affordable finance' offers an excellent website allowing you to view finance opportunities in specific regions, and gives details of the nearest Community Development Finance Institutions (CDFIs), and information listing success stories.
Finding Finance
Website: www.findingfinance.org.uk

Foundation East

Foundation East provides 'loans to business owners of start-up and growing enterprises in the Bedfordshire, Cambridgeshire, Essex, Hertfordshire, Norfolk, Suffolk and neighbouring areas.
Foundation East.
Email: info@foundationeast.org Website: www.foundationeast.org

Fredericks Foundation

Fredericks Foundation offers loans to people starting up or running a business in Berkshire, Bristol and Bath, Buckinghamshire, Cambridgeshire, Cornwall, Devon, Gloucestershire, Hampshire, Isle of Wight, Isles of Scilly, Kent, Lincolnshire, London, Northamptonshire, Surrey and Wiltshire, and who are unable to secure funding from high street banks.
Fredericks Foundation
Email: mail@fredericksfoundation.net   Website: www.fredericksfoundation.org/

Government Grants

Visit the Government grants website to use Funding Finder programmes to help locate funding for businesses, alongside many useful resources on offer at the Business Resource Centre.
Government Grants
Website: www.governmentfunding.org.uk

GRANTnet

GRANTnet is a free-to-use service from GRANTfinder, which can help small businesses and charitable and community groups find suitable funding.
GRANTnet
Website: www.grantsnet.co.uk

HEFCE - Higher Education Funding Council for England

The Higher Education Funding Council (HEFCE) 'works closely with, and provides funding to, the Higher Education Academy to promote innovation and excellence in teaching and to enhance students' experiences and their engagement throughout the higher education system'. Visit the HEFCE website for details of news and events, publications and reports, and for funding opportunities in the Higher Education (HE) sector across research, teaching and knowledge exchange.
Funding for the Development of Teaching and Learning (FDTL)
HEFCE
Email: hefce@hefce.ac.uk   Website: www.hefce.ac.uk

Jerwood Charitable Foundation (JCF)

The Jerwood Charitable Foundation (JCF) is 'dedicated to imaginative and responsible funding of the arts, with a particular focus on supporting emerging talent and excellence'. Visit the Foundations website for details about what they do, the Foundations current and past projects; job opportunities and bursaries; news and reviews; artist opportunities such as the Jerwood Drawing Prize; Jerwood Makers Open; Jerwood Painting Fellowships; awards and small grants; professional development and research.
Jerwood Charitable Foundation 171 Union Street, London, SE1 0LN
Tel: 020 7261 0279
Email: info@jerwood.org   Website: http://jerwoodcharitablefoundation.org

Leverhulme Trust

The Leverhulme Trust was established by the Will of William Hesketh Lever, the Founder of Lever Brothers. The Trust provides grants and scholarships for research and education. Visit the Trust's excellent website for details of grant funding including research leadership awards, research project grants, research fellowships and arts scholarships, artist in residence grants and for details of awards made. The Trust's website includes useful links detailing organisations and resources of further research councils, funding bodies, arts funding bodies, Higher Education funding, news and advice.
Leverhulme Trust
Website: www.leverhulme.ac.uk

NESTA (National Endowment for Science and Technology)

Nesta is an innovation charity with a mission to 'help people and organisations bring great ideas to life'. They have a superb website highlighting areas of their work, news and features, projects, publications, events and funding including details of NESTA's Creative Business Mentor Network.
NESTA
Website: www.nesta.org.uk

Pasold Research Fund

The Pasold Research grants are 'awarded to fund high quality research, relating to all branches of textile history including the history of dress and fashion'. Grants are awarded from small self-contained research projects to research activity grants, MA grants, PhD grants, publication grants, to the Raine grant and Pasold Research Fellowships. Visit the website for details on publications, events, conferences, resources, grants and Fellowships.
Pasold Research Fund
Website: www.pasold.co.uk

The Pitch

Founded in 2008, The Pitch is 'Britain's biggest small business' competition with a prize package that includes business support worth thousands of pounds up for grabs'. To enter The Pitch you need to have a trading business, which is less than three years old, or have a great business idea. See wesbite for further details.
The Pitch
Website: www.thepitchuk.com

Prince's Scottish Youth Business Trust

Youth Business Scotland supports young people aged 18 to 30 years old to start-up and grow in business, by providing essential funding, practical advice and professional mentoring support. The Trust works closely with partners across the Enterprise Network in Scotland and organises regular Elevator events for young people. Visit the website for further details of the Trust's work and activities.
Prince's Scottish Youth Business Trust.
Website: www.princes-trust.org.uk

Prowess

Support for women in business, Prowess has a growing membership network, and offers business support and services, a women's business network, a calendar of events and information on funding and business.
Prowess
Website: www.prowess.org.uk

Queen Elizabeth Scholarship Trust (Qest)

QEST is an organisation that supports education and excellence in Craft in the UK. The Trust funds 'talented people, whether at entry level in to the industry via a QEST Apprenticeship Scheme, or when they are trying to reach a level of excellence to further their career, via QEST Scholar awards'.
Queen Elizabeth Scholarship Trust (Qest).
Email: info@qest.org.uk   Website: www.qest.org.uk

Seed Enterprise Investment Scheme (SEIS)

The Seed Enterprise Investment Scheme (SEIS) aims to 'encourage investment in small and early stage companies by reducing the risk to investors of investing in these types of companies. The Government introduced SEIS as a way to promote new enterprise and boost economic growth in the UK'. SEIS offer an informative website for both the new and experienced investor, and entrepreneurs.
Seed Enterprise Investment Scheme (SEIS). Somerset House, Strand, London, WC2R 1LA
Email: info@seiswindow.org   Website: www.seiswindow.org.uk

Shell LiveWire Awards

Launched in 1982, Shell LiveWIRE offers an online community for young entrepreneurs aged 16-30. Shell LiveWIRE offer an awards programme for young entrepreneurs aged 16-30, based in the UK. See the website for full details of awards (New Awards, Young Entrepreneur of the Year Award and the Grand Ideas Award), and to sign up for the Shell LiveWire newsletter providing the latest information about how to enter.
Shell LiveWIRE UK.
Tel: 0191 423 6229
Email: enquiries@shell-livewire.org   Website: www.shell-livewire.org

Smarta Start Up Loans

Smarta Start Up Loans are government backed funds that are specifically for start-ups that have been trading for less than 12 months enabling and encouraging them to grow and develop their businesses, with the help of mentor support.
Smarta Start-up Loans
Website: https://startuploans.smarta.com

Theo Moorman Trust for Weavers

The Theo Moorman Trust for Weavers is a valuable resource for both young and experienced weavers. The Trust offers grants to 'enable weavers to purchase special equipment to pursue their craft, to undertake a specific project or projects in the development of their craft which might not normally be possible or for time out to develop their work'.
Theo Moorman Trust for Weavers. Lisa Harms. 46 Church Road, Abbots Leigh, Bristol, BS8 3QU
Website: www.theomoormantrust.org.uk

Trustfunding.org.uk

Trustfunding.org.uk is a useful subscription based fundraising tool identifying trusts and foundations.
Trustfunding.org.uk
Website: www.trustfunding.org.uk

UK Business Angels Association

The UK Business Angels Association is the national trade association representing angel and early stage investment in the UK. They provide policy and regulatory updates, market research, resources and tools, a UK Business Angels Association Members Directory listing all organisations. The Association gives lots of useful information on the website: Introducing Angel Investment, Accessing Angel Finance and Understanding the Angel Investment Process.
UK Business Angels Association.
Email: info@ukbusinessangelsassociation.org.uk Website: www.ukbusinessangelsassociation.org.uk

The UK Crowd Funding Association

The UK Crowdfunding Association was formed in 2012 by fourteen crowdfunding businesses. See website for full details of Associations members, UK and international supporters, and the aims of the Association. The Association has also published a code of practice that is adopted by UK crowd funding businesses.
The UK Crowd Funding Association
Email: info@ukcfa.org.uk Website: www.ukcfa.org.uk

The UK Research Office (UKRO)

The UK Research Office (UKRO) is the European office of the UK Research Councils, whose mission is 'to promote effective UK engagement in EU research, innovation and higher education activities'.
The UK Research Office (UKRO)
Website: www.ukro.ac.uk

Wellcome Trust

The Wellcome Trust is a global charitable foundation dedicated to 'improving health by supporting bright minds in science, the humanities and social sciences, and public engagement'. The Trust's funding focuses on 'supporting outstanding researchers, accelerating the application of research and exploring medicine in historical and cultural contexts'.

Wellcome Trust.

Website: www.wellcome.ac.uk

The Winston Churchill Memorial Trust

Each year The Winston Churchill Memorial Trust offers over 100 British Citizens Fellowships for a wide range of projects to travel overseas, to 'bring back knowledge and best practice for the benefit of others in their UK professions and communities'. Fellows receive a travel grant to cover return and internal travelling, daily living and insurance within the countries visited. Further details of the aims and objectives of the Trust, and examples of previous Fellowship awards are available to view on the Trusts website.

Winston Churchill Memorial Trust.

Tel: 020 7799 1660

Email: office@wcmt.org.uk   Website: www.wcmt.org.uk

Women in Business Loan Fund

'A dedicated loan fund for female entrepreneurs across the North West region, Women in Business Loan Fund seeks to raise finance to start or grow a business'. Visit the website for further details.

Women in Business Loan Fund.

Email: sp@bbvonline.net   Website: www.bbvonline.net

The Worshipful Company of Cordwainers

Cordwainers dates 1272, making the company one of the oldest Liveries in the City. Today, they have a strong charitable ethos, working to support talent in the footwear and leather industries through grants, awards, scholarships and bursaries, and other assistance.

The Worshipful Company of Cordwainers

Email: office@cordwainers.org   Website: www.cordwainers.org

Legal Support

ACID
ACID (Anti-copying in Design) is a membership trade organisation, established 'by designers for designers'. ACID is 'committed to raising awareness and encouraging respect for intellectual property rights within individual and corporate responsibility'. ACID has an excellent website that is informative and includes membership details, case studies, details of services, news and events, and lots of information to help its members in understanding and protecting their rights.
ACID. PO Box 5078, Gloucester, GL19 3YB
Email: info@acid.uk.com   Website: www.acid.uk.com

British Library Business and IP Centre
Launched in 2006, the Business and IP Centre aims to support businesses, entrepreneurs and inventors develop their organisations across a range of industries. They provide business advice, support and resources, and offer a programme of workshops, webinars, advice sessions and other events. They also have a comprehensive collection of databases, publications and industry guides offering an excellent resource to all new and developing businesses.
British Library Business and IP Centre. 96 Euston Road, London, NW1 2DB
Website: www.bl.uk/bipc

Business Companion
Business Companion is the Trading Standards Institutes website sponsored by the government Department for Business, Innovation and Skills. The website provides free advice for businesses about trading standards legislation and general business guidance.
Business Companion
Website: www.businesscompanion.info

The Chartered Institute of Patent Attorneys (CIPA)
The Chartered Institute of Patent Attorneys (CIPA) is the professional and examining body for patent attorneys in the UK. Any new manufacturing process or new invention can be protected by law. See the CIPA website to learn more about intellectual property rights such as patents and trademarks, design and copyright.
The Chartered Institute of Patent Attorneys. 95 Chancery Lane, London WC2A 1DT
Tel: 020 7405 9450
Email: mail@cipa.org.uk   Website: www.cipa.org.uk

The Chartered Trading Standards Institute (CTSI)
The Chartered Trading Standards Institute (CTSI) is a not-for-profit membership organisation that offers a resource for consumer protection and advice on the most recent legislation and policies, and represent trading standards professionals in the UK and overseas.
The Chartered Trading Standards Institute (CTSI)
Website: www.tradingstandards.gov.uk

Citizens Advice Bureau
Citizens Advice Bureaus are located across England, Scotland, Ireland and Wales. They provide free, independent, confidential and impartial advice to everyone on their rights and responsibilities. Visit their website for further information and to find your local Citizens Advice Bureau.
Citizens Advice Bureau
Website: www.citizensadvice.org.uk

Companies House – Gov.UK
Companies House is the UK's register of companies and is a Government Department for Business, Innovation and Skills (BIS) and provides a range of services and information on starting and running a company and changing your company details.
Companies House
Website: www.companieshouse.gov.uk

The Design and Artists Copyright Society (DACS)

The Design and Artists Copyright Society (DACS) is a membership based organisation representing fine artists, photographers, illustrators, craftspeople, cartoonists, architects, animators and designers. The Society offer an informative website providing excellent links and information on copyright and collective licensing, news and events and artist opportunities.
Design and Artists Copyright Society (DACS)
Tel: 020 7336 8811
Email: info@dacs.org.uk Website: www.dacs.org.uk

The Department for Work and Pensions (DWP)

The Department for Work and Pensions (DWP) is responsible for welfare and pensions including State Pension eligibility, claims and payments, and child maintenance policy.
The Department for Work and Pensions
Website: www.gov.uk/contact-pension-service

The European Patent Office (EPO)

The European Patent Office (EPO) is the patent office for Europe whose main activity is the examination of patent applications and the grant of European patents. See the EOP website for further information on their mission, activities taking place, advice relating to the process of applying for a patent and details of the European patent register.
The European Patent Office (EPO)
Website: www.epo.org

The Fashion and Design Protection Association (FDPA)

Established in 1974, The Fashion and Design Protection Association (FDPA) was founded to 'protect and uphold the rights of originators of fashion and other original designs'. The FDPA provides many services including legal consultations, copyright and design systems, an arbitration service, trade mark registration and brand consultancy and legal documentation.
The Fashion and Design Protection Association (FDPA). 94-96 Great North Road, London, N2 0NL
Tel: 0208 8837288
Email: info@fdpa.co.uk   Website: www.fdpa.co.uk

Federation of Small Businesses (FSB)

The Federation of Small Businesses (FSB) is a non-profit making UK membership organisation, with approximately 200,000 members. The FSB was founded to 'promote and protect the interests of the self-employed and owners of small firms'. Membership benefits include information on employment law, legal advice, tax protection and insurance cover for legal and professional fees.
Federation of Small Businesses (FSB)
Tel: 0808 20 20 888 (Head Office Customer Services)
Website: www.fsb.org.uk

HM Revenue and Customs (HMRC)

HMRC is the UK's tax and customs authority. Visit the HMRC website for details regarding National Insurance; self-employment; Self-Assessment; Tax and Revenue; Tax Guidance for Employers and much more.
HM Revenue and Customs (HMRC)
Website: www.hmrc.gov.uk

Ideas 21

Ideas 21 is supported by Government and industry, and offers information and resources to innovators, both corporate and individual. See the Ideas 21 website to view the Directory of Specialists, workshops and surgeries, and to access their 'Ask an Expert Online' offering advice ranging from protection of your idea, design and prototyping to licensing and manufacture.
Ideas 21
Website: www.ideas21.co.uk

Intellectual Property Awareness Network (IPAN)

Founded in 1993, IPAN was formed to support greater awareness and understanding of property rights including patents, trademarks, designs, copyright in commerce and industry, especially in the UK. See website for further details.

Intellectual Property Awareness Network (IPAN).
C/o The Chartered Institute of Patent Attorneys, 3rd Floor, 95 Chancery Lane, London, WC2A 1DT
Tel: 0207 4409360
Email: ipan@ipaware.net   Website: www.ipaware.net

Intellectual Property Office (IPO)

The UK Intellectually Property Office (IPO) is the official government body who can help in getting the right type of protection for your creation or/and invention. The IPO website provides information concerning intellectual property (IP) rights, patents and applying for a patent, trademarks, designs, copyright, law practice and other protection, including Intellectual property for businesses. There are also guidance tools and case studies available.

Intellectual Property Office
Tel: 0300 300 2000
Email: information@ipo.gov.uk   Website: www.ipo.gov.uk

Smallbusiness.co.uk

Smallbusiness.co.uk is an online service that provides resources, products and help for small business owners and start-ups. The website offer lots of free online advice, news articles, guides and features for small businesses.

Smallbusiness.co.uk
Website: www.smallbusiness.co.uk

UK Trade and Investment (UKTI)

UK Trade and Investment (UKTI) works with UK based businesses to help grow internationally achieving success in international markets through export trading. See the UKTI website for further details of international trade services, to register for business opportunities and to access details of all UKTI events, trade fairs and webinars.

UK Trade and Investment (UKTI)
Tel: 020 7215 5000
Email: enquiries@ukti.gsi.gov.uk   Website: www.ukti.gov.uk

Museums, Research Centres, Collections and Galleries

The museums and galleries included in this section house fashion, costume and textile collections, archives and displays housing historical artefacts and memorabilia, providing excellent sources of inspiration for artists and designers. Many museums and centres offer exhibited collections and additional resources including archives, study centres, library facilities, educational programmes, workshops, tours, daily activity programmes and venues for exhibitions.

If you are intending to visit a museum, gallery, mill or research centre always contact or check for details, dates and times of opening including admission charges before your visit to avoid any disappointment. Occasionally some centres have to close for periods due to refurbishment, maintenance and changing of exhibitions and displays. Some of the museums listed are relatively small independent museums and are managed and run entirely by teams of volunteers, and therefore have limited opening times, with some centres only being open by appointment. Many museums and galleries are only able to display a very small selection of their collection. Therefore, if you are a researcher it is essential to contact the museum before visiting to discuss your requirements and the possibility of access to specific stored collections or items.

Aberdeen Art Gallery and Museum
The Applied Art Collection comprises of over 15,000 items including applied and decorative art, design, craft and costume and textiles. The Collection includes the work of designer Bill Gibb (1943-1988), along with an archive of over 2,000 fashion sketches, working drawings and notes.
Aberdeen Art Gallery and Museum. Aberdeen Art Gallery, Schoolhill, Aberdeen, AB10 1FQ
Tel: 01224 523700
Email: info@aagm.co.uk   Website: www.aagm.co.uk

Abington Museum
Abington Museum is housed in a 15th century manor house, once the home of Shakespeare's granddaughter, Elizabeth Bernard. It is now a museum telling the history of the house, and has a 19th century Costume Gallery, and room of Victorian curiosities.
Abington Museum. Park Avenue South, Northampton, NN1 5LW
Tel: 01604 838110
Email: museums@northampton.gov.uk   Website: www.northampton.gov.uk/museums

Allhallows Museum
Situated in a town famous for lacemaking, Allhallows Museum houses one of the most comprehensive collections of Honiton Lace in the world, with displays feature examples of 16th to early 20th century.
Allhallows Museum. High Street, Honiton, EX14 1PG
Tel: 01404 44966
Email: info@honitonmuseum.co.uk   Website: www.honitonmuseum.co.uk

American Museum in Britain
The collection at the Museum is extremely varied, ranging from quilts to Renaissance maps, Shaker furniture to ancient Native American tools. There is an internationally famous collection of American quilts, Navajo weavings, American hooked rugs, woven coverlets, and embroideries. The Museum's library holds a collection of over 11,000 specialist books relating to American History and culture, and is open only by prior appointment.
American Museum in Britain. Claverton Manor, Bath, BA2 7BD
Tel: 01225 460503
Email: enquiries@americanmuseum.org   Website: www.americanmuseum.org

Armagh County Museum
The Armagh County Museum Costume Collection contains an array of ladies clothes, including wedding dresses, day dresses, evening gowns and accessories including fans and purses many dating from the Victorian period.
Armagh County Museum. The Mall East, Armagh, BT61 9BE
Tel: +44 (0) 28 3752 3070
Website: www.nmni.com/acm/Collections/Art/Costume

Bankfield Museum

Bankfield Museum (Calderdale Museums) has over 14,000 items of costume and textiles including 18th to 20th century women's clothing and ethnographic collections from around the world. Textiles include spinning and weaving to dyeing and sample books.
Bankfield Museum. Boothtown Road, Halifax, West Yorkshire, HX3 6HG
Tel: 01422 352334
Email: collections@calderdale.gov.uk
Website: www.calderdale.gov.uk/museums

The Beamish Museum, County Durham

Beamish open air living and working museum tells the story of people living in the North East England in the Georgian, Victorian and Edwardian times.
Beamish Museum. Beamish, County Durham, DH9 0RG
Tel: 0191 370 4000
Email: museum@beamish.org.uk   Website: www.beamish.org.uk

Beck Isle Museum of Rural Life

The Beck Isle Museum of Rural Life illustrates life over 200 years specialising in the Victorian period. There is a costume room housing clothes from the 18th, 19th and 20th centuries. The Museum also has a print room housing a working Columbian printing press that was once used by a local printer in Pickering, and over 160 years old letterpress printing equipment.
Beck Isle Museum. Beck Isle, Pickering, North Yorkshire, YO18 8DU
Tel: 01751 473653
Website: www.beckislemuseum.org.uk

Bexhill Museum

Bexhill Museum houses collections from local history and archaeology to fashion and Bexhill's motoring heritage. The Museum's unique fashion and costume collections date from the 17th century
to the modern day, with displays exhibiting corsets to stunning evening dresses.
Bexhill Museum. Egerton Road, Bexhill on Sea, East Sussex, TN39 3HL
Tel: 01424 787950 (General enquiries)
Website: www.bexhillmuseum.co.uk

Birmingham City Museum and Art Gallery (BMAG)

Birmingham City Museum and Art Gallery (BMAG) has over 40 galleries displaying art, applied art, social history, archaeology and ethnography. The Art Gallery is famous for its 'Pre-Raphaelite paintings forming part of the largest public Pre-Raphaelite collection in the world'. See the BMAG website to view their online collections.
Birmingham Museum and Art Gallery. Chamberlain Square, Birmingham, B3 3DH.
Tel: 0121 348 8000 (General enquiries)
Website: www.birminghammuseums.org.uk

Blairs Museum

Blairs Museum offers a unique insight into Scotland's Catholic history and heritage with collections spanning more than 500 years. Highlights include church textiles, hand embroidered vestments and ceremonial clothing.
Blairs Museum. South Deeside Road, Blairs, Aberdeen, Scotland, AB12 5YQ
Tel: 01224 863767
Email: manager@blairsmuseum.com   Website: www.blairsmuseum.com

Blaise Castle House Museum

Blaise Castle House Museum is housed in a late 18th Century mansion with a Victorian school room, situated in Blaise Castle Estate at Henbury. The Museum houses a large collection of 20th century women's everyday wear. They also house a small collection of costume and accessories from 1800 to 1970s, which is on public display. Viewing is by appointment.
Blaise Castle House Museum. Henbury Road, Bristol, BS10 7QS
Website: www.bristolmuseums.org.uk/blaise-castle-house-museum

The Blandford Fashion Museum

The Blandford Fashion Museum has an extensive collection of day wear, evening wear and wedding dresses dating from 1730 to 1970s including a large collection of accessories: shoes, hats, parasols, bags and many other items. The Museum has a resource room for use by students studying fashion and textiles.
The Blandford Fashion Museum. Lime Tree House, The Plocks, Blandford Forum, Dorset, DT11 7AA
Tel: 01258 453006
Website: www.theblandfordfashionmuseum.com

Borders Textile Towerhouse

Borders Textile Towerhouse houses a range of artefacts and archives celebrating the 'past, present and the future of the Borders knit, tweed and textile industries'. Collections include vintage and contemporary fashions, mill machinery and tools, and over a century of textile fabric and design samples from some of Scotland's best-known brands.
Borders Textile Towerhouse. 1 Tower Knowe, Hawick, TD9 9EN
Tel: 01450 377615
Email: textiletowerhouse@scotborders.gov.uk
Website: www.museumsgalleriesscotland.org.uk/member/borders-textile-towerhouse

The Bowes Museum

The Bowes Museum houses artwork, ceramics, metalwork, sculpture, a permanent Fashion and Textile Gallery and other items of historical interest. The Fashion and Textile Collection includes women's, children's and men's clothing and accessories from the late 18th century to the 1960s. The collections consist of wedding dresses, and evening gowns by Paquin, Madeleine Vionnet, and Victor Steibel. The Museum also houses excellent examples of embroidery, tapestry, quilts, home textiles and holds the Blackborne Lace Collection.
The Bowes Museum, Barnard Castle, Co Durham DL12 8NP
Tel: 01833 690606
Email: info@thebowesmuseum.org.uk   Website: www.thebowesmuseum.org.uk

Bradford Museums and Galleries - Industrial

Bradford Industrial Museum is housed in an original Victorian worsted spinning mill 'Moorside Mills, built around 1875. The Museum houses costume collections reflecting the local history and culture, with industrial textile samples and items relating to the history of manufacturing.
Bradford Museums and Galleries, Industrial Moorside Mills, Moorside Road, Eccleshill, Bradford, BD2 3HP
Tel: 01274 435900
Website: www.bradfordmuseums.org

Brighton Museum and Art Gallery

Brighton Museum and Art Gallery houses wide-ranging collections, which include galleries of 20th Century Decorative Art and Design; a Performance Gallery exhibiting puppets, masks, costume and musical instruments; a fashion and style Gallery; two local history galleries and much more.
Brighton Museum and Art Gallery. Royal Pavilion Gardens, Brighton, East Sussex, BN11EE
Tel: 03000 290900 (General enquiries)
Email: visitor.services@brighton-hove.gov.uk   Website: http://brightonmuseums.org.uk

British Airways Heritage Collection

The British Airways Heritage Collection includes a large archive of documentation recording the formation, development and management of BOAC, BEA, BSAA, the pre-war Imperial Airways Ltd and British Airways Ltd. The Museum has over 400 uniforms from the 1930s to the present day. For further information about the Heritage Collection and to arrange a visit to the Centre see website for details.
British Airways Heritage Collection
Tel: 020 8562 5777/020 8562 5737
Website: www.britishairways.com

The British Museum

The British Museum was founded in 1753, the first national public museum in the world. The Museum houses a collection of over seven million objects representing the rich history of human cultures. See the Museum's website for details of collections, exhibitions, events, tours and Museum activities. They also

offer a programme of higher education courses, ESOL programmes and opportunities for adult learning, on-line research catalogues, publications, libraries and archives.
British Museum, Great Russell Street, WC1B 3DG
Tel: 020 7323 8299
Email: information@britishmuseum.org   Website: www.britishmuseum.org

Calverton Museum

Calverton Museum is a folk museum located in a stockinger's cottage dedicated to William Lee and the local industry of Calverton; where in 1851 over 200 framework knitters were recorded. There is a frameworker's knitting machine dated approximately 1700 with displays and information on the history of framework knitting.
Calverton Museum. Main Street, Calverton, Nottinghamshire, NG14 6LU
Tel: 0115 8417832

Central Saint Martins Museum and Study Collection

Central Saint Martins Museum and Study Collection acts as the College archive with work from the 13th century to the present day. The Collection includes early printed books, prints, illuminated manuscripts, embroideries, theatre costume design, textiles, garments, and much more. Details of their collections, their online catalogue and visiting times are available on their website.
Museum and Study Collection. Central Saint Martins, Granary Building, 1 Granary Square, London, N1C 4AA
Tel: 020 7514 7146
Email: museum.collection@csm.arts.ac.uk   Website: www.csm.arts.ac.uk/museum

Charleston

Charleston is the country home of the Bloomsbury Group and shows Vanessa Bell and Duncan Grant's decorative style and represents 'the fruition of over sixty years of artistic creativity'. Charleston presents examples of the decorative art of the Bloomsbury artists with murals, painted furniture, ceramics and objects from the Omega Workshops, paintings and textiles. Search and view their collections, Photo Gallery and resources online.
Charleston. Firle, Lewes, East Sussex, BN8 6LL
Tel: 01323 811626 (Office)   Tel: 01323 811265 (Visitor information)
Email: info@charleston.org.uk   Website: www.charleston.org.uk

The Charles Wade Costume Collection

The Charles Wade Costume Collection consists of over 2,200 items collected by Charles Paget Wade in the early 20th century. The Collection has an excellent range of 18th and early19th century costume and accessories, including a good representation of men's embroidered coats and waistcoats. Military uniforms and a small ethnographic collection and Samurai armour are also represented.
The Charles Wade Collection. Berrington Hall, Leominster, Herefordshire, HR6 0DW
Tel: 01568 615721
Email: althea.mackenzie@nationaltrust.org.uk

Chertsey Museum

The Chertsey Museum houses collections from the history of the area, to fine art and decorative art collections including the Olive Matthews Collection of Dress and Textiles. This Collection contains over 4,000 men's, women's and children's fashionable clothes dating from c1700 to the present. There is also a fashion gallery and library providing an excellent resource for students and researchers of dress, textile and design history.
Chertsey Museum. The Cedars, 33 Windsor Street, Chertsey, Surrey, KT16 8AT
Tel: 01932 565764
Email: enquiries@chertseymuseum.org.uk   Website: www.chertseymuseum.org.uk

Coggeshall Museum

Coggeshall Museum is located in the Village Hall. It has a working wool loom and also a collection of Coggeshall lace including lace-making tools and patterns to mark out the design. Other collections include Edwardian costume, wedding dresses, agricultural clothing and war time uniforms. They also have library and study facilities.
Coggeshall Museum. Village Hall, Stoneham Street, Coggeshall, CO6 1RH
Tel: 01376 563003 (Curator Contact)
Email: coggeshallmuseum@btinternet.com Website: www.coggeshallmuseum.org.uk

Coldharbour Mill Working Wool Museum

Coldharbour Mill Museum is located in an 18th century spinning mill and tells the story of the Devon wool and textile industry with displays of machinery and artefacts associated with the wool trade, along with weaver's cottage, dyers and carpenters workshops. Guided tours of the Mill are available along with activities, workshops and tuition.

Coldharbour Mill. Uffculme, Cullompton, Devon, EX15 3EE.

Tel: 01884 840960

Email: info@coldharbourmill.org.uk   Website: www.coldharbourmill.org.uk

Colne Valley Museum

Colne Valley Museum is located in traditional handloom weavers' cottages built in the 1840s, and houses a Loom Chamber, Spinning and Cropping rooms and a clog-maker's workshop with a full range of period tools. The Museum is run entirely by volunteers, so please check their website or telephone for full details of opening times or for organising a visit.

Colne Valley Museum

Tel: 01484 659762

Email: info@colnevalleymuseum.org.uk Website: www.colnevalleymuseum.org.uk

Colour Experience

Formerly the Museum of Colour, the Colour Experience is an educational activity of the Society of Dyer's and Colourists with interactive galleries and displays exploring the world and science of colour. There are regular workshops and downloadable resources available.

The Colour Experience. 1 Providence Street, Bradford, West Yorkshire, BD1 2PW

Tel: 01274 390 955

Email: info@sdc.org.uk Website: www.sdc.org.uk/education/colour-experience

The Constance Howard Gallery & The Goldsmiths Textile Collection

The Constance Howard Gallery is home to the Goldsmiths Textile Collection comprising of textile art, embroidery and dress from all continents, and has a specialist reference library open to the public.

The Constance Howard Gallery & the Goldsmiths Textile Collection.

Goldsmiths University of London, Deptford Town Hall Building, New Cross Road, London, SE14 6AF

Tel: 020 7717 2210

Email: textiles@gold.ac.uk Website: www.gold.ac.uk/textile-collection

The Courtaulds Institute of Art

The Courtauld Institute of Art is an independent college of the University of London based at Somerset House, and one of the world's leading centres for the study of the history and conservation of art and architecture. Collections range from paintings, prints and drawings to textiles and fashion.

The Courtaulds Institute of Art. Somerset House, Strand, London, WC2R 0RN

Tel: 020 7872 0220

Website: www.courtauld.ac.uk

Crafts Study Centre

The Crafts Study Centre is a specialist university museum open to the public as well as a research centre of the University for the Creative Arts. The Centre's collections include modern and contemporary calligraphy, ceramics, textiles (print, woven and needlework), furniture and wood as well as makers' diaries, working notes and photographs dating from the 1920s. Exhibitions and gallery talks by leading artist-makers are held throughout the year. The Centre's research library is available by appointment.

Crafts Study Centre. University for the Creative Arts, Falkner Road, Farnham, Surrey, GU9 7DS

Tel: 01252 891450

Email: craftscentre@ucreative.ac.uk Website: www.csc.ucreative.ac.uk

Design Museum

The Design Museum Collection comprises of over 3000 objects ranging from early Modernism of the 1900s to the cutting edge of contemporary design. The Collection tells the history of design in mass production and includes furniture, lighting, domestic appliances and communications technology, and provides an insight in to 20th century design and looks at how design affects our lives.

Membership details and exhibition programme are available on the Museum's website.

Design Museum. Shad Thames, London, SE1 2YD
Tel: 0207 403 6933
Email: info@designmuseum.org   Website: http://designmuseum.org

Dorset County Museum

Dorset County Museum houses a costume and textile collection of men's, women's and children's clothes from between 1650 to 1950, and includes baby robes, smock-frocks, Dorset sun-bonnets, wedding gowns, embroidery samplers, Dorset buttons and Dorset feather stitchery. Other items include dress accessories (including footwear, fans, jewellery, millinery and beadwork), lace, quilts, school uniforms and later 18th century fashionable male clothing.
Dorset County Museum. High West Street, Dorchester, Dorset, DT1 1XA
Tel: 01305 262735
Website: www.dorsetcountymuseum.org

The Dover Museum

The Dover Museum holds the Deal Costume and Accessories Collection, comprising of over 500 items ranging from the beginning of the 19th century to the post-war period of the 1950's, 60's and 1970's, along with its own collection. Collections includes clothes for men, women, children and babies, with representative examples of underwear, uniforms, wedding dresses, bathing costumes, decorative waistcoats, and accessories.
The Dover Museum. Market Square, Dover, Kent, CT16 1PB
Tel: 01304 201066
Website: www.dovermuseum.co.uk

Embroiderers' Guild

The Guild has a superb collection of embroidery dating from Coptic times to the present, comprising of over 11,000 catalogued items, covering more than six centuries and many countries. Catalogued items include designs, threads and needlework tools. The Embroiders' Guild also has a library housing a fantastic resource of approximately 3,000 books from over 30 countries published in the last 200 years, and over 500 magazines. See the Guild's website for details of their Collection, resources and library opening times.
Embroiderers' Guild.
Postal Address: Embroiderers' Guild House. 1 Kings Road, Walton on Thames, Surrey, KT 12 2RA
Tel: 01932 260738   Ext: 29 (General Enquiries)
Email: administrator@embroiderersguild.com   Website: www.embroiderersguild-secure.co.uk

Fairfield Mill

Fairfield Mill is housed in a restored Victorian woollen mill on the edge of Cumbria and Yorkshire, and tells the history of the woollen and textile industry in the Sedbergh area. The Mill has working looms, exhibitions, craft demonstrations, workshops and a programme of events.
Fairfield Mill. Garsdale Road, Sedbergh, Cumbria, LA10 5LW
Tel: 015396 21958
Email: admin@farfieldmill.org   Website: www.farfieldmill.org

The Fan Museum

The Fan Museum is the only museum in the UK dedicated to the history of fans and the art of fan making, and houses a collection of over 5,000 fans from around the world, dating from the 12th century to the present day. The Museum also houses rare publications and fan-making tools displayed inside two restored Grade II listed Georgian townhouses. The Museum's study facilities and reference library are available for use by appointment.
The Fan Museum. 12 Crooms Hill, Greenwich, London, SE10 8ER
Tel: 0208 305 1441
Email: j.mundy@thefanmuseum.org.uk   Website: www.fan-museum.org

Fashion Museum

The Fashion Museum holds a 'world-class collection of contemporary and historic dress and is housed in the magnificent Assembly Rooms'. There are almost 100,000 objects in the Museum's collection, and over 165 dressed figures on display in the Fashion Museum galleries from the 17th century to the

present day. The Collection is stunning with examples of menswear, womenswear, accessories, dresses, coats, jackets, corsets, knitwear, fashion photography, pockets, shirts, blouses, waistcoats, fans. See Museum's website for further details of collections, exhibitions and events, the facilities, opening times and admission.
Fashion Museum. The Assembly Rooms, Bennett Street, Bath, BA1 2QH
Tel: 01225 477789
Email: fashion_bookings@bathnes.gov.uk   Website: www.museumofcostume.co.uk

Fashion & Textile Museum (FTM)
Founded by the British designer Zandra Rhodes, the Fashion and Textile Museum (FTM), London is a centre for contemporary fashion, textiles and jewellery, housing permanent and changing exhibitions from 1947 to the present day. It also houses the Zandra Rhodes Collection spanning 40 years of work and is an excellent and inspirational resource. The FTM is now operated by Newham College, and the Academy runs a programme of talks, events, and courses for students and businesses.
Fashion & Textile Museum (FTM). 83 Bermondsey Street, London, SE1 3XF

Tel: 020 7407 8664
Email: info@ftmlondon.org   Website: www.ftmlondon.org

The Fitzwilliam Museum
The Fitzwilliam Museum was described by the Standing Commission on Museums and Galleries in 1968 as "one of the greatest art collections of the nation and a monument of the first importance". The Department of Applied Arts is responsible for about 20,000 pieces of decorative arts and sculpture from Europe, the Middle East, India and the Far East. See details of the Museum's collections online.
The Fitzwilliam Museum. Trumpington Street, Cambridge, CB2 1RB
Tel: 01223 332900
Email: fitzmuseum-enquiries@lists.cam.ac.uk   Website: www.fitzmuseum.cam.ac.uk

The Forge Mill Needle Museum
The Forge Needle Mill Museum, Redditch tells the story of needlemaking and how Redditch dominated the world needle market. The Museum includes models and recreated scenes illustrating the heritage of the needle and how needles were made, and also the fishing tackle industries. The Museum also houses a collection of needle cases produced by the Redditch needle companies, and a collection of photographs relating to the needle industry. The Museum regularly hosts exhibitions from the country's leading textile artists.
Forge Mill Needle Museum. Needle Mill Lane, Riverside, Redditch, Worcestershire, B98 8HY
Email: info@forgemill.org.uk   Website: www.forgemill.org.uk

Framework Knitters Museum
The Framework Knitters Museum features two preserved frameshops, cottages, chapel and outbuildings located around Britain's only preserved Knitter's Yard, and illustrates the lives and working conditions which led to the Luddite Riots. Visits include machine demonstrations and an opportunity to make a knitted souvenir. A shop promotes local textile makers.
Framework Knitters Museum. Chapel Street, Ruddington, Nottingham, NG11 6HE
Tel: 0115 984 6914
Email: office@frameworkknittersmuseum.org.uk   Website: www.frameworkknittersmuseum.org.uk

Gawthorpe Hall
Gawthorpe Hall houses a specialist collection of lace, embroidery and European textiles collected by Miss Rachel B. Kay-Shuttleworth (1886 – 1967), who was renowned for her knowledge and expert skills in needlework. She turned her ancestral home Gawthorpe Hall into a Craft House in order to 'keep alive the textile skills and techniques she feared were being lost'. See the website for further details of the Collection, opening times and their online Gallery.
Gawthorpe Hall. Burnley Road, Padiham, near Burnley, Lancashire, BB12 8UA
Tel: 01282 771004
Email: gawthorpehall@nationaltrust.org.uk
Website: www.nationaltrust.org.uk/gawthorpe-hall   www.gawthorpetextiles.org.uk

Glasgow Museums

The Glasgow Museums collections include a few early pieces of 17th century costume in the Burrell Collection. The majority dates from about 1760 and is particularly strong with regards to late 19th century to early 20th century womenswear.

Glasgow Museums. Glasgow Museums Resource Centre, 200 Woodhead Road, South Nitshill Industrial Estate, Glasgow, G53 7NN

Tel: 0141 276 9300

Email: museums@glasgowlife.org   Website: www.glasgowmuseums.com

The Goldsmiths Textile Collection & Constance Howard Gallery

The Constance Howard Gallery is home to the Goldsmiths Textile Collection comprising of textile art, embroidery and dress from all continents, and has a specialist reference library open to the public. The Constance Howard Gallery holds exhibitions of textiles. These include pieces from the Collection or from associated research projects, or work by textile artists, students and alumni.

The Goldsmiths Textile Collection & Constance Howard Gallery. Goldsmiths University of London, Deptford Town Hall Building, New Cross Road, London, SE14 6AF

Tel: 020 7717 2210

Email: textiles@gold.ac.uk   Website: www.gold.ac.uk/textile-collection

Grosvenor Museum

Grosvenor Museum has a range of collections from art, social history, and archaeology to natural history, and it also has a small Costume Gallery.

Grosvenor Museum. 27 Grosvenor Street, Chester, CH1 2DD

Tel: 01244 972197

Email: grosvenormuseum@cheshirewestandchester.gov.uk

Website: www.cheshirewestmuseums.org

Hampshire Museums and Archives

Hampshire Museum Services manage 19 museums and specialist sites across Hampshire. Their collections represent Hampshire's archaeology, history, natural sciences, art and cultural life. They hold a large collection of bags and purses from the 18th century to the present day, and a large Fan collection, which have been collected over a period of 50 years. See their Museums Service website for further information for details on specific museums and collections.

Hampshire Museums Service. Chilcomb House, Chilicomb Lane, Winchester, Hampshire, SO23 8RD

Tel: 0845 603 5635

Email: musmsw@hants.gov.uk Website: www.hants.gov.uk/museums

Hands on History Museum

The Museum store holds a selection of costume dating from the 18th century, with a particular emphasis on Victorian and 20th century women's fashion. Access to the Collection is restricted, although details of items in the collection can be viewed online.

Hands on History Museum. South Church Side, Hull, HU1 RR

Tel: 01482 613902

Email: museums@hullcc.gov.uk

Website: wwwhullcc.gov.uk/museums   Website: www.hullcc.gov.uk/museumscollections

Harris Museum and Art Gallery

The Harris Museum and Art Gallery is an important regional museum which holds collections of fine art, decorative arts, costume and textiles of regional, national and international significance. The Costume and Textile Collection includes over 6,000 costumes, 600 textiles and 2,000 fashion plates, dating from 1600s to the present day. Notable pieces include their collection of 1800s dresses, the collection and archive of Horrockses Fashions, a sampler collection, and the Forbes Watson pattern books. See links for pattern books: www.tmoi.org.uk

Harris Museum and Art Gallery. Market Street, Preston, Lancashire, PR1 2PP

Tel: 01772 258248

Email: harris.museum@preston.gov.uk Website: www.harrismuseum.org.uk

Haslemere Educational Museum

Haslemere Educational Museum is one of the largest natural history museums in central southern England with over 240,000 specimens, along with over 140,000 Human History artefacts from around the world. They also have a broad-ranging clothing and accessories, and historic textile collection. See highlights of the collections on the Museum's website and online database.

Haslemere Educational Museum. 78 High Street, Haslemere, Surrey, GU27 2LA
Tel: 01428 642112
Email: enquiries@haslemeremuseum.co.uk   Website: www.haslemeremuseum.co.uk

Hat Works

The Hat Works is located in Wellington Mill, which was once a hat factory, and is the UK's only museum dedicated solely to the hatting industry, hats and headwear. The Museum includes a collection of headwear from around the world, and includes a recreated hat factory with twenty Victorian-style machines, which have been restored to show how hats were made.

Hat Works. Wellington Mill, Wellington Road, Stockport, SK3 0EU
Tel: 0161 474 2399
Website: www.stockport.gov.uk/services/leisureculture/museumsandgalleries/hatworks

Helmshore Textile Museum

Helmshore Textile Museum exhibits embrace many aspects of Lancashire textile industry including handlooms to the power loom, tracing the history of weaving. There are many original machines displayed, with some still in working order. To discover more about weaving and steam power, visit their sister museum - the Queen Street Mill Textile Museum in Harle Syke, which is the last remaining steam powered weaving mill in the world.

Helmshore Textile Museum. Holcombe Road, Helmshore Rossendale, Lancashire, BB4 4NP
Tel: 01706 226459
Email: helmshoremuseum@lancashire.gov.uk   Website: www.helmshore.com

Hereford Museum Resource and Learning Centre

The Hereford Museum's costume and textile collection span from the 17th century to the present day. It includes male, female and children's costume, military uniforms, flat textiles, sewing accessories, lace and fashion plates.

Hereford Museum Resource and Learning Centre. 58 Friar Street, Hereford, HR4 0AS
Tel: 01432 383033
Email: amackenzie@herefordshire.gov.uk

The Higgins Art Gallery & Museum, Bedford

The Museum has a collection of over 2500 items of costume includes accessories and also a collection of lace. See website for details and images of the collections.

The Higgins Art Gallery & Museum, Bedford, Castle Lane, Bedford, MK 40 3RP
Email: thehiggins@bedford.gov.uk   Website: www.thehigginsbedford.org.uk

Historic Royal Palaces

Historic Royal Palaces is an independent charity that looks after the Tower of London, Hampton Court Palace, the Banqueting House, Kensington Palace, Kew Palace and Hillsborough Castle. The Royal Ceremonial Dress Collection, based at Hampton Court Palace and Kensington Palace includes royal court dress from the 17th century onwards. Items from the Collection are included in permanent displays and temporary exhibitions at Kensington Palace.

Historic Royal Palaces. Hampton Court Palace, East Molesey, Surrey, KT8 9AU
Tel: 0844 482 777 (from the UK) Tel: +44 (0)20 3166 6000 (from outside the UK)

Hull Museums Collection

The Costume Collection at Hull Museums contain over 6,000 items ranging from bodices to boots and waistcoats to whalebone corsets and accessories including hand held fans. The Collection represents every major historical period from the Georgian period to the last decades of the 20th century. Only a very small selection of this collection is on display at any time. Access to stored collections can be arranged for research purposes.

Hull Museums. Ferens Art Gallery, Queen Victoria Square, Kingston-upon-Hull, HU1 3RA
Tel: 01482 300300
Email: museums@hullcc.gov.uk   Website: www.hullcc.gov.uk/museumcollections

Imperial War Museum (IWM)

The Imperial War Museum (IWM) houses a wealth of military reference material including a large exhibition hall and art galleries from the First World War to the present day. The Museum has its main London location, but there are four further branches: the Churchill War Rooms, London, the historic ship HMS Belfast moored in the Pool of London, Imperial War Museum, Duxford near Cambridge, and the Imperial War Museum North in Manchester. See website listing full details of permanent displays and exhibitions.

Imperial War Museum (IWM) London. Lambeth Road, London, SE1 6HZ
Imperial War Museum North. The Quays, Trafford Wharf Road, Manchester, M17 1TZ
Imperial War Museum Duxford. Cambridgeshire, CB22 4QR
Churchill War Rooms. Clive Steps, King Charles Street, London, SW1A 2AQ
HMS Belfast. The Queen's Walk, London, SE1 2JH
Website: www.iwm.org.uk

Irish Linen Centre & Lisburn Museum

The Irish Linen Centre and Lisburn Museum houses the permanent exhibition featuring the story of the Irish linen industry, which includes demonstrations 'Living Looms' and original looms. Visitors can see costume, dress and household linens. Details of their collections, library facilities, education services and current exhibitions are available on the Museums website.

Irish Linen Centre & Lisburn Museum. Market Square, Lisburn, BT28 1AG, County Antrim
Northern Ireland
Tel: +44 28 9266 3377
Website: www.lisburnmuseum.com

Kelvingrove Art Gallery and Museum

Kelvingrove Art Gallery and Museum has 22 galleries displaying over 8,000 objects, brought together from across Glasgow Museums' varied collections. The displays include the Charles Rennie Mackintosh and the Glasgow Style Gallery. More of Mackintosh's work can be seen at Scotland Street School Museum.

Kelvingrove Art Gallery and Museum. Argyle Street, Glasgow, G3 8AG
Tel: 0141 276 9500
Email: museums@glasgowlife.org.uk   Website: www.glasgowlife.org.uk/museums/kelvingrove

Killerton House, Devon

Killerton House is home to an extensive Costume Collection of over 9,000 outfits, which includes men's, women's and children's clothing and accessories with shoes, jewellery, fans, hats, samplers, fine lace and beadwork ranging from mid-17th century to the present day. Killerton House is also home to the 'Paulise de Bush' Costume Collection.

Killerton House. Broadclyst, Exeter, Devon, EX5 3LE
Tel: 01392 881345
Email: killerton@nationaltrust.org.uk   Website: www.nationaltrust.org.uk/killerton

Knitting Together

The Knitting Together website tells the story of the East Midlands knitting industry over the past four hundred years. In addition to the history of the industry, the content includes a range of objects from museum collections across the region, interactives, oral histories and links to further information.

Knitting Together. Room 2.23, Town Hall, Town Hall Square, Leicester, LE1 9BG
Telephone: 0116 4543528
Email: davidorton@leicester.gov.uk   Website: www.knittingtogether.org.uk

The Lace Guild Museum

The Lace Guild's Collection became a registered museum in 2001, and contains over 15,000 objects including all types of lace, bobbins, shuttles, netting needles, threads and much more. All artefacts are recorded on a database. An appointment is required to visit the Museum. For further details contact the Lace Guilds Headquarters by post or email.

The Lace Guild Museum. The Hollies, 53 Audnam, Stourbridge, West Midlands, DY8 4AE
Tel: 01384 390739
Website: www.laceguild.org/museum

The Lace Research Network

The Lace Research Network is a centre based at UCA Farnham for the study and research of lace and covers all types and aspects of lace from the historical to the contemporary including hand and machine made, the digital and the conceptual.
The Lace Research Network
Email: laceresearchnetwork@ucreative.ac.uk   Website: www.ucreative.ac.uk/laceresearchnetwork

The Leather Museum

Walsall Leather Museum is situated in a restored factory and houses workshops where you can watch skilled leather workers in the process of hand-crafting leather goods. The Museum tells the stories of the Walsall leather trade and features examples of local craftsmen past and present.
The Leather Museum. Littleton Street West, Walsall, WS2 8EW
Tel: 01922 652288
Email: leathermuseum@walsall.gov.uk   Website: http://cms.walsall.gov.uk/leathermuseum

Leeds Industrial Museum

Housed in what was once the world's largest woollen mill, Leeds Industrial Museum tells the story of the industrial history of Leeds from manufacturing textiles and clothing to printing, engineering and locomotives.
Leeds Industrial Museum. Canal Road, Leeds, LS12 2QF
Tel: 0113 378 3173
Email: armley.mills@leeds.gov.uk
Website: www.leeds.gov.uk/museumsandgalleries/Pages/armleymills

London College of Fashion: Cordwainer's College Historic Shoe Collection

The Cordwainer's Historic Shoe Collection has approximately 650 items consisting mainly of women's shoes with some men's shoes and a few children's dating from 1870 to the 1990s.
Cordwainer's College Historic Shoe Collection. The Archives. London College of Fashion, 20 John Princes Street, London, WIG OBJ
Email: archives@fashion.arts.ac.uk

London College of Fashion – The Woolmark Company

The International Wool Secretariat, now The Woolmark Company was founded in 1937 to carry out research and promote wool internationally. In the 1980s the Woolmark Collection was donated to the London College of Fashion, and is a fantastic resource, comprising of over 4000 of promotional photographs and press releases providing examples of the fashion and photographic styling dating from the 1940's to the early 1980's.
The Archives. London College of Fashion, 20 John Princes Street, London, WIG OBJ
Email: archives@fashion.arts.ac.uk

Lotherton Hall

Lotherton Hall houses a costume and textile collection in its new Fashion Galleries, which includes 18th century dresses and suits, to designers such as Zandra Rhodes and Vivienne Westwood. The Hall also houses the Sanderson Collection purchased by Leeds City Art Galleries in 1949.
Lotherton Hall. Off Collier Lane, Aberford, Leeds, LS25 3EB
Tel: 0113 378 2959
Email: Lotherton.hall@leeds.gov.uk
Website: www.leeds.gov.uk/museumsandgalleries/Pages/lothertonhall

Macclesfield Silk Museums

The Macclesfield Museums are devoted to silk and tell the story of the history of the silk industry. The Macclesfield Museum Trust operates four sites: Paradise Mill, The Old Sunday School, the Silk Museum and West Park Museum.
Macclesfield Silk Museums
Website: www.macclesfield.silk.museum

Maidstone Museum and Bentif Art Gallery

Maidstone Museum is housed in an Elizabethan Manor House in Maidstone, Kent. The collections consists of 7,800 pieces. The Costume and Textile Collection spans the 17th to 20th centuries, and is exhibited in chronological order with displays including underwear, accessories, children's garments and dolls clothes from each decade. The Museum includes the private wardrobe of Lady Doreen Brabourne; couture and designer garments; high street fashion, uniforms, wedding dresses and accessories. The Needlework Collection also contains a number of outstanding pieces.

Maidstone Museum and Bentif Art Gallery. St Faith Street, Maidstone, Kent, ME14 1LH
Tel: 01622 602854
Email: museuminfo@maidstone.gov.uk   Website: www.museum.maidstone.gov.uk

Masson Mills

Masson Mills is a working textile museum at Matlock Bath, Derbyshire, and is renowned for being 'the finest surviving and best preserved example' of an Arkwright cotton mill.

Masson Mills. Sir Richard Arkwright's Masson Mills, Working Textile Museum, Derby Road,
Matlock Bath, Matlock, Derbyshire, DE4 3PY
Tel/Fax: 01629 581001
Website: www.massonmills.co.uk

Museum of Carpet

The Museum of Carpet is dedicated to the history of Kidderminster's carpet industry, and is run by the Carpet Museum Trust, and supported by the Friends Association. The Museum houses an extensive collection including more than 5000 carpet designs, from designers such as Charles Voysey, Edouard Glorget, Lucienne Day and Bernat Klein, paper designs, samples of rugs and carpets, books and photographs relating to the carpet industry dating from the 18th century to the present.

Museum of Carpet. Stour Vale Mill, Green Street, Kidderminster, DY10 1AZ
Tel: 01562 69028
Website: http://museumofcarpet.org

Museum of Domestic Design & Architecture (MoDA)

The Museum of Domestic Design & Architecture (MoDA) is part of Middlesex University. The collections include textiles, wallpapers, magazines, books and emphemera mainly relating to the British home from 1880 to 1960. Most of the textiles in the MoDA collections were designed for the British home, with many produced for manufacturers such as Liberty & Co and Sandersons. MoDA houses examples of both printed and woven furnishing fabrics and some examples of dress fabrics.

MoDA is open to all by appointment, and MoDA's collections are available to view by appointment in the Study Room at their Collections Centre in Beaufort Park, and are also available online.

Museum of Domestic Design & Architecture (MoDA). Postal Enquires: MoDA Collections Centre. Middlesex University, 9 Boulevard Drive, Beaufort Park, Colindale, London, NW9 5HF
Tel: 020 8411 5244
Email moda@mdx.ac.uk   Website: www.moda.mdx.ac.uk

The Museum of Leathercraft

Founded in 1946, the Museum of Leathercraft has a collection of over 5000 items that cover several centuries, cultures and crafts reflecting the development of leathercraft across the world. See the Museum's website for further details about their collections and resources.

Abington Museum, Abington Park, Northampton, NN1 5LW
Website: www.museumofleathercraft.org

Museum of London – (Dress and Textile Collection)

The Museum of London is the largest city museum in the world, and houses collections of paintings, drawings, decorative arts, social and working history illustrating London society and culture past and present. The Fashion and Textiles Collection includes over 25,000 items from the late 18th century to the present day. The Museum also houses the Harry Matthews Collection of costume and fashion plates consisting of almost 4,000 prints dating from the 16th century to 1829, and textiles manufactured in London. Visit the Museum's excellent website online search facility, and to view all available resources.

Museum of London. 150 London Wall, London, EC2Y 5HN
Tel: 020 7001 9844
Email: info@museumoflondon.org.uk   Website: www.museumoflondon.org.uk

Museum of Science and Industry

The Museum of Science and Industry's collections include textile designs, fabric samples, pattern books, textile research and development papers, and business records of textile merchants, and pictorial trademarks, as well as other visual material that can act as inspiration to students, designers and researchers of textiles and fashion.

Museum of Science and Industry. Liverpool Road, Manchester, M3 4FP
Tel: 0161 606 0127
Email: collections@mosi.org.uk   Website: www.msim.org.uk

Natural History Museum

A fantastic source of inspiration to any artist or designer, the National History Museum has over 70 million specimens, and is home to the largest and most important natural history collection in the world. They also have the world's finest natural history library, which include books, periodicals, paintings and prints, original drawings, manuscripts and maps.

Natural History Museum. Cromwell Road, London, SW7 5BD
Tel: 020 7942 5000
Website: www.nhm.ac.uk

The National Museum of Ireland

The National Museum of Ireland has three locations in Dublin and one in County Mayo. Collections include almost four million objects, focusing primarily on Ireland, but include material from all over the world. Items in the Art and Industry collections include: Arms and Armour; a Childhood collection, a costume and accessories collection of approximately 2,000 items, comprising of mainly Irish and English costume from the 18th Century to the present. There are also examples of religious vestments, court dress, legal and academic robes, and ephemera relevant to the design, production, marketing and use of Irish designed/manufactured clothing. A collection of Irish and European lace accessories ranging from the 17th century to the early 20th century, and textile collections include exhibits associated with the Irish silk and poplin industries of the 18th, 19th and 20th centuries. See website for further details of the collections, resources and activities across all four museums.

The National Museum of Ireland.
Tel: +353 1 6777444
Website: www.museum.ie

National Museums Liverpool

National Museums Liverpool includes the Walker Art Gallery and the World Museum, Liverpool; Museum of Liverpool; the Merseyside Maritime Museum; International Slavery Museum; Seized, Border Force National Museum; Piermaster's House; Sudley House and the Lady Lever Art Gallery. Collections contain everything from Impressionist paintings to a lifejacket from the Titanic. The Walker Art Gallery has a collection of Western European men's and women's costume and fashionable dress comprising of approximately 10,000 items dating from about 1700 to the present day. There is a collection of Western European textiles divided between the Walker Art Gallery and the Lady Lever Art Gallery. This includes tapestries, embroideries, lace and household furnishings, dating from about 1600 to the present day. See the Museums website for further details of the Museum's collections, events calendar and their education programme and resources.

National Museums Liverpool. 127 Dale Street, Liverpool, L2 2JH
Tel: 0151 207 0001
Website: www.liverpoolmuseums.org.uk

National Museums Northern Ireland

National Museums of Ireland present collections across four sites, which include: Ulster Museum, Ulster Folk and Transport Museum, Ulster American Folk Park and Armagh County Museum. The present collections reflect the 'creativity, innovation, history, culture and people of Northern Ireland'.

National Museums Northern Ireland. Cultra, Holywood, Northern Ireland, BT18 0EU
Tel: 0845 608 0000
Email: info@nmni.com   Website: www.nmni.com

National Museums of Scotland

The National Museums of Scotland comprises of the National Museum of Scotland, the National Museum of Flight, the National War Museum and the National Museum of Rural Life providing an illustrated history of Scotland. In 2016 the Museum will open ten new galleries showcasing its internationally important collections of decorative art, design, fashion, science and technology. Collections include embroideries by May Morris and clothing by fashion designers Zandra Rhodes and Vivienne Westwood. The Museum remains open, but some galleries have been closed to make way for this transformation. Full details are available on the Museums website along with details of their exhibition and events programme.
National Museums of Scotland. Chambers Street, Edinburgh, EH1 1JF
Tel: 0300 123 6789
Email: info@nms.ac.uk   Website: www.nms.ac.uk

National Wool Museum

The National Wool Museum is located in the historic Cambrian Mills and tells the story of the Welsh woollen Industry and explain the process from fleece to fabric. See the Museum's website for details of workshops, events and guided tours.
The National Wool Museum. Dre-Fach Felindre, Llandysul, Carmarthenshire, SA44 5UP
Tel: 029 2057 3070
Email: wool@museumwales.ac.uk   Website: www.museumwales.ac.uk/wool

Newtown Textile Museum

Housed in an early 19th century weaving shop, Newtown Textile Museum focuses on the history of the woollen industry in Newtown from 1790 to the early 20th century, along with exhibits from other related industries. The Museum exhibits include four hand weaving looms and spinning wheels, explaining the processes from shearing through to weaving.
Newtown Textile Museum. 5-7 Commercial Street, Newtown, Powys, SY16 2BL
Tel: 01938 554656
Email: powysland.museum@powys.gov.uk
Website: www.powys.gov.uk/en/museums/visit-your-local-museum/newtown-textile-museum

Northampton Central Museum and Art Gallery

Northampton Central Museum and Art Gallery is the home of the world famous shoe collection and the largest collection of shoe heritage in the world. The Collection contains over 12,000 shoes from Egyptian footwear to contemporary British design, and includes machines, tools, trimmings, trade journals and archive material along with permanent and temporary exhibitions. The Museum also houses 7000 items of non-shoe costume dating from 1750 to the present day. Study facilities are available by appointment.
Northampton Museum and Art Gallery. 4-6 Guildhall Road, Northampton, NN1 1DP
Tel: 01604 838111
Email: museums@northampton.gov.uk   Website: www.northampton.gov.uk/museums

Nottingham Castle Museum and Gallery

Nottingham Castle Museum and Gallery is located in a 17th century ducal mansion built on the site of the original Medieval Castle. The Museum and Gallery offer regional, national and international art. They have permanent collections showcasing costume and textiles, silverware, glass and jewellery..
Nottingham Castle Museum and Gallery. Lenton Road, Nottingham, NG1 6EL
Tel: 0115 876 1400
Email: nottingham.castle@nottinghamcity.gov.uk
Website: www.nottinghamcity.gov.uk

Nottingham Industrial Museum

Nottingham Industrial Museum is located in the 17th century stables block of Wollaton Hall, Nottingham and houses collections from transport to textiles. The Textile Gallery features some of the earliest machinery of its type in the country, and includes three examples of hand knitting frames, Jacquard card machines, a card punching machine and much more.
Nottingham Industrial Museum. Wollaton Hall, Nottingham, NG8 2AE
Email: info@nottinghamindustrialmuseum.co.uk   Website: www.nottinghamindustrialmuseum.co.uk

The Old Sunday School

Built in 1814, The Old Sunday School presents the history of the building and the people associated with it, and tells the story of how a market town developed its silk industry, and shows the range of mills that once thrived there.

The Old Sunday School. Heritage Centre, Roe Street, Macclesfield, Cheshire, SK11 6UT
Tel: 01625 613210
Email: info@silkmacclesfield.org.uk Website: www.silkmacclesfield.org.uk

Paisley Museum and Art Galleries

Paisley Museum is located in a building designed by the architect John Honeyman and was financed by Sir Peter Coats of the Coats thread manufacturing family. The Museum and Art Gallery houses collections of local and natural history, ceramics and Scottish paintings, along with the 'world famous collection' of Paisley shawls and many original pattern books. There are displays tracing the history of the Paisley pattern, providing an excellent resource for fashion and textile artists and designers.

Paisley Museum and Art Galleries. High Street, Paisley, Renfrewshire, PA1 2BA
Tel: 0141 618 2598
Website: www.museumsgalleriesscotland.org.uk

Paradise Mill

Paradise Mill is devoted to the history of the silk industry and has twenty-six restored Jacquard Looms and silk handlooms with Jacquard. Hear about the silk industry and watch a weaving demonstration. Guided tours are available demonstrating the process of silk weaving and factory life in the 1930's.

Paradise Mill. Park Lane, Macclesfield, SK11 6TJ
Tel: 01625 613210
Email: info@macclesfield.org.uk   Website: www.silkmacclesfield.org.uk

Penlee House Gallery and Museum

Founded in 1839, Penlee House Gallery and Museum collection covers over 6000 years of history of West Cornwall. Displays reflect the unique history of the area, including local fishing, farming, mining and tourism industries. Penlee House has a good collection of Crysede fabrics, an internationally acclaimed textile firm based in Newlyn in the 1920s and 1930s.

Penlee House Gallery and Museum. Morrab Road, Penzance, Cornwall, TR18 4HE
Tel: 01736 363625
Email: info@penleehouse.org.uk   Website: www.penleehouse.org.uk

People's History Museum

The People's History Museum tells the 'history of working people in Britain and has the largest collection of political material in Britain'. It has an important collection of over 400 historic trade union and political banners with some on display. Visit the Museum and observe the work of conservators working on the conservation and preservation of textiles and banners at the Textile Conservation Studio, established to work on the Museum's collection of banners, and who also work on commissions.

People's History Museum. Left Bank, Spinningfields, Manchester, M3 3ER
Tel/Fax: 0161 838 9190
Email: info@phm.org.uk (General Enquiries)   Website: www.phm.org.uk

Petersfield Museum and the Flora Twort Gallery

Petersfield Museum and the Flora Twort Gallery hold exhibitions relating to local history, historic costume and work by the local artist Flora Twort. The Museum holds artefacts contributing to the social, industrial and agricultural history of the town, villages and surrounding area. The Costume Gallery houses dress from the first two decades of the 20th century.

Petersfield Museum Limited. The Old Courthouse, St Peter's Road, Petersfield, GU32 3HX
Tel: 01730 262601
Flora Twort Gallery, Church Path Studio, 21 The Square, Petersfield, GU32 3HS
Tel: 01730 260756
Website: www.petersfieldmuseum.co.uk

Pitt Rivers Museum

Founded in 1884, Pitt Rivers Museum displays of ethnographic and archaeological objects, originally donated to the University of Oxford by General Pitt Rivers, an ethnologist and archaeologist. The

Museum's collection has over half a million objects including items such as Hawaiian feather cloaks; a range of hand-woven textiles and looms; costumes from North America including Inuit fur parkas, painted coats from the Northeastern Woodlands and a range of decorated moccasins; magic objects including amulets and charms; jewellery and body decoration, and musical instruments. See the website for full details of the Museum's collections and online databases, their education programme, resources, present research and their latest news.
Pitt Rivers Museum. South Parks Road, Oxford, OX1 3PP
Tel: 01865 270927
Email: prm@prm.ox.ac.uk   Website: www.prm.ox.ac.uk

The Quaker Tapestry Exhibition Centre
The Quaker Tapestry is an award winning visitor attraction comprising of panels of embroidery providing a visual chronicle of Quaker life, movement and its development through the centuries. There are temporary and interactive displays, events, films, audio guides, children's activities and many artefacts on display.
The Quaker Tapestry Exhibition Centre. Friends Meeting House, Stramongate, Kendal, Cumbria, LA9 4BH
Tel: 01539 722975
Email: info@quaker-tapestry.co.uk   Website: www.quaker-tapestry.co.uk

Quarry Bank Mill
Quarry Bank Mill is a Georgian cotton mill built in 1784, and now a living, working museum telling the story of 'King Cotton from bale of raw cotton to bolt of finished cotton'. Exhibits show the progression of the cotton industry from the mediaeval era through to the 19th century.
Quarry Bank Mill Trust (Enterprises) Ltd. Styal, Wilmslow, SK9 4LA
Tel: 01625 527468
Email: quarrybankmill@nationaltrust.org.uk   Website: www.nationaltrust.org.uk

Queen Street Mill Textile Museum
Queen Street Mill Textile Museum is based in the last 19th century steam powered weaving mill, and holds a collection of machinery preserved in situ, and in full working order. Machines include the original Lancashire boiler, the 500 horse power tandem compound steam engine, the line shafting and the 19th century looms connected to it. Other machines include a collection of machinery which demonstrates the development of weaving including Dobby looms, and a Hattersley Jacquard (tapestry) loom, and other items connected to the textile industry. The Museum also houses a library containing over 7,000 books, journals and other items relating to Lancashire's textile industry.
Queen Street Mill Textile Museum. Queen Street, Harle Syke Burnley, Lancashire, BB10 2HX
Tel: 01282 412 555
Email: queenstreetmill@lancashire.gov.uk
Website: http://new.lancashire.gov.uk/leisure-and-culture/museums/queen-street-mill-textile-museum

Quilt Museum and Gallery
The Quilt Museum and Gallery is Britain's first museum dedicated to quilt making and textile arts. The Quilters' Guild Collection has over 800 quilts from the earliest known dated British patchwork - the 1718 silk patchwork coverlet to items of costume, quilted clothing, miniature pieces and small domestic items such a tea cosies and night dress cases, templates, tools and quilting equipment.
Quilt Museum and Gallery.
Email: curator@quiltmuseum.org.uk   Website: www.quiltmuseum.org.uk

Royal Albert Memorial Museum (RAMM)
Exeter's world-class Museum has a stunning displays and galleries, exhibitions and modern amenities. The displays reveal Devon and Exeter's rich history and global connections. Exotic animals, birds and insects and the world cultures galleries display stunning items and collections from all over the world. The Costume and Textile Collection is one of the most important outside London and is particularly strong in lace. Specialist textile conservation services are available. They have also have a reference collection of magazines, fashion plates and dress patterns.
Royal Albert Memorial Museum (RAMM). Queen Street, Exeter, EX4 3RX
Tel: 01392 265858
Website: www.exeter.gov.uk/RAMM

Conservator preparing the Joanna Southcott quilt for an exhibition at the V&A. © 2015 Royal Albert Memorial Museum & Art Gallery, Exeter City Council.

Shoes from England in the 1760s, © 2015 Royal Albert Memorial Museum & Art Gallery, Exeter City Council

Royal Armouries Museum
The Royal Armouries Collection has over 70,000 examples of arms, armour and artillery dating from antiquity to the present day. The collections include royal armours of the Tudor and Stuart kings, arms and armour of the English Civil Wars, British and foreign military weapons from the Board of Ordnance and MOD Pattern Room Collection, as well as a collection of oriental arms and armour, plus much more.
The Royal Armouries Museum. Armouries Drive, Leeds, LS10 1LT
Tel: 0870 034 4344
Website: www.royalarmouries.org

Royal Cornwall Museum
The Royal Cornwall Museum holds collections from fine art and world cultures to classical Greek and Roman objects. The majority of collections relate mainly to Cornwall, but there are others from the rest of the UK and abroad. The Textile and Costume Collection includes clothing made or worn in Cornwall mainly from the 18th to 20th centuries, with a few early 16th century pieces. They also have an archive of 1920s-1930s block printed silk costumes and woodblocks of the Cryséde textile company including fabrics and ephemera.
Royal Cornwall Museum. River Street, Truro,
Cornwall, TR1 2SJ
Tel: 01872 272205
Email: enquiries@royalcornwallmuseum.org.uk
Website: www.royalcornwallmuseum.org.uk

Royal Opera House Collections (Online)
The Royal Opera House Collections (online) records the history of the three Covent Garden sited theatres and the performances that they housed. The Collections are divided into three categories: the online Royal Opera House Collections; the Specials Collections and the Commissioned Collections, all providing a fantastic and inspirational resource.
Royal Opera House Collections (ROH)
Tel: 020 7212 9353
Email: archive.enquiries@roh.org.uk   Website: www.rohcollections.org.uk

Ruddington Framework Knitter's Museum
Ruddington Framework Knitter's Museum comprises of a unique surviving Victorian knitters yard, furnished cottages and frame shops located in a garden courtyard, depicting the working and living conditions of a bygone knitting community. There are sock machines, and historic frames including Griswolds and a collection of handframes.
Ruddington Framework Knitter's Museum. Chapel Street, Ruddington, Nottingham, NG11 6HE
Tel: 01159 846 914
Website: www.frameworkknittersmuseum.org.uk

Saddleworth Museum and Art Gallery
The Museum covers the history of textile production in the Saddleworth area with textile machinery from the 18th and 19th centuries, and demonstrations of textile processes. There is also an extensive archive

of textile company records. For further details of the collections, archives, exhibition programme, events and latest news see the Museum's website.
Saddleworth Museum and Art Gallery. High Street, Uppermill, Saddleworth, Yorkshire, OL3 6HS
Tel: 01457 874093
Website: www.saddleworthmuseum.co.uk

Salisbury and South Wiltshire Museum
The Museum's collections span the history and archaeology of Salisbury and South Wiltshire from prehistoric times to the present day. The clothing and textile collections include wedding dresses, uniforms and formal wear from the past 250 years, and lace samples produced by the Downton lace industry.
Salisbury and South Wiltshire Museum. The King's House, 65 The Close, Salisbury, Wiltshire, SP1 2EN
Tel: 01722 332151
Email: museum@salisburymuseum.org.uk   Website: www.salisburymuseum.org.uk

Scottish Registers of Tartans
The Scottish Register of Tartans was established in 2008 by an act of the Scottish Parliament 'to protect, promote and preserve tartan'. The Register is maintained by the National Records of Scotland, and provides a database of tartan designs, which can be searched by tartan name or colour, and gives information with reference to 1000s of tartans.
Scottish Registers of Tartans
Website: www.tartanregister.gov.uk

Scottish Tartans Museum
The Scottish Tartans Museum has exhibits of weaponry to weaving, and has over 500 tartan samples on display representing tartans for clans, families, districts and various organisations from the late 16th century till today, with a collection of kilts dating back over 200 years.
Scottish Tartans' Museum. The Institute Hall, Mid Street, Keith, Moray, AB55 5BJ, Scotland
Tel: 01542 888 419
Website: www.scottishtartans.org

Shetland Museum & Archives
The Shetland Museum houses collections relating to all aspects of the islands history from the trade and industry to customs and folklore along with their important collection of textiles. Exhibits include examples of Fair Isle knitting, fine laces, textile tools and equipment, and a collection of commercial weaving equipment. See website for further details.
Shetland Museum & Archives. Hay's Dock, Lerwick, Shetland, ZE1 0WP
Tel: 01595 695057
Website: www.shetland-museum.org.uk

Shetland Textile Museum
The Shetland Museum is dedicated to Shetland's textile culture and heritage. The Museum's collection includes approximately 500 knitted and woven textile items, and about 500 knitting patterns. The Museum is a community museum and holds regular demonstrations by volunteers, exhibitions and events.
Shetland Textile Museum. Böd of Gremista, Lerwick, Shetland, ZW1 0PX
Tel: 01595 694386
Email: shetlandtextilemuseum@gmail.com   Website: http://shetlandtextilemuseum.wordpress.com

The Shoe Museum
The Shoe Museum houses a collection of more than 1500 shoes from Roman to modern day, and tells 'the story of Clarks Shoes from its beginnings in the early 19th century'. Exhibits include advertising materials, shoe-making machinery and tools.
The Shoe Museum. High Street, Street, Somerset, BA16 0EQ
Tel: 01458 842243
Website: http://the-shoe-museum.org

Shugborough Hall
Shugborough Hall is located in a working historic Estate with a Georgian mansion house, servants quarters and working farm. The Costume Collection features costume and accessories from the past 400 years, which includes a unique collection of shoes and boots from Lotus Ltd, Stafford and Stone's last shoe manufacturers. Other highlights of the costume and textiles collection include the cap presented

by Charles I to the Bagot family of Blithfield, and a collection of women's costume, wedding dresses samplers and servants' costume.
Shugborough Hall. Shugborough Estate, Shugborough, Milford, Stafford, ST17 0XB
Tel: 01889 881388 or 0845 459 8900
Email: shugborough.promotions@staffordshire.gov.uk   Website: www.shugborough.org.uk

Silk Museum

The Silk Museum is operated by Maccelsfield Trust along with Paradise Mill, The Old Sunday School and West Park Museum. The Silk Museum is dedicated to the history of Macclesfield's silk industry with exhibits showing the industrial process of silk making 'from cocoon to loom'. The Macclesfield Museums: Paradise Mill, The Old Sunday School, the Silk Museum and West Park Museum offer the most complete representation of the story of silk in the UK. There are guided tours, costumes, displays and demonstrations of hand loom weaving. See website for further details of each individual museum, events and forthcoming exhibition programme.
Silk Museum. Park Lane, Macclesfield, SK11 6TJ
Tel: 01625 612045
Website: www.macclesfield.silk.museum

Stott Park Bobbin Mill

Stott Park Bobbin Mill, Cumbria was built in 1835 to produce millions of wooden bobbins essential to the spinning and weaving industries of Lancashire. The Bobbin Mill is a working mill, with exhibits and guided tours telling the story of the industry. Visitors can see the bobbins being made using the Mill's original belt driven machinery.
Stott Park Bobbin Mill. Finsthwaite, Ulverston, Cumbria, I A12 8AX
Website: www.english-heritage.org.uk/daysout/properties/stott-park-bobbin-mill

Stroudwater Textile Trust

Stroudwater Textile Trust was established in 1999 by local people wanting to promote awareness of the woollen industry in the Stroud valleys and to celebrate contemporary textiles. Working machinery, weaving, cloth finishing and waterwheels tell the story of Cotswold cloth industry. The cloth sample collection can be viewed by arrangement. Demonstrations of historical textile machinery are available at the Dunkirk Mill Centre and the Gigg Mill, Nailsworth. See the Trust's website for further details.
Stroudwater Textile Trust. Chalford Grove, Marle Hill, Chalford, Stroud, Gloucestershire, GL6 8PW
Tel: 01453 766540
Email: info@stroud-textile.org.uk   Website: www.stroud-textile.org.uk

Strutt's North Mill

Strutt's North Mill, Belper was built in 1804, and is located in a grade 1 listed mill, which is one of the oldest surviving examples of an industrialised, iron framed 'fire proof' building. The Museum demonstrates how the small town of Belper was transformed into the 'world's first factory community', and tells stories of cotton spinning, stocking making, the Strutt family and the Belper Mill workers.
Strutt's North Mill. North Mill, Bridgefoot, Belper, Derbyshire, DE56 1YD
Tel: 01773 880474
Website: http://belpernorthmill.org

Textiles Collection - University for the Creative Arts at Farnham

The Textiles Collection, University for the Creative Arts, Farnham is a working collection consisting of over 3,000 artefacts originally established by Ella McLeod. See website for further details.
The Textiles Collection. University for the Creative Arts at Farnham, Falkner Road, Farnham, Surrey, GU9 7DS
Tel: 01252 892778
Email: lbrassington.s1@ucreative.ac.uk   Website: www.vads.ac.uk/collections

Totnes Fashion and Textile Museum

Totnes Fashion and Textiles Museum houses the Devonshire Collection of Period Costume and includes men's, women's and children's clothing dating from the 18th century to the 21st century.
Totnes Fashion and Textile Museum. Bogan House, 43 High Street, Totnes, Devon, TQ9 5NP
Website: www.devonmuseums.net/Totnes--Fashion-and-Textiles-Museum

Trowbridge Museum

Trowbridge Museum is a specialist textile museum housed in the last working woollen cloth mill in Wiltshire, and which focuses on the west of England woolen cloth industry. The Museum houses nearly

19,000 objects, including 18th and 19th century looms and associated woollen cloth manufacture machinery, and over 5,000 photographs.
Trowbridge Museum. The Shires, Court Street, Trowbridge, Wiltshire, BA14 8AT
Tel: 01225 751339
Email: hannah.lyddy@trowbridge.gov.uk   website: www.trowbridgemuseum.co.uk

Tuckers Hall, Exeter

Tuckers Hall was built in 1471 as a chapel for the Guilds of the woollen cloth workers in Exeter. It is the home of the Incorporation of Weavers, Fullers & Shearmen. Tuckers Hall tells the story of the history of Exeter's historical woollen cloth. See website for further details.

Tuckers Hall. 140 Fore Street, Exeter, Devon, EX4 3AN
Website: www.tuckershall.org.uk

Tullie House Museum and Art Gallery Trust

Tullie House Museum and trust houses an important collection of works by Pre-Raphaelite artists and their heirs, relating to the Arts and Crafts Movement. The Collection consists of textiles, ceramics, metalwork, furniture and costume. Highlights include works by Dante Gabriel Rossetti, Elizabeth Siddal, Edward Burne-Jones, Ford Madox Brown and textiles by William Morris.
Tullie House Museum and Art Gallery Trust. Castle Street, Carlisle, Cumbria, CA3 8TP
Tel: 01228 618718
Email: enquiries@tulliehouse.co.uk   Website: www.tulliehouse.co.uk

Ulita

Ulita holds a collection of world textiles, which includes Chinese embroideries; Kashmir shawls; Mediterranean embroideries; Javanese batiks; Japanese textiles; Qing Dynasty textiles; West African weaves; European sample books; glass photographic plates and the Louisa Pesel and Marchini Collections; the Tibor Reich Collection and colour chemistry sample boards. The purpose of the archive is to 'collect, preserve and document textiles and other related items from many of the textile producing areas of the world for the benefit of scholars, researchers and the general public'.
ULITA - An Archive of International Textiles.
St.Wilfred's Chapel, Maurice Keyworth Building, University of Leeds, Leeds, LS2 9JT
Tel: 0113 343 3919
Email: ulita@leeds.ac.uk   Website: www.leeds.ac.uk/ulita

The Ulster Museum. National Museums of Northern Ireland (UFTM)

The Ulster Folk and Transport Museum (UFTM) has a large costume, accessories and textile collection including Irish and continental lace, embroidery and household linens. The Costume Collection has over 1,000 garments dating from 1840 to 1910. The Museum also has Irish lace ranging from the early 18th to late 20th century, and a comprehensive collection of patchwork and quilted bedcovers dating from 1790 to the mid-1990s. The Children's Costume Collection contains over 100 christening robes and examples of 1900s sailor suits and pinafores.
The Ulster Museum. National Museums of Northern Ireland. Cultra, Holywood, BT18 0EU
Tel: +44 (0) 28 9042 8428
Website: www.nmni.com/uftm

Victoria and Albert Museum (V&A)

The V&A holds one of the largest collections of Decorative Arts, with 146 galleries containing unrivalled collections dating from 3000BC to the present day, spanning 2000 years of art and design around the world.'The V&A's Fashion Collection is the largest and most comprehensive collection of dress in the world' and includes 17th century gowns to post-war couture and with exhibits from many prominent 21st century designers. The textile collections and the permanent Fashion Collection ranges from 18th century court dress to contemporary dress. The Museum has a superb database providing online access to over 1.1 million catalogue records and over 293,000 images of objects in their Online Collection. See the Museum's website for further details of their research facilities, activities, events and forthcoming exhibitions.
Victoria and Albert Museum (V&A). Cromwell Road, London, SW7 2RL
Tel: 020 7942 2000
Website: www.vam.ac.uk

V&A Museum of Childhood
The V&A Museum of Childhood in London's Bethnal Green houses the Victoria and Albert Museum's collection of childhood-related objects and artefacts, spanning the 1600s to the present day. It houses the UK's premier public collection of children's clothing, covering 400 years, and holds over 6000 items, telling the diverse stories of British childhood.
V&A Museum of Childhood. Cambridge Heath Road, London, E2 9PA
Tel: 020 8983 5200
Email: moc@vam.ac.uk   Website: www.vam.org.uk/moc

The Wandle Industrial Museum
The Wandle Industrial Museum was founded in 1983 to 'preserve, keep and share the history and heritage of the industries and people of the River Wandle'. The Museum pays homage to Morris and Liberty, and has a collection of Liberty and Morris textiles, hand printed blocks and silk screens. Research facilities are available.
The Wandle Industrial Museum. Vestry Hall, London Road, Mitcham, Surrey, CR4 3UD
Tel: 020 8648 0127
Email: office@wandle.org   Website: www.wandle.org

Wardon Park Museum
The Wardon Park Museum has displays highlighting Luton's history and the traditional crafts of the area such as lace making and hat making. The Museum hosts exhibits of fine arts, costumes and a collection that features hats and displays of decorative arts including several Victorian room settings.
Wardon Park Museum. Old Bedford Road, Luton, LU2 7HA
Tel: 01582 746722
Email: museum.gallery@luton.gov.uk   Website: www.luton.gov.uk/museums

Warner Textile Archive
The Warner Textile Archive is housed in an original Warner and Sons mill building, and holds an extensive collection of more than 60,000 textiles, 10,000 paper designs, pattern books, record books, photographs and documentary material. There is a permanent gallery exhibiting some of the collection, including the creations of renowned 20th century designers such as Alec Hunter and Eddie Squires, and the silks woven for royal coronations. See website for details of the Warner Textiles Archives, facilities and times of opening.
Warner Textile Archive. Silks Way, Braintree, Essex, CM7 3GB
Tel: 01376 557741
Email: info@warnertextilearchive.co.uk   Website: www.warnertextilearchive.co.uk

The Weavers' Cottage Museum
The Weavers' Cottage Museum is set in a restored 18th century craftsman's cottage, depicting the living and working conditions of a typical handloom weaver. See how traditional tartan was made by hand using original equipment from 200 years ago, and see hundreds of small hand-woven tartan fabric samples on display, along with examples of Paisley designs. The cottage has period furnishings, household objects, photographs and parish records, giving an insight into everyday life in Scotland before the Industrial Revolution.
The Weavers' Cottage Museum. The Cross, Kilbarchan, Renfrewshire, PA10 2JG
Email: www.nts.org.uk/Property/Weavers-Cottage
Website: www.nts.org.uk/Property/Weavers-Cottage

Whitby Museum
The Whitby Museum houses a wide range of collections and exhibits. The Costume and Textile Collection consists of approximately 200 dresses and accessories including fans, gloves, parasols, undergarments and hats, which are mainly Victorian and Edwardian in date with some earlier pieces.
There is also a large collection of Chantilly, Maltese and Nottingham lace, and samplers from 1714.
Whitby Museum. Pannett Park, Whitby, North Yorkshire, YO21 1RE
Tel: 01947 602908
Email: keeper@whitbymuseum.org.uk   Website: www.whitbymuseum.org.uk

Wigston Framework Knitters Museum
The Museum is located in an original late 17th century Master Framework Knitter's house and workshop, and is a unique example, preserved as when the last master hosier, Edgar Carter died in 1952. Inside on the ground floor were eight knitting-frames for making gloves, mittens and fancy ribbed tops for golf

hose, together with all the needle moulds and tools associated with each machine.
Wigston Framework Knitters Museum. 42-44 Bushloe End, Wigston, Leicestershire, LE18 2BA
Tel: 0116 288 2632
Website: http://wigstonframeworkknitters.org

The William Morris Gallery

The William Morris Gallery is devoted to the 'life and legacy of William Morris: designer, craftsman and socialist'. The Museum is set in the historic Georgian house, Morris's family home from 1848 to 1856. Details of the collections, the Gallery's resources and image library are available on the Gallery's website
The William Morris Gallery. Lloyd Park, Forest Road, Walthamstow, London, E17 4PP
Tel: 020 8496 4390
Email: wmg.enquiries@walthamforest.gov.uk   Website: www.wmgallery.org.uk

Wimbledon Lawn Tennis Museum

The Museum details the history of lawn tennis, and includes fashion, costume and tennis exhibits and memorabilia.
Wimbledon Lawn Tennis Museum. Church Road Wimbledon, London SW19 5AE
Website: www.wimbledon.com/en_GB/museum

Winchester School of Art Knitting Reference Library (KRL)

The Knitting Reference Library (KRL) is based at Winchester School of Art, and offers a superb collection of books, journals, knitted objects and over 12,000 knitting patterns, and includes the Collections of Richard Rutt, Montse Stanley and Jane Waller. See website for further details.
Winchester School of Art Library. University of Southampton, Highfield Campus, Southampton SO17 1BJ
Tel: 023 8059 2180
Email: wsaenqs@soton.ac.uk   Website: www.southampton.ac.uk/intheloop

The Whitworth: University of Manchester

The Whitworth has an extensive collection comprising of over 55,000 artworks alone. They have a textile collection consisting of around 20,000 dress and textile items from around the world from the 3rd century AD to the present day. They have a wallpaper collection of over 5,000 examples. See the Whitworth website for full details of their collections, exhibitions and events programme, and facilities including the Whitworth Research and Study Centre.
The Whitworth, University of Manchester, Oxford Road, Manchester, M15 6ER
Tel: 0161 275 7450
Email: whitworth@manchester.ac.uk   Website: www.whitworth.manchester.ac.uk

Worthing Museum and Art Gallery

The Worthing Museum and Art Gallery houses collections ranging from archaeology to the decorative arts. It also houses one of the largest costume collections in the UK, alongside items of local history. The Textile Collection dates from the 17th century to the present day, and comprises of decorative textiles including embroidery, beadwork, white work, samplers, fabric samples, apprentices' miniature garments, darning specimens and a large hand-made and machine-made lace collection. Examples of domestic textiles date from 1800.
Worthing Museum and Art Gallery. Chapel Road, Worthing, West Sussex, BN11 1HP
Tel: 01903 221448
Email: museumadur-worthing.gov.uk   Website: www.worthingmuseum.co.uk

York Castle Museum

York Castle Museum collections include social history, military, costume and textiles. See the Museum's excellent online catalogue providing images of the costume and textile collections including men's, women's and children's clothes and accessories, household furnishings and needlework dating back nearly 300 years. The Collection also includes 19th century women's magazines, dressmaking patterns, fashion-plates, shop and mail order catalogues and photographs. The Textile Collection includes patchwork quilts, samplers, lace and embroidery examples.
York Castle Museum. Eye of York, York, YO1 9RY
Tel: 01904 687687
Website: www.yorkcastlemuseum.org.uk

Organisations, Societies, Guilds, Networks and Associations

The organisations, societies, guilds, networks and associations listed in this section represent a wide spectrum of interests and disciplines. Whether you are interested in fashion writing, journalism, designing, illustration, retail, the gift industry, education or fashion photography and styling there is a professional association or body that will meet your needs. Many of the organisations listed have very informative websites giving details of awards, events, news up-dates, business support and membership benefits, and provide excellent networking opportunities to meet like-minded people with similar interests and business ventures.

Arts Council of England
Arts Council England supports, develops and invests in the arts from theatre to digital art to dance, music to literature, and crafts to collections. See website for full details of Arts Council areas, funding, advice and guidance, news, conferences and much more.
Arts Council of England
Tel: 0845 300 6200
Website: www.artscouncil.org.uk

Arts Council of Northern Ireland
The Arts Council of Northern Ireland is the development and funding agency for the Arts in Northern Ireland. See website for full details of activities, events, funding and opportunities.
Arts Council ot Northern Ireland
Tel: 028 9038 5200
Website: www.artscouncil-ni.org

Arts Council of Scotland
The Scottish Arts Council is the leading funding body and development agency, supporting, funding, developing and promoting the arts in Scotland. See website for full further details of activities, events, funding and opportunities.
Scottish Arts Council
Tel: 0131 226 6051
Website: www.scottisharts.org.uk

Arts Council of Wales
The Arts Council for Wales is the leading funding body and development agency, supporting, funding, developing and promoting the arts in Wales. See website for full details of activities, events, funding and much more.
Arts Council of Wales
Tel: 0845 8734 900 / 029 2044 1300
Website: www.artswales.org.uk

Art Workers Guild
Members of the Art Workers Guild are artists, craftsmen and designers with a common interest in the interaction, development and distribution of creative skills. See website for details of membership, craft apprenticeships and a calendar of forthcoming events.
Art Workers Guild. 6 Queen Square, Bloomsbury, London, WC1N 3AT
Website: www.artworkersguild.org

The Association of Dress Historians
The Association of Dress Historians is dedicated to 'supporting and promoting the study and professional practice of dress and textile history'. See website for details of membership, the history of the Association, news, events, and useful links.
The Association of Dress Historians
Website: www.dresshistorians.co.uk

Association of Degree Courses in Fashion and Textile (FTC)
The Association of Degree Courses in Fashion and Textile (FTC) aims are to 'promote and develop fashion and textiles through academic debate, education and research'. The Association has extensive networks with industrial, public and professional bodies, and represents over 50 member institutions in

the UK. The FTC website provides details of member institutions, research, key events and activities.
Association of Degree Courses in Fashion and Textile (FTC). School of the Arts, Loughborough University
Tel: 01509 228935
Website: www.ftc-online.org.uk

The Association of Guilds of Weavers, Spinners and Dyers (AGWSD)

The Association of Guilds of Weavers, Spinners and Dyers have over 100 affiliated Guilds to promote
and maintain excellence of craftsmanship, the exchange of information and to develop the aims of the
individual through achievement. See website for details of member groups, individual membership, news
and events.
Association of Guilds of Weavers, Spinners and Dyers (AGWSD)
Website: www.wsd.org.uk

Association of Model Agents (AMA)

The Association of Model Agents (AMA) is the trade association of the UK model industry. The AMA
website lists members details, and information and advice on becoming a model, reports on the latest
news and also details the code of practice within the industry.
Association of Model Agents. 11-29 Fashion Street, London, E1 6PX
Tel: 020 7422 0699
Email: amainfo@btinternet.com   Website: www.associationofmodelagents.org

Association of Photographers (AOP)

Association of Photographers (AOP) is a membership based organisation comprising of professional
photographers, agents, assistants and students, including affiliated colleges and companies. See website
listing details of activities, exhibitions and events, news and annual AOP Awards.
Association of Photographers (AOP). Studio 9, Holborn Studios, 49/50 Eagle Wharf Road London, N1 7ED
Tel: 020 7739 6669
Email: info@aophoto.co.uk   Website: www.the-aop.org

Association of Suppliers to the British Clothing Industry (ASBCI)

The Association of Suppliers to the British Clothing Industry (ASBCI) unites the clothing industry from fibre
and garment manufacture, to retail and aftercare. See the ASBCI website for details of services, activities,
events, news, the ASBCI Design Competition and awards, and details of membership. Members range
from large multi-national companies to individual students.
Association of Suppliers to the British Clothing Industry (ASBCI).
Unit 5, 25 Square Road, Halifax, West Yorkshire, HX1 1QG
Tel: 01422 354666
Email: office@asbci.co.uk   Website membership and: www.asbci.co.uk

The Batik Guild

The Batik Guild was founded in 1986, to promote and improve education in the field of batik, and to
encourage and support the Guild's members who include professional artists, amateur artists, teachers,
students and those that simply enjoy doing batik. Membership details are available on the Guild's website
with information about the history of batik and a list of suppliers for batik equipment and materials.
The Batik Guild
Website:www.batikguild.org.uk

The Bead Society

Formed in 1989, the Bead Society is a subscription-based organisation. Details of forthcoming
workshops, events and membership are listed on the Society's website.
The Bead Society of Great Britain
Website: www.beadsociety.org.uk

The Beadworkers Guild

The Beadworkers Guild is a registered charity founded to 'promote beadwork and to facilitate the
exchange of ideas, knowledge amongst beadworkers'. The Guild organises the Great British Bead Show
and the Beading Festival.
Postal: The Beadworkers Guild. 4 Honor Oak Road, London, SE23 3SF
Tel: 07837 649712
Email: enquiries@beadworkersguild.org.uk   Website: www.beadworkersguild.org.uk

BLC Leather Technology Centre

Established for over 90 years, the BLC is the leading independent Leather Technology Centre, working with many companies in over 40 countries. They offer a range of leather related services including consultancy, research, testing, training and much more.

BLC Leather Technology Centre Ltd. Kings Park Road, Moulton Park, Northampton, NN3 6JD

Tel: 01604 679999

Website: www.blcleathertech.com

The Braid Society

The Braid Society aims to promote 'the education and practice of the art and craft of making braids and narrow bands'. Members include professional craftsmen, teachers, collectors, researchers, authors, students and people who are interested in the craft of making braids and narrow bands from across the UK and around the world. Full details of membership and activities are available on the Society's website.

The Braid Society

Website: www.braidsociety.com

British Agents Register

The British Agents Register 'brings together companies with professional sales agents to form successful and mutual beneficial business partnerships'.

British Agents Register

Website: www.agentsregister.com

British Allied Trades Federation (BATF)

The British Allied Trades Federation (BATF) comprises of five trade associations, which collectively represent approximately 2,500 enterprises from jewellery, giftware, surface engineering, and travel goods to the accessories industry sector. BATF membership comprises of micro to medium size companies, and includes manufacturers, designers, craftworkers, wholesalers, distributors and also retailers. See website for further details of membership and activities.

British Allied Trades Federation (BATF). Federation House, 10 Vyse Street, Birmingham, B18 6LT

Tel: 0121 236 2657

Email: enquiries@batf.uk.com   Website: www.batf.uk.com

British Bridal Retailers Association (BBRA)

The British Bridal Retail Association (BBRA) was founded in 2011 to provide a voice and network to Bridal retailers. See the Association's website for details of membership.

British Bridal Retailers Association (BBRA)

Website: www.britishbridalretailersassociation.co.uk

British Bridalwear Suppliers Association (BBSA)

British Bridalwear Suppliers Association (BBSA) members are UK based companies supplying wedding attire to retailers in the UK and Ireland. The Association supports its members and the bridal industry staging events, lobbying government and in the exchange of business and trade information.

British Bridalwear Suppliers Association (BBSA)

Email: info@bridalsuppliers.co.uk   Website: www.bridalsuppliers.co.uk

British Button Society

The British Button Society promotes the study and collection of buttons: uniform, fashion and costume. Full membership details are available on the Society's website.

British Button Society

Website: www.britishbuttonsociety.org

British Costume Association (BCA)

The British Costume Association (BCA) works on behalf of its members and provides links to all its member companies through the Associations Store Directory, which lists all business names, business types and location.

British Costume Association (BCA)

Website: www.incostume.co.uk

British Council

The British Council is 'the UK's international organisation for educational opportunities and cultural relations' with a worldwide network of colleagues and international partners. The Council has an excellent

website detailing projects in the arts and in education, funding grants, research fellowships, events, opportunities and resources, and much more.
British Council Customer Service UK. 10 Spring Gardens, London, SW1A 2BN
Tel: +44 (0) 20 7389 4385
Email: arts@britishcouncil.org   Website: www.britishcouncil.org

British Display Society (BDS)

The British Display Society 'encourages and promotes the highest standards of visual merchandising design and display installation throughout commerce and industry'. This includes display techniques used in retail windows, point-of-sale display, exhibitions and museum displays, design and training. Visit the Society's website for details of membership, courses, training and professional awards.
British Display Society (BDS)
Tel: 020 8856 2030
Website: www.britishdisplaysociety.co.uk

British Fashion Council (BFC)

The British Fashion Council (BFC) was formed in 1983 with aims to 'showcase British designers and to develop London's position as a major player in the international fashion arena'. They have an excellent website providing details of designer support, press gallery and business support network, the BFC Colleges Council initiative forming links between industry and fashion graduates from the UK's leading colleges, and the BFC Education Foundation. The BFC are the organisers of the British Fashion Awards See website for further details.
British Fashion Council (BFC)
Website: info@britishfashioncouncil.com

British Footwear Association (BFA)

The British Footwear Association (BFA) supports the British footwear industry helping its members in all aspects of their businesses, and supplying members with specialist advice, ranging from start-ups, exporting, product sourcing, import regulations, health and safety, employment queries and lots more. Details of all services and membership are available on the BFA website.
British Footwear Association (BFA). 3 Burystead Place, Wellingborough, NN8 1AH
Tel: 01933 229005
Email: info@britishfootwearassociation.co.uk   Website: www.britishfootwearassociation.co.uk

British Independent Retailers Association (bira)

The British Independent Retailers Association (bira) is a trade association for independent retailers in the UK. It represents single retail outlets to small chains, dealers, suppliers, manufacturers and distributors. See the Association's website for details of business services, events and exhibitions, and membership benefits.
British Independent Retailers Association (bira)
Email: info@bira.co.uk   Website: www.bira.co.uk

British Interior Textiles Association (BITA)

British Interior Textiles association (BITA) is a trade association for the UK interior textiles industry. It seeks to 'promote and safeguard the interests of its members, who range from large, well-known brands, to small companies with only a few employees'. The product range supplied by members includes all aspects of the interior industry.
British Interior Textiles Association. (Head Office) 134 Dunthorne Way, Grange Farm, Milton Keynes, MK8 0LW
Tel: 01904 410598
Email: marketing@norfolkhouse-uk.com   Website: www.interiortextiles.co.uk

British Menswear Guild

Founded in 1959, the British Menswear Guild represents a portfolio of high quality British menswear brands. See the BMG website for details of the Guild's history, events and membership.
British Menswear Guild Ltd
Website: www.british-menswear-guild.co.uk

British Retail Consortium (BRC)

The British Retail Consortium (BRC) is a trade association for the British retail industry including large multiples, independents, high streets and out of town stores to online retailers, selling products across all sectors.
British Retail Consortium. 21 Dartmouth Street, Westminster, London, SW1H 9BP
Tel: 020 7854 8900
Email: info@brc.org.uk   Website: www.brc.org.uk

British Standards Institute (BSI)

The British Standards Institute (BSI) is the business standards company whose main activity is 'the production of standards and the supply of standards-related service'. See the BSI's website for details of services including developing standards, training, certification and verification, supply chain solutions, events and international projects.
British Standards Institute
Tel: 020 8996 9000
Email: cservices@bsigroup.com   Website: www.bsigroup.co.uk

British Tapestry Group (BTG)

The British Tapestry Group (BTG) 'promotes and explores the concept of woven tapestry as a contemporary art form', and has both national and international members. See the Group's website for full membership details, news and events, BTG Gallery of members work and exhibition archive.
British Tapestry Group
Email: info@thebritishtapestrygroup.co.uk   Website: www.thebritishtapestrygroup.co.uk

British Textile Machinery Association (BTMA)

The British Textile Machinery Association (BTMA) is a non-profit making membership organisation. See website for details of membership, shows and events, buyers guide and news.
British Textile Machinery Association (BTMA)
Tel: 0161 775 5740
Email: btma@btma.org.uk   Website: www.btma.org.uk

British Textile Technology Group (BTTG)

The British Textile Technology Group (BTTG) was founded in 1989 by the merger of the Shirley Institute and Wool Industry Research Association, and offers independent testing, certification and consultancy services.
British Textile Technology Group (BTTG)
Email: info@bttg.co.uk   Website: www.bttg.co.uk

British Travelgoods and Accessories Association (BTAA)

The British Travelgoods and Accessories Association (BTAA) is a membership organisation and represents companies from across the travelgoods and fashion accessories industry, including manufacturers, designers, wholesalers, importers, exporters, agents and retailers.
British Travelgoods and Accessories Association (BTAA). Federation House, 10 Vyse St, Birmingham, B18 6LT
Tel: 0121 236 2657
Website: www.btaa.org.uk

The British Wool Marketing Board (BWMB)

Established in 1950 The British Wool Marketing Board (BWMB) was founded to operate a central marketing system for UK fleece. The Board works on behalf of around 60,000 registered wool producers and works alongside the textile industry to raise the profile and promote British wool. See the BWMB website for further details of services.
The British Wool Marketing Board (BWMB). Wool House, Sidings Close, Canal Road, Bradford, West Yorkshire, BD2 1AZ
Tel: 01274 688666
Email: mail@britishwool.org.uk   Website: www.britishwool.org.uk

Candid Arts Trust

Candid Arts Trust is a self-funded, registered charity founded to 'promote the arts and art education with special emphasis placed on helping newly graduated artists and designers in their first years out of college'. Candid Arts Trust events include the Islington Contemporary Art and Design Fair, the Angel Christmas Fair as well as various group shows and film screenings throughout the year. It also hosts a number of college degree shows and solo and group exhibitions.
Candid Arts Trust. 3-5 Torrens Street, Angel, Islington, EC1V 1NQ
Tel: 020 7837 4237
Email: office@candidarts.com   Website: www.candidarts.com

CAPITB Trust

CAPITB Trust is an independent charity providing support and funding for "people employed or about to be employed in the British Clothing Industry". The Trust is formerly the Clothing and Allied Products

Industry Training Board. Each year the Trust strives to make donations to projects that will enhance skills within the British Clothing Industry. See website for further details.
RTITB. Access House, Halesfield 17, Telford, Shropshire, TF7 4PW
Tel: 01952 588533
Email: enquiries@capitbgrants.com   Website: capitbgrants.com

Charles Rennie Mackintosh Society (CRM)

The Charles Rennie Mackintosh Society (CRM) was founded to 'promote and encourage awareness of the Scottish architect and designer, Charles Rennie Mackintosh'. The Society has an excellent website providing information on Mackintosh, the Society's aims, news, events, education and learning, and membership details.
Charles Rennie Mackintosh Society (CRM). Queen's Cross Church, 870 Garscube Road, Glagow, G20 7EL
Tel: 0141 946 6600
Email: info@crmsociety.com   Website: www.crmsociety.com

Chartered Society of Designers (CSD)

The Chartered Society of Designers (CSD) is the 'world's largest chartered body of professional designers with members in 33 countries and represents designers in all disciplines, including fashion and textile design'. The Society offers chartered status, membership services and benefits, career advice and training. Student membership is available for those studying on a recognised design course. Visit the CSD website for further details of services and activities, training and professional development, awards, the CSD library, membership and membership benefits.
Chartered Society of Designers
Tel: +44 (0)20 7357 8088
Email: info@csd.org.uk   Website: www.csd.org.uk

Costume Society

The Costume Society promotes the study and preservation of historic and contemporary dress. Visit the Society's website for further details of activities, events, conference, awards, bursaries and membership.
Costume Society
Email: membership@costumesociety.org.uk   Website: www.costumesociety.org.uk

Costume Society of Scotland

The Costume Society of Scotland was established in 1966 with the aim of 'fostering an interest in every aspect of costume historical and contemporary in Scotland'. The Society encourages research and study by means of regular monthly lectures held throughout the academic year, a programme of events and news.
Costume Society of Scotland
Website: www.costumesocietyofscotland.btik.com

Costume and Textile Association for Norfolk Museums (C&TA)

Established in 1989, the Costume and Textile Association (C&TA) is an independent charity that raises funds to enrich and expand the Museum's collection through a varied programme of talks, workshops, activities and events. Full membership details are available on the Association's website along with details of activities and forthcoming events.
Costume and Textile Association for Norfolk Museums (C&TA). C/o Shire Hall, Market Avenue, Norwich, Norfolk, NR1 3JQ
Email: ctacostume@gmail.com   Website: www.ctacostume.org.uk

The Costume and Textile Society of Wales / Cymdeithas Gwisgoedd a Thecstilau Cymru

The Costume and Textile Society of Wales was founded to 'promote and encourage the study, preservation and documentation of costume and textiles in the region of Wales and the Marches'.
The Costume and Textile Society of Wales
Website: www.costumeandtextilesocietyofwales.org.uk

Crafts Council

The Crafts Council is the national development agency for contemporary craft. See the Council's excellent website for details of resources; opportunities; awards; competitions; residencies; exhibitions; workshops; seminars and conferences; collaborations and research. See details of the Council's Professional and Business Development programme: Hothouse for emerging designers and Injection for established

businesses. They also have an online Crafts Council Directory of makers across the UK.
Crafts Council. 44a Pentonville Road, Islington, London, N1 9BY
Tel: +44 (0) 207 806 2500
Email: makerdev@craftscouncil.org.uk   Website: www.craftscouncil.org.uk craft and makers

Creative Skillset

Creative Skillset is the industry skills body for the creative industries, including fashion and textiles. Led by research into the skill needs of the industries, they devise solutions that increase productivity and foster growth. One such solution for the fashion and textile industry has been the development of a broad range of apprenticeships, which enable smaller companies to scale-up and mould skills to fit their own business needs. They offer consultation for accessing funding and training and offer industry accreditation for HE and apprenticeship courses to help businesses identify the best quality graduates and talent. You can find this talent on Hiive.co.uk (Connect, Collaborate, Grow).
Creative Skillset. Focus Point, 21 Calendonian Road, London, N1 9GB
Tel: 020 7713 9800
Email: Info@creativeskillset.org   Website: http://creativeskillset.org

The Creative Society

The Creative Society is an arts employment charity that helps young people gain employment in the creative and cultural industries. They work with a range of creative partners around the country. See the Society's website for further details of projects, partners and research.
The Creative Society
Tol: 020 7845 5830
Email: contact@thecreativesociety.co.uk   Website: www.thecreativesociety.co.uk

Cross Stitch Guild (CSG)

The Cross Stitch Guild (CSG) is a worldwide organisation with a committed and enthusiastic membership. The CSG deals with cross stitch and all other forms of counted embroidery including blackwork, hemstitch, pulled and drawn threadwork, Hardanger and canvas work. Full details of membership and forthcoming events are available on the Guild's website.
Cross Stitch Guild (CSG). Pinks Barn, London Road, Fairford, Gloucestershire, GL7 4AR
Tel: 01285 713678
Email: jane@crossstitchguild.com   Website: www.thecrossstitchguild.com

Design and Artists Copyright Society (DACS)

Design and Artists Copyright Society (DACS) is a not-for-profit visual artists' rights management organisation that 'campaigns for artists' rights, championing their sustained contribution to the creative economy'. See the Society's website for details of their work, services, management schemes and events.
Design and Artists Copyright Society (DACS). 33 Old Bethnal Green Road, London, E2 6AA
Tel: 020 7336 8811
Email: info@dacs.org.uk   Website: www.dacs.org.uk

The Design Business Association (DBA)

The Design Business Association (DBA) is a 'trade association for the design industry in the UK; building the bridge between designers and businesses, and championing effective design'. See the DBA website for range of membership services, training courses, events, and useful guides and tools.
The Design Business Association. 35-39 Old Street, London, EC1V 9HX
Tel: 020 7251 9229
Website: www.dba.org.uk

The Design & Crafts Council of Ireland (DCCoI)

The Design & Crafts Council of Ireland (DCCoI) is 'the main champion of the design and craft industry in Ireland, promoting its growth and trade, and stimulating quality design, innovation and competitiveness'. DCCoI's activities are funded by the Department of Jobs, Enterprise and Innovation via Enterprise Ireland. See the Council's website for details of the Council's support and development programme, workshops, online tools, membership organisations and opportunities such as professional development residencies, awards and much more.
The Design & Crafts Council of Ireland (DCCoI) Castle Yard, Kilkenny, Ireland
Tel: +353 56 776 1804
Website: www.dccoi.ie

Design Council

The Design Council is 'a centre of new thinking and insight into new ways to do business', and offers events, practical demonstrations and support programmes for private industry and the public sector, investing in the future of UK design. The Council has an informative website providing the history of the Council, details of services, projects, knowledge, resources, a calendar of events, case studies, news and useful links.

Design Council. Angel Building, 407 St John Street, London, EC1V 4AB

Tel: 020 7420 5200

Email: info@designcouncil.org.uk   Website: www.designcouncil.org.uk

Design Factory

Design Factory is a resource that supports and develops designer-makers through programmes of opportunities and a national network of peer support. See the Design Factory website for details of their membership scheme which is available at three levels: 'new, mid-career and established maker'.

Design Factory. The National Centre for Craft & Design, Navigation Wharf, Sleaford, Lincolnshire, NG34 7TW

Tel: 01529 414532

Email: info@designfactory.org.uk   Website: www.designfactory.org.uk

Design-Nation

Design Nation is an organisation that aims to 'promote excellence of British design, craft and product whilst enabling and supporting commercial collaborations between entrepreneurs, industry, retailers and the wider creative economy'. Visit their website for further details.

Design Nation. The National Centre for Craft & Design, Navigation Wharf, Sleaford, Lincolnshire, NG34 7TW

Tel: 01529 414532

Email: info@designnation.co.uk   Website: www.designnation.co.uk

Design Research Society (DRS)

The Design Research Society (DRS) is 'committed to promoting and developing design research'. Visit the DSR website for details of the Society, membership, activities, events and awards, and also the monthly online Design Research Newsletter, and other publications.

The Design Research Society (DRS)

Website: www.designresearchsociety.org

The Design and Technology Association (D&T)

The Design and Technology Association (D&T) is an association that represents those who are involved in design and technology education. It organises conferences, training and events, and offers a range of resources and publications including the A3 magazine Designing. See the D&A website for research, consultants, local branches, resourses and further information.

The Design and Technology Association (D&T)

Website: www.data.org.uk

Dress and Textile Specialists (DATS)

Dress and Textile Specialists (DATS) is a 'museum subject specialist network' providing links and mutual support for professionals working with specialist collections of fashion, dress and textiles, and wider museum collections that include these materials, located in the United Kingdom and Ireland. See DATS website for details of membership, news, events and their annual conference.

Dress and Textile Specialists (DATS)

Website: www.dressandtextilespecialists.org.uk

East Midlands Textiles Association (EMTEX) Ltd

East Midlands Textiles Association (EMTEX) is an association founded to 'assist the regions clothing and textile businesses, and supports individual designers through to established businesses'. See the EMTEX website for membership details, EMTEX projects, news and events.

East Midlands Textiles Association (EMTEX) Ltd

Tel: 0115 9473613

Email: enquiries@emtex.org.uk   Website: www.emtex.org.uk

East Midlands Visual Arts Network (EMVAN)

East Midlands Visual Arts Network (EMVAN) is an open network for all those working in the visual arts, particularly in the East Midlands, with a remit to strengthen the sector. It celebrates and promotes the making and presenting of contemporary visual art and contributes to a flourishing arts habitat in the region. It seeks to broker useful and inter-dependent relationships between artists and organisations; initiate a range of activities designed to meet the needs of the sector; and tackle common issues resulting in new ways of working. Emvan is part of the national contemporary visual arts network and aims to take full advantage of the knowledge, skills and assets of this wider network.

East Midlands Visual Arts Network (EMVAN)
Tel: 0115 914 1320
Email: coordinator@emvan.net   Website: www.emvan.net

The Embroiderers Guild

The Embroiderers' Guild - the objectives of the charity is 'to promote and encourage the art of embroidery and related crafts'. They have over 200 branches nationwide, and over 9,000 Guild members with varying levels of ability. They offer online courses, exhibitions, a workshop programme and competitions, and publish two magazines Stitch, and Embroidery magazine. Membership details are available on the Guild's website along with their latest news and their programme of events.

Embroiderers' Guild. Embroiderers' Guild House, 1 Kings Road, Walton on Thames, Surrey, KT12 2RA
Tel: 01932 260738
Email: administrator@embroiderersguild.com   Website: www.embroiderersguild.com

Ethical Fashion Forum (EFF)

The Ethical Fashion Forum (EFF) is the industry body for sustainable fashion, representing its members in more than 100 countries, and supporting their members through SOURCE, 'the Global Platform for Sustainable Fashion'. SOURCE offers valuable information, reporting on business resources, trends, legal information, skills, development and training, events calendar, Source awards and fellowships, and consultancy. See the EFF website for membership details and network contacts.

Ethical Fashion Forum. Rich Mix, Unit C02, 35-47 Bethnal Green Rd, London, E1 6LA
Tel: 020 7739 7692
Email: info@ethicalfashionforum.com   Website: www.ethicalfashionforum.com

European Textile Network (ETN)

The European Textile Network (ETN) is an organisation established to 'promote European cooperation and cultural interchanges in textiles'. See the ETN website for membership details (Institutional, group and individual) and information on events and activities.

European Textile Network (ETN). ETN Secretariat, Friedenstr. 5, D-30175 Hannover, Germany
Tel: +49-511/817006
Email: ETN@ETN-net.org   Website: www.etn-net.org

Fashion Awareness Direct (FAD)

Fashion Awareness Direct (FAD) provides young people with an understanding into fashion, 'bridging the gap between education and working in the industry'. FAD organises fashion workshops, industry days and competitions. See FAD's website for details of the Leadership Academy, competitions and awards, FAD projects and Fashion Futures.

Fashion Awareness Direct (FAD). 10a Wellesley Terrace, London, N1 7NA
Tel/Fax: 020 7490 3946
Email: info@fad.org.uk   Website: www.fad.org.uk

Fan Circle International (FCI)

The Fan Circle International (FCI) was founded to 'promote interest in, and understanding of, all aspects of fans'. Members include collectors, fan makers, costume designers, historians, artists, students, antique dealers, lace makers and interior designers. They have many members in Europe, the USA, and now Asia.

Fan Circle International (FCI)
Website: www.fancircleinternational.org

The Fashion and Design Protection Association (FDPA)

Established in 1974, The Fashion and Design Protection Association (FDPA) was founded to 'protect and uphold the rights of originators of fashion and other original designs'. The FDPA provides many services including legal consultations, copyright and design systems, an arbitration service, trade mark registration and brand consultancy and legal documentation.

The Fashion and Design Protection Association (FDPA). 94-96 Great North Road, London, N2 0NL
Tel: 0208 8837288
Email: info@fdpa.co.uk   Website: www.fdpa.co.uk

Fashion & Textiles Children's Trust (FTCT)

The Fashion & Textile Children's Trust (FTCT) is a registered charity which provides grants to children (0-18yrs) whose parents or carers work, or have previously worked, in any aspect of the UK fashion and textile industry. 'Our grants support all aspects of a child's education and wellbeing. Call our friendly team who are here to help'.

Fashion & Textile Children's Trust
Tel: 0300 123 9002
Email: grants@ftct.org.uk   Website: www.ftct.org.uk

The Fashion and Textile Group Training Association (GTA)

The Fashion and Textiles Group Training Association (GTA) offers a service to employers providing training provision, working with companies and businesses to identify their requirements and to find solutions. See the GTA website for further details relating to training, apprenticeships, industry and sector information, events, case studies and membership.

F&T Group Training Association (GTA)
Tel: 01484 346500
Email: info@fashionandtextiles-gta.co.uk   Website: http://fashionandtextiles-gta.co.uk

The Giftware Association (GA)

The Giftware Association (GA) is a national trade representative body and is 'the only UK trade association serving the gift and home industry'. Members range from retailers to suppliers, high street brand names to individual craftspeople.

The Giftware Association (The GA)
Email: simone.rose@ga-uk.org   Website: www.ga-uk.org

Glass Beadmakers UK (GBUK)

The Glass Beadmakers UK (GBUK) was established to share and publicise information about making glass beads through networking and educational opportunities. A full list of members and a Members Gallery is available for viewing on the Glass Beadmakers UK website.

Glass Beadmakers UK
Website: www.gbuk.org

The Goldwork Guild

The Goldwork Guild promotes 'the specialist art of goldwork, and presents information for the expert, teacher, designer, museum curator, beginner and the inexperienced'.

The Goldwork Guild.   Penkridge Hall, Leebotwood, Shropshire, SY6 6LZ
Tel: 01694 751390 / 07974308743
Email: tcbee@btinternet.com   Website: www.thegoldworkguild.com

The Guild of Machine Knitters

The Guild of Machine Knitters is a charitable organisation run 'by machine knitters for machine knitters, and is devoted to supporting and raising the standards of machine knitting'. The Guild consists of designers, manufacturers, educators and other interested people. See the Guild's website for details of the work of the Guild, regional officers, courses, resources, links, events and news.

The Guild of Machine Knitters
Email: membership@guild-mach-knit.org.uk   Website: www.guild-mach-knit.org.uk

The Guild of Master Craftsmen

The Guild of Master Craftsmen aims to 'provide the public with a list of skilled, trustworthy and dependable individuals and companies who are masters of their particular trade'. Full details of membership are available on the Guild's website, in addition to consumer advice, and also a Directory of Craftsmen listed by location, trade and profession.

The Guild of Master Craftsmen
Website: www.guildmc.com

Guild of Needle Laces

The Guild of Needle Laces is a non-profitmaking organisation set up to 'promote the interest, skills, teaching, conservation, history and exhibition of all needle made laces'. See the Guild's website for gallery, diary dates of events and activities, and membership details.
Guild of Needle Laces
Website: www.guildofneedlelaces.org

Guild of Silk Painters

The Guild of Silk Painters is an international, non-profit making organisation, based in Great Britain whose aim is to 'promote and inspire the art of silk painting'. Full membership details are available on the Guild's website along with information listing classes and workshops, resources and associated links. The Guild are organisers the biennial Silk Painting Festival.
Guild of Silk Painters
Email: membership@silkpainters-guild.co.uk   Website: www.silkpainters-guild.co.uk

Guild of Traditional Upholsterers

The Guild of Traditional Upholsterers was formed in 1987 to 'maintain standards of excellence, and to promote the craft of traditional handmade upholstery'. Visit the Guild's website for membership details, the Directory of Members, and for information about the Guild's activities and news.
Guild of Traditional Upholsterers
Website: www.gtu.uk

Harris Tweed Authority

The Harris Tweed Authority is a legal body who 'protect, maintain and promote the authenticity, standard and reputation of the world famous Harris Tweed cloth'. The Authority provides leaflets, brochures and DVD's, and have an archive in Stornoway holding a wealth of historical items and images. See the Authority's website for details of the history, the heritage, and authenticity of Harris Tweed, the mills and producers, and much more.
Harris Tweed Authority. Town Hall, 2 Cromwell Street, Stornoway, Isle of Lewis, HS1 2DB
Tel: 01851 702 269
Email: enquiries@harristweed.org   Website: www.harristweed.org

Heritage Crafts Association

The Heritage Crafts Association is the advocacy body that safeguards and promotes traditional heritage craft skills. See the Associations website for information and advice, opportunities, research, the Heritage Craft Awards, courses, support, news, events and membership details and also the Association's Craft Directory.
Heritage Crafts Association
Email: info@heritagecrafts.org.uk   Website: www.heritagecrafts.org.uk

Independent Footwear Retailers Association (IFRA)

The Independent Footwear Retailers Association (IFRA) is a trade membership association for shoe retailers. Visit the Association's website for further details.
Independent Footwear Retailers Association (IFRA). PO Box 123, Banbury, Oxfordshire, OX15 6WB
Tel: 01295 738726
Email: admin@shoeshop.org.uk   Website: www.shoeshop.org.uk

International Council for Museums Costume Committee (ICOM)

The International Council for Museums Costume Committee (ICOM) are committed to 'the study of all aspects of presenting, preserving researching and collecting dress'. Members are museum professionals and costume historians from all over the world who share their expertise through presentations at annual meetings and publications.
International Council of Museums Costume Committee
Website: http://network,icom.museum/costume

International Council of Tanners (ICT)

The International Council of Tanners (ICT) is a membership organisation of the world's leather trade associations. See the ICT website for excellent information on leather, legislation, labelling, statistics and sources of information, and link sites.
International Leather Council (ICT)
Email: see@tannerscouncilict.org   Website: www.leathercouncil.org

International Feltmakers Association (IFA)

The International Feltmakers Association (IFA) is a not for profit organisation that seeks to 'promote worldwide interest in the art and ethnography of felt making in all its forms, to facilitate the exchange of knowledge and ideas, and to promote networking and exhibition opportunities for members'. Full details of membership are available on the Association's website.

International Feltmakers Association

Email: secretary@feltmakers.com   Website: www.feltmakers.com

International Sewing Machine Collectors' Society (ISMACS)

The International Sewing Machine Collectors' Society (ISMACS) is a sewing machine collector's group. Details of membership and ISMACS newsletter are available on the Society's website.

International Sewing Machine Collectors' Society (ISMACS)

Website: http://ismacs.net

Irish Linen Guild

The Irish Linen Guild is a promotional organisation, representing its members in the linen industry, 'promoting and protecting Irish Linen in national and international markets'. See the Guild's website for details of membership and membership benefits, activities and events.

Irish Linen Guild

Website: www.irishlinen.co.uk

Knitting and Crochet Guild

Founded in 1978, the Knitting and Crochet Guild works to 'raise standards, and to promote and preserve the practice, development and continuance of skills in knitting and crochet'. See the website for details of the Guilds history and Collection; membership benefits; events and activities; workshops and courses; the Guilds Knitting Convention and AGM; news and quick links to find your local branch; and details of Slipknot: The Journal of the Knitting and Crochet Guild.

The Knitting and Crochet Guild

Email: secretary@kcguild.org.uk   Website: www.kcguild.org.uk

Lace Guild

Founded to promote the study, collection and use of lace, the Lace Guild offers an informative website detailing the history of lace, with an online Museum of Lace, a database collection containing over 15,000 objects including examples of lace, bobbins, shuttles, netting needles, threads and much more. An appointment can be made to view the Lace Guild Collection, which became a registered museum in 2001. See the Guild's website featuring forthcoming events and details of membership.

Lace Guild. The Hollies, 53 Audnam, Stourbridge, West Midlands, DY8 4AE

Website: www.laceguild.org

Lace Society

The Lace Society is a membership organisation that 'promotes and supports all types of lace making and an interest in lace in general and offers a wide-range of lace related activities'. The Society has a library of over 600 lace books and offers a range of activities, courses events and specialist visits each year.

Lace Society

Website: www.thelacesociety.org.uk

Lancashire Textile Manufacturers' Association (LTMA)

The Lancashire Textile Manufacturers' Association (LTMA) provides 'practical help and advice to its textile industry member companies, promoting the benefits to the regional economy of a strong and healthy textile industry'. See the LTMA website for details of membership, services, news and events, and excellent resource links.

Lancashire Textile Manufacturers' Association. 4 St Andrew's Street, Blackburn, Lancashire, BB1 8AE

Tel: 01254 580248

Email: enquiries@ltma.co.uk   Website: www.ltma.co.uk

The Leather Conservation Centre

Founded in 1978, The Leather Conservation Centre offers a comprehensive service in the conservation and restoration of leather objects of historical and cultural significance. Areas include: conservation, restoration, education and research including various specialist publications.

The Leather Conservation Centre. Boughton Green Road, Northampton, NN2 7AN

Tel: 01604 719766

Email: lcc@northampton.ac.uk   Website: www.leatherconservation.org

The International Footwear Foundation (IFF)

The International Footwear Foundation (IFF) brings together the contemporary footwear industry and the footwear heritage sector in Northamptonshire, 'to recognise and promote their strengths in footwear design and manufacturing and in acknowledgement to their leading position in leather technology'. See the IFF website for details of events and exhibitions, education and training, the Foundation's Trade Directory and resources.
The International Footwear Foundation (IFF)
Website: www.international-footwear-foundation.co.uk

Made Up Textiles Association (MUTA)

The Made Up Textiles Association (MUTA) is a trade association for the UK temporary structures and technical textile industries. The Association 'informs, promotes best practice, facilitates and represents' suppliers and manufacturers of textile products used in diverse areas, such as marquees, healthcare, aerospace, inflatable structures, tarpaulins, covers and bags.
Made Up Textiles Association (MUTA)
Email: info@muta.org.uk   Website: www.performancetextiles.org.uk

The Medieval Dress and Textile Society (MeDaTS)

The Medieval Dress and Textile Society (MeDaTS) was founded to provide a forum for those interested in European clothing and textiles, from the end of the Roman Empire in Western Europe until about 1600. MeDaTS members include dress and textile historians, designers for the theatre, museum curators, re-enactors, economic and social historians, art historians, archaeologists, conservators, dyers and weavers, and all who are interested in the history of dress and textiles.
The Medieval Dress and Textile Society (MeDaTS)
Website: www.medats.org.uk

Midlands Textile Forum

The Midlands Textile Forum was founded to 'encourage and to promote the textile arts across the Midlands, and provide a supportive network for members and a platform to showcase the textile arts within the region'. Further details of membership and the application process are available on the Forum's website.
Midlands Textile Forum
Email: info@midlandstextileforum.com   Website: http://midlandstextileforum.com

National Association of Disabled Craft Workers

The National Association of Disabled Craft Workers was established to assist disabled people to develop hobbies and crafts, providing information to enable the provision of training in a local area where possible, through their network of practicing craft workers, and to provide sources of materials for craftwork, and to help and offer advice on setting up craft venture, covering all aspects of development.
National Association of Disabled Craft Workers
Website: www.update.org.uk

National Childrenswear Association (NWCA)

The National Childrenswear Association (NCWA) is a membership association that supports and assists members in providing expert advice and lobbying on all aspects of childrenswear on the industries behalf.
National Childrenswear Association. 3 Queen Square, Bloomsbury, London, WC1N 3AR
Tel: 020 7843 9488
Email: enquiries@ncwa.co.uk   Website: www.ncwa.co.uk

National Society for Education in Art and Design (NSEAD)

The National Society for Education in Art and Design (NSEAD) is the leading national authority relating to art, craft and design across all levels of education in the UK. The NSEAD has an excellent website full of information providing details of regional networks; Continuing Professional Development (CPD); events, conferences and training; curriculum resources and the NSEAD Consultant Members Database.
National Society for Education in Art and Design (NSEAD).
3 Masons Wharf, Potley Lane, Corsham, Wiltshire, SN13 9FY
Tel: 01225 810134
Email: info@nsead.org   Website: www.nsead.org

NESTA

NESTA (National Endowment for Science Technology and the Arts) is a public body designed to 'promote creativity, talent and innovation across a wide spectrum of areas and interests, founded with a mission 'to help people and organisations bring great ideas to life'. They have an excellent website full of information, listing events, news and features, publications, funding opportunities, an Enterprise Resource Toolkit and much more.
NESTA (Headquarters). 1 Plough Place, London, EC4A 1DE
Tel: 020 7438 2500
Email: information@nesta.org.uk Website: www.nesta.org.uk

Non Wovens Network

The Nonwovens Network comprises of industry professionals, with over 170 members who are all associated with the nonwovens industry. Members include manufacturers, suppliers, converters and product users to researchers from across the UK and beyond.
Non Wovens Network. Centre for Technical Textiles, University of Leeds, Leeds, LS2 9JT
Tel: 0113 343 3758
Website: www.nonwovensnetwork.com

Northern Ireland Textile and Apparel Association (NITA)

Northern Ireland Textile and Apparel Association Ltd (NITA) is a trade association and representative body of the textiles and clothing industry in Northern Ireland. Members are from across all sectors, from fibres and yarns to fabrics, clothing and other textile products. See the NITA website for details of membership, the latest industry news, awards, directories, publications and forthcoming events.
Northern Ireland Textile and Apparel Association Ltd (NITA)
Tel: 028 9268 9999
Email: info@nita.co.uk

Northern Society of Costume and Textiles (NSCT)

The Northern Society of Costume and Textiles (NSCT) was founded to 'encourage the study, research and preservation of costume and textiles'.
Northern Society of Costume and Textiles
Email: info@nsct.org.uk Website: www.nsct.org.uk

Norwich Cathedral Broderers' Guild

The Broderers' Guild is responsible for the care and repair of ecclesiastical textiles, in addition to designing and making new frontals and vestments for Norwich Cathedral. The Guild also provides services such as restoration expertise, alterations and repairs to existing ecclesiastical work. They also design and make new textile items for other parishes and private individuals.
Norwich Cathedral Broderer's Group
Tel: 01603 218326 (Workshop Supervisor)
Website: www.cathedral.org.uk/cathedral-life/broderers-guild-broderers-guild

Oriental Rug and Textile Society (ORTS)

The Oriental Rug and Textile Society (ORTS) was founded in 1977 to encourage enthusiasm and interest in the carpets and textiles of the Orient; and now of the whole world. They also aim to advance the understanding of the processes involved in the creation of Oriental rugs and textiles and to promote knowledge of the traditional centers of weaving. See website for details of the Society's membership, current programme and past activities.
Oriental Rug and Textile Society (ORTS)
Email: membership@orientalrugandtextilesociety.org.uk
Website: www.orientalrugandtextilesociety.org.uk

The Quilt Association Ltd

The Quilt Association is a membership organisation formed with the aim of promoting quilting and patchwork from its base in Mid Wales. See website for membership details.
The Quilt Association Ltd. Minerva Arts Centre, Llanidloes, Powys, Wales, SY18 6BY
Email: quilts@quilt.org.uk Website: www.quilt.org.uk

The Quilters' Guild

The Quilters Guild is a national membership organisation for people involved and interested in patchwork and quilting. See the Guild's website for details of membership, activities and events including seminars and study days, awards, bursaries, and the Guild's magazine The Quilter.

The Quilters' Guild of the British Isles. St Anthony's Hall, Peasholme Green, York, YO1 7PW
Tel: 01904 613242
Email: admin@quiltersguild.org.uk   Website: www.quiltersguild.org.uk

Real Sheepskin Association (RSA)

The Real Sheepskin Association (RSA) 'represents tanners, manufacturers and merchants, retailers, after carers and designers specialising in real sheepskin products and services, and was founded to promote the use of sheepskin, and provides a forum for the whole UK Sheepskin Industry'.

Real Sheepskin Association (RSA)
Tel: 01604 714103
Email: info@realsheepskin.org.uk   Website: www.realsheepskin.org.uk

Retail Trust

Retail Trust is the charity 'looking after the needs of all the three million people working in retail and related industries in the UK'. The Trust offers a wide range of advice, help and support from career development to mentoring, counselling, hardship grants and retirement housing.

Retail Trust (Head Office). Marshall Hall, Marshall Estate, Hammers Lane, London, NW7 4DQ
Tel: 020 8201 0110 (Head Office)
Website: www.retailtrust.org.uk

Ring of Tatters

The Ring of Tatters is an organisation which 'supports and promotes the craft of tatting, encouraging both new and experienced tatters to enjoy their craft and develop their skills'.

Ring of Tatters
Email: secretary@ringoftatters.org.uk   Website: www.ringoftatters.org.uk

Royal Society for the Encouragement of the Arts, Manufacture and Commerce (RSA)

The Royal Society for the Encouragement of the Arts, Manufacture and Commerce (RSA) is an organisation with a 27,000-strong Fellowship 'committed to finding innovative practical solutions to today's social challenges'. The RSA offers a superb website with information outlining the history and the work of the RSA, including details of cutting-edge research, Fellowships, the latest news and RSA events. Their key themes include Public Services and Communities; Creative Learning and Development; Economy, Enterprise and Manufacture.

Royal Society for the Encouragement of the Arts, Manufacture and Commerce.
8 John Adam Street, London, WC2N 6EZ
Tel: 020 7930 5115
Email: general@rsa.org.uk   Website: www.thersa.org

Royal School of Needlework (RSN)

Founded in 1872, the Royal School of Needlework (RSN) is 'the international centre for excellence dedicated to teaching, practising and promoting the art of hand embroidery in the 21st century'. Based at Hampton Court Palace, the RSN offers a range of embroidery courses from day classes for beginners to a Degree programme – BA (Hons) Hand Embroidery for Fashion, Interiors, Textile Art. The RSN also teaches Exeter, Bristol, Rugby, Durham and Glasgow and internationally in the USA and Japan. See RSN website for further details.

Royal School of Needlework. Apartment 12a, Hampton Court Palace, Surrey, KT8 9AU
Tel: 020 3166 6943
Email: enquiries@royal-needlework.org.uk   Website: www.royal-needlework.org.uk

SATRA Technology

SATRA is an independent research and testing organisation. They have specialist technical facilities, laboratories and resources allowing them to test products and components to European and international standards across a wide range of industry sectors. Sectors include clothing, fabrics, leather, footwear and floorings, along with Personal Protective Equipment (PPE) and workwear testing, and other technical

services. See website for further information on product research, facilities, consultancy, technical training, SATRA membership, and their programme of events, courses and seminars.
SATRA Technology Centre (Registered Office), Wyndham Way, Telford Way, Kettering, Northamptonshire, NN16 8SD
Tel: 01536 410000
Email: info@satra.co.uk Website: www.satra.co.uk

The Sampler Guild (TSG)
The aim of The Sampler Guild (TSG) is to offer a forum for the research of sampler history, to continue the art of sampler making, and to promote the preservation of antique samplers.
The Sampler Guild
Email: linda@thesamplerguild.co.uk   Website: www.thesamplerguild.co.uk

The Schoolwear Association (SA)
The Schoolwear Association (SA) represents all those involved in the supply of school specific uniform, from retailers, direct to school suppliers, manufacturers, distributors, wholesalers, suppliers, decorators, agents and schools.
The Schoolwear Association (SA)
Email: info@schoolwearassociation.co.uk   Website: www.schoolwearassociation.co.uk

Scottish Machine Knitters Association
The Scottish Machine Knitters Association aims 'to promote machine knitting and to raise the standard of the craft by means of exhibitions, workshops, lectures and publications'. A bi-monthly newsletter is available to all its members, and membership is open to all machine knitters worldwide.
Scottish Machine Knitters Association
Email: Chairperson@scottishmachineknitters.org.uk   Website: www.scottishmachineknitters.org.uk

Scottish Textile & Leather Association (STLA)
The Scottish Textile & Leather Association (STLA) supports Scotland's textile design and manufacturing sector. Visit the Association's website for specifics of membership and the Membership Directory, along with details of resources, skills development, news, industry overview, events and job opportunities.
Scottish Textile & Leather Association (STLA)
www.stla.uk.com

Sewing Machine Trade Association (SMTA)
Established in the 1930s, the Sewing Machine Trade Association (SMTA) aims to 'serve and guide the public to SMTA members who are able to assist in finding and recommending sewing machines, overlockers, embellishers, embroidery and cover stitch machines, and spare parts'.
Sewing Machine Trade Association (SMTA)
Email: info@smta.org.uk Website: www.sewingmachine.org.uk

Shetland Heritage Association (SHA)
Founded in 2000, the Shetland Heritage Association (SHA) is a network of voluntary groups established throughout Shetland as an umbrella group to 'give a voice to the voluntary heritage sector in the islands'. Areas of specialist interest include all aspects of Shetland heritage, such as Textiles, Crofting, Shetland Dialect, Storytelling, Family History and the Norwegian Connection.
Shetland Heritage Association
Website: www.shetlandheritageassociation.com

Silk Association of Great Britain (SAGB)
The Silk Association of Great Britain (SAGB) exists to 'further the aims of the UK silk industry and to promote silk in general'. Full details and benefits of membership are provided on the Association's website, along with information about the history of the silk industry, the production of silk, fabric types and details of the Associations education service and resources.
The Silk Association of Great Britain. 3 Queen Square, London, WC1N 3AR
Tel: 020 7843 9460
Email: info@silk.org.uk   Website: www.silk.org.uk

The 62 Group of Textile Artists

Established in 1962, The 62 Group is an artist led organisation who aim to 'incorporate and challenge the boundaries of textile practice through an annual programme of exhibitions'. The Group are recognised internationally for their stunning and innovative work.

The 62 Group of Textile Artists
Website: www.62group.org.uk

Society of Designer Craftsmen Ltd (SDC)

The Society of Designer Craftsmen (SDC) is a Society for designers and makers to 'promote and encourage excellence in professional practice, workmanship, design and to develop the status of all those who work in the crafts'. Licentiateship and membership schemes are available with opportunities to exhibit. See the Societies website for membership details, a list of present members, exhibitions, the Societies Licentiate Mentoring Scheme and additional links.

Society of Designer Craftsmen. 24 Rivington Street, London, EC2A 3DU
Tel: 07531 798983
Email: info@societyofdesignercraftsmen.org.uk   Website: www.societyofdesignercraftsmen.org.uk

Society of Dyers and Colourists (SDC)

The Society of Dyers and Colourists (SDC) is the world's leading independent education charity dedicated to colour. The Society's mission is to 'educate the changing world in the science of colour'. The SDC is a professional, chartered society with an international network of regions and activities. See the SDC website for further details of activities, workshops, events, training and education courses, and internationally recognised qualifications.

Society of Dyers and Colourists. Perkin House, 82 Grattan Road, Bradford, West Yorkshire, BD1 2LU
Tel: +44 (0)1274 725138
Email: info@sdc.org.uk   Website: www.sdc.org.uk

Surface Design Association (SDA)

Founded in America in 1976, the Surface Design Association (SDA) now has branches all over the world with nearly 4000 members worldwide. The Association aims to 'promote awareness and appreciation of textile-inspired art and design'. See the Association's website for details of membership, news, exhibitions and conferences, calendar of events and opportunities, publications, and SDA grants and awards section.

Surface Design Association
Website: www.surfacedesign.org

TechniTex

TechniTex is a research and knowledge transfer organisation for the UK's Technical Textiles and Advanced Materials Sector. The Organisation focuses on 'research, design and development of new technologies and applications for the technical textile industry', and offers consultancy services for a wide range of technical textile requirements. See the TechniTex website for further details of services.

TechniTex. Arch 30, North Campus Incubator, Altrincham Street, off Sackville Street, Manchester, M1 3NJ
Tel: 0161 306 8500
Website: www.technitex.org

Texprint

Texprint is an organisation run by industry professionals with the aim to 'select, mentor and promote the best of the UK's newly graduated textile designers, providing an opportunity for realistic development, and a vital bridge between higher education and the real, commercial world'. See the Texprint website for details of their Mission, Texprint history, events diary and awards, list of sponsors, designers, internships, and resources.

Texprint
Email: info@texprint.org.uk   Website: www.texprint.org.uk

Textile Centre of Excellence

The Textile Centre of Excellence is a not-for-profit company based in West Yorkshire. The Centre delivers a wide range of training and development support. Training provided includes apprenticeships and NVQs, Leadership and Management training, Health and Safety and IT. See the Centre's website for details of

training programmes, technical support, conferencing and projects.
Textile Centre of Excellence. Textile House, Red Doles Lane, Huddersfield, HD2 1YF
Tel: 01484 346500
Email: enquiries@textilehouse.co.uk   Website: www.textilehouse.co.uk

The Textile Institute – UK

The Textile Institute is a textiles, clothing and footwear organisation whose aim is to 'enable learning, to recognise achievement, to reward excellence and to disseminate information'. The Institute has individual and corporate members in up to 80 countries covering all sectors and disciplines in textiles, clothing and footwear industries. They have an excellent website providing details of membership,
news, events, awards, publications, TI Professional Qualifications, accredited programmes, a jobs page and much more.
The Textile Institute, UK. 1st Floor, St. James's Buildings, Oxford Street, Manchester, M1 6FQ
Tel: +44(0)161 237 1188.
Email: tiihq@textileinst.org.uk Website: www.textileinstitute.org

Textile Recycling Association

Textile Recycling Association is the UK's trade association for used clothing and textile collectors, sorters and reprocessors. Members include collectors, graders and reprocessors of second hand clothing, textiles and shoes operating throughout the United Kingdom.
Textile Recycling Association. PO Box 965, Maidstone, Kent, ME17 3WD
Email: info@ textile-recycling.org.uk   Website: www.textile-recycling.org.uk

Textile Services Association (TSA)

The Textile Services Association (TSA) is the trade association for the laundry, dry cleaning and textile rental industries in the UK. Membership varies from large multi-site public companies to smaller family businesses.
Textile Services Association. 3 Queen Square, Bloomsbury, London, WC1N 3AR
Tel: 020 7843 9490
Email: tsa@tsa-uk.org Website: www.tsa-uk.org

The Textile Society

The Textile Society aims to 'connect scholars, designers, researchers, teachers, artists, collectors and others who share an interest in the study of textile design and history'. Meetings, visits and student bursaries are available. The Society's publishes the journal TEXT and a member's newsletter. Full details of membership are available on the Societies website.
The Textile Society
Website: www.textilesociety.org.uk

UK Creative Industries

UK Creative Industries are a partnership of government and industry promoting the UK's creative industries to trade audiences worldwide. Their website highlights the UK's creative industries by collating statistics, case studies, news, commentary, event details, contact and other resources related to the creative sectors.
UK Creative Industries
Tel: 0207 235 7020
Email: info@creativeindustries.co.uk   Website: www.thecreativeindustries.co.uk

UK Fashion and Textile Association (UKFT)

The UK Fashion and Textile Association (UKFT) work to 'support fashion, clothing and knitting, UK businesses offering advice and guidance to its members on all aspects of running a business including export advice through UKFT Exports Division'. The UKFT offers a superb website providing information relating to business, regulations, export, trade fairs, funding, employment and training, and membership details and much, much more.
UK Fashion and Textile Association (UKFT). 3 Queen Square, Bloomsbury, London, WC1N 3AR
Tel: +44 (0) 20 7843 9460
Email: info@ukft.org   Website: www.ukft.org

UK Handknitting Association

The UK Handknitting Association is dedicated to hand knitting and the promotion of knitting. The Association was formerly known as the British Handknitting Confederation. The website offers an

excellent resource providing details on 'What's happening in Groups', events, projects, careers and information on the Knitted Textile Awards and competitions, knitting statistics and details listing suppliers and retailers.
UK Handknitting Association
Website: www.ukhandknitting.com

UK Leather Federation (UKLF)

The UK Leather Federation (UKLF) is a trade association for the UK leather industry. They are a membership-based organisation with the aims to 'represent, promote and protect the UK leather Industry'. See the Federation's website for membership details, events and links.
UK Leather Federation
Tel: 01604 679999
Website: www.ukleather.org

Wallpaper History Society

Founded in 1986, the Wallpaper History Society was established to 'promote an awareness and understanding of historic and contemporary wall coverings'. The Society organises a programme of events, including lectures and seminars, visits to wallpaper collections, historic houses and towns, design studios and manufacturers archives.
The Wallpaper History Society
Website: wallpaperhistorysociety.org.uk

West of England Costume Society (WECS)

Formed in 1973, the West of England Costume Society (WECS) is a group of enthusiasts who 'share the same interests in the study costume, the decorative arts and their history, and to preserve important and significant items of dress from the past and present'. See the Society's website for details of past and forthcoming events, the Society's magazine WECS Wardrobe and Spin a Yarn, and details of membership.
West of England Costume Society (WECS)
Website: www.wofecostumesociety.org

The William Morris Society and Museum

The William Morris Society aims to 'make the life of Morris and his associates better known and has worldwide membership open to all'. The Society publishes books, pamphlets, the William Morris Society Newsletter and The Journal of William Morris Studies. See the Society's website for membership details, and calendar listing its lecture programme, educational activities, conferences, tours, museum visits and social gatherings.
The William Morris Society and Museum
Website: www.williammorrissociety.org

The Worshipful Company of Broderers

The Worshipful Company of Broderers was formed to 'promote and protect the art of embroidery, a major City trade in the Middle Ages'. Today they continue to support the industry and encourage excellence.
The Worshipful Company of Broderers
Email: clerk@broderers.co.uk   Website: www.broderers.co.uk

The Worshipful Company of Cordwainers

Cordwainers dates back to 1272, making the company one of the oldest Liveries in the City of London. Today, they have a highly regarded charitable ethos and support and encourage talent in the footwear and leather industries through grants, awards, scholarships and bursaries, and other help.
The Worshipful Company of Cordwainers
Email: office@cordwainers.org   Website: www.cordwainers.org

The Worshipful Company of Drapers

Founded over 600 years ago, the Drapers' Company was a trade association of wool and cloth merchants, and is one of the 'Twelve Great Livery Companies in the City of London. The Organisation has evolved and today has new significance through its charitable role'. See the website for details of the Company's history, membership, charitable work and grant-making trusts.
The Worshipful Company of Drapers
Email: mail@thedrapers.co.uk   Website: www.thedrapers.co.uk

The Worshipful Company of Dyers
The Worshipful Company of Dyers present-day activities focus on the continuing development of the craft of dyeing. The Company has developed strong connections with the Society of Dyers and Colourists in Bradford, and many education institutions. See the website for further information.
The Worshipful Company of Dyers
Email: clerk@dyerscompany.com   Website: www.dyerscompany.co.uk

The Worshipful Company of Fan Makers
The Worshipful Company of Fan Makers has an informative website providing details of the Livery company's history, news, events, resources, affiliations and charities in education and the community.
Worshipful Company of Fan Makers
Email: clerk@fanmakers.com   Website: www.fanmakers.com

The Worshipful Company of Feltmakers
Visit the Worshipful Company of Feltmakers website for details of the Company's history, charities, the Livery's magazine and their annual Design Awards.
The Worshipful Company of Feltmakers
Website: www.feltmakers.co.uk

The Worshipful Company of Framework Knitters
The Worshipful Company of Framework Knitters traces its origins to 1589 when William Lee of Calverton in Nottinghamshire invented a method of knitting mechanically. Today, the Framework Knitters 'no longer control its trades but continues close association with its industry'. See the website for details of the Company's heritage, affiliations, activities, events, charities, and student bursaries.
The Worshipful Company of Framework Knitters
Website: www.frameworkknitters.co.uk

The Worshipful Company of Girdlers
The Worshipful Company of Girdlers was involved with the making of girdles (or belts). Visit the Company's website featuring the Company's history and today's principal activities.
The Worshipful Company of Girdlers
Website: www.girdlers.co.uk

The Worshipful Company of Glovers
The Worshipful Company of Glovers of London traces its history back to medieval times. Today, they still continue close links with the glove industry, working to 'promote the wearing of gloves and the businesses, training and education connected with glove-making'. They are the organisers of the annual Student Glove Design Completion.
The Worshipful Company of Glovers
Email: clerk@thegloverscompany.org   Website: www.thegloverscompany.org

The Worshipful Company of Haberdashers
The Worshipful Company of Haberdashers traces back its origins to medieval times. Today it has developed into a significant supporter of schools and education in England and Wales. See the website for the Company's history, activities, events, charities, and affiliations.
The Worshipful Company of Haberdashers
Email: enquiries@haberdashers.co.uk   Website: www.haberdashers.co.uk

The Worshipful Company of Leathersellers
Founded by royal charter in 1444, The Leathersellers' Company is one of the ancient Livery Companies of the City of London, with authority to control the sale of leather within the City. Today the Company devotes its energies and resources to 'supporting charities, education and the British leather trade'. See the website for details of activities, events, news, services and affiliations, charitable grants and education awards.
The Worshipful Company of Leathersellers
Email: enquiries@leathersellers.co.uk   Website: www.leathersellers.co.uk

The Worshipful Company of Pattenmakers
The Worshipful Company of Pattenmakers is one of the ancient Livery Companies City of London awarded its Royal Charter in 1670. Today the Patten makers' Charitable Foundation has developed a new role in funding the design and bespoke manufacture of orthopaedic shoes, particularly for the

UK's injured servicemen. Today, the Company's main activities focus on 'charity, fellowship and the participation in the life of the City of London'. See the website for details of the Company's history and Charitable Foundation.

The Worshipful Company of Pattenmakers
Email: clerk@pattenakers.co.uk   Website: www.pattenmakers.co.uk

The Worshipful Company of Weavers

An original textile Guild, the Worshipful Company of Weavers is one of the ancient Livery Companies of the City of London. Today it works as a 'charitable organisation, contributing to textile education through a variety of awards, scholarships and bursaries'. See the Company's website featuring the Company's history, membership details and their competitions, charitable grants and awards.

The Worshipful Company of Weavers
Email: weavers@weavers.org.uk   Website: www.weavers.org.uk

The Worshipful Company of Woolmen

The Worshipful Company of Woolmen is one of the oldest of the Livery Companies of the City of London tracing its roots to 1180. Originally it was the body that managed woolpackers and wool merchants making sure there was consistency in the standards for wool producers and wool merchants throughout the wool industry. View details of the Company's history, City Wool project, Charitable Trust accounts, events and awards on the Company's website.

The Worshipful Company of Woolmen
Website: http://woolmen.com

Young Embroiderers

The Young Embroiderers is part of the Embroidery Guild, and is dedicated to encouraging and supporting young people who want to take up embroidery and textiles to those just making their first stitches to students wanting to base their careers in this area of art and design. See the Guild's website for membership details, projects, competitions and local groups.

Young Embroiderers. Embroiderers' Guild. 1 Kings Road, Walton-on-Thames, Surrey, KT12 2RA
Tel: 01932 260738
Email: yeadministrator@embroiderersguild.com   Website: www.youngembroiderers.com

A selection of costume on display at Bankfield Museum, Halifax. Courtesy of Calderdale Museums

Recruitment Agencies, Consultancies and Services

Listed in this section are details of fashion and textile consultants and recruitment agencies which specialise in a wide range of industry sectors and job roles. Many agencies have detailed websites offering CV, career advice and guidance in completing application forms and writing speculative applications, covering letters and providing expert advice. Some agencies provide example aptitude, psychometric and personality tests together with interview advice and guidelines in negotiating your salary.

If looking for a new position, a number of agencies listed offer the opportunity to upload CV's onto their website and to sign-up for 'job alerts'. This allows you to hear about positions which match your abilities and career requirements, as soon as they are advertised. Whether you are looking for your first job within the industry or Graduate Programme, a promotional position or you are an employer and need to find and recruit the right person for a position there will be something here for you.

Angela Harper Resourcing

Angela Harper Resourcing is an independent specialist recruitment agency. Their main focus as a business is to provide good quality, experienced and reliable permanent and temporary staffing to manufacturers, wholesalers, importers and retailers within the, clothing, textiles and homewares industries. From graduates to director level they are equally important to Angela Harper Resourcing.

Angela Harper Resourcing
Tel: 07881 520 720
Email: resourcing@angelaharper.co.uk   Website: www.angelaharper.co.uk

CVUK

CVUK is an international recruitment partner for the fashion and retail sectors with offices located in Central London, Birmingham and Melbourne, Australia. The CVUK Group is made up of seven divisions: CVUK Group; CVInternational; CVExecutive; CVDigital; CVHospitality; Bespoke Recruitment Solutions; HR Solutions. They recruit for retail, buying, merchandising, marketing, production, technical, design, wholesale and E-commerce, and recruit for roles across a wide range of brands including fashion, beauty, home, lifestyle and general merchandise.

CVUK
Website: web.cvukgroup.com

Denza Ltd

Denza Ltd is an international recruitment company who recruit for womenswear menswear and childrenswear design, lingerie, accessories and footwear design, and home and textile design. They also recruit for areas of non-design, such as product development, studio management, pattern cutting, production, garment technology, fabric sourcing, marketing, wholesale/sales account management, visual merchandising, brand management, licensing and consultancy.

Denza Ltd. 4-5 Park Place, London, SW1A 1LP
Tel: +44 (0) 20 3008 7898
Email: denza@denza.co.uk   Website: wwwdenza.co.uk

Elite Associates

Elite Associates is a specialist in the luxury recruitment industry with offices in London and New York.

Elite Associates. 102-108 Clerkenwell Road, London, EC1M 5SA
Email: info@eliteassociates.co.uk   Website: www.eliteassociates.co.uk

Fashion Appointments

Fashion Appointments is an independent fashion recruitment consultancy specialising in the permanent and contract placement of personnel to a whole range of fashion roles including design, technical, production and sales.

Fashion Appointments
Tel: 0203 6519 440
Email: info@fashionappointments.com   Website: www.fashionappointments.com

Fashion Enter

Fashion Enter is a not for profit, and strives to be a centre of excellence for sampling, grading, production, and learning and development of skills within the fashion and textiles industry.
Fashion Enter Ltd. Unit 14, Crusader Estate, 167 Hermitage Road, London, N4 1LZ
Tel: 0208 8093311
Email: info@fashion-enter.com   Website: fashioncapital.co.uk

Fashion Innovation Agency

Visit the Fashion Innovation Agency website for further information on projects, designers, partners and news.
Fashion Innovation Agency. 20 John Prince's Street, London, W1G 0BJ
Tel: 020 7514 7518
Website: www.fialondon.com

FashionInsightJobs.co.uk

FashionInsightJobs.co.uk lists jobs in the fashion and beauty industry and includes PR and communications, marketing, media, retail, internships and graduate employment opportunities.
FashionInsightJobs.co.uk
Tel: +44 (0)7946 121 043
Email: info@fashioninsight.co.uk   Website: www.fashioninsightjobs.co.uk

Fashion and Retail Personnel

Fashion Personnel works in the sectors of design; wholesale and technical; buying and merchandising; marketing and Head Office; retail operations; marketing; fashion temps and executive appointments. They have two offices one based in London and the other in the Midlands.
Fashion Retail Personnel
Email: info@fashionpersonnel.co.uk   Website: www.fashionpersonnel.co.uk

Fashion Workie

Fashion Workie is a self-service portal for finding and advertising jobs, internships, work placements, castings and collaborations within the fashion industry.
Fashion Workie
Website: www.fashionworkie.com

Four Seasons Recruitment Ltd

Four Seasons Recruitment Ltd specialise in the areas of design (fashion, graphics and print), CAD, production managers and developers, retail management, retail sales, fashion wholesale, fashion buying, merchandising, visual merchandising, marketing, PR, temp retail and E-commerce positions.
Four Seasons Recruitment Ltd
Website: www.fsrl.co.uk

Freedom Recruitment

Freedom Recruitment offers a recruitment service to the retail and fashion industries. Divisions include accounting and finance, buying and merchandising, design, digital, HR, recruitment and training, marketing, PR and e-commerce, production, technical and wholesale, and retail operations and visual merchandising.
Fashion Recruitment. 22 Stukeley Street, London, WC2B 5LR
Tel: +44 (0)20 7734 9779
Email: info@freedomrecruit.com   Website: www.freedomrecruit.com

Fusion Associates

Launched in 1998, Fusion Associates is an international 'executive search firm' operating exclusively within the luxury, designer, fashion and performance sportswear sectors providing recruitment services and consultancy to brands and retailers across Europe, Asia and the USA.
Fusion Associates
Website: www.fusionassociates.eu

Graduate Jobs

Graduate jobs is a specialist employment and recruitment agency for graduates. Visit the Graduate Jobs website to view internships, graduate schemes, jobs by sector, jobs by location, jobs by degree and jobs by industry, and a section on employment advice and guidelines.
Graduate Jobs
Email: thosenicepeople@graduate-jobs.com   Website: www.graduate-jobs.com

Harpers Recruitment Ltd

Harpers Recruitment Ltd., works across the areas of merchandising, buying, design, technical, sales HR, marketing and legal.

Harpers Recruitment Ltd. Shaw Park Business Center, Shaw Park, Off Silver Street, Aspley, Huddersfield, HD5 9AF

Tel: 0203 542 8883

Email: info@harpers-recruitment.com   Website: harpersrecruitment.co.uk

InDesign

Founded in 1968, InDesign is an international fashion recruitment agency, and who also undertake executive searches, freelance places and graduate appointments. See their website for full details of services, career opportunities and to access their current database of jobs.

In Design. 1 Ashland Place, London, W1V 4AQ

Tel: +44 (0) 20 7935 7485

Email: i@indesignrecruitment.co.uk   Website: www.indesignrecruitment.co.uk

InRetail

InRetail is a recruitment agency working in the sectors for retail and hospitality. Job categories include distribution, buying, marketing and E-Commerce, merchandising, visual merchandising, shop floor and sales assistants, wholesale, technical and design, administration, and graduate retail jobs,

InRetail. Langstone Technology Park, Langstone Road, Havant, PO9 1SA

Website: www.inretail.co.uk

Janou Pakter

Janou Pakter recruits for international leading businesses, design consultancies, advertising and branding agencies, fashion and luxury goods houses. See their website for details of their London and international offices in Paris, Milan and Los Angeles, and their New York headquarters.

Janou Pakter

Website: www.pakter.com

People Marketing Fashion Recruitment LLP

People Marketing Fashion Recruitment is a specialist recruitment agency for the fashion industry (UK and internationally). They manage a wide range of vacancies including jobs in clothing, footwear, accessories, sportswear, corporate wear and fashion retail. Their consultants have industry experience, and their extensive network of contacts has been built up over 25 years.

People Marketing. 4 Bowden Drive, Boulevard Industrial Park, Beeston, Nottingham, NG9 2JY

Tel: 0115 922 3335

Email: sales@peoplemarketing.co.uk   Website: www.peoplemarketing.co.uk

Planet Personnel Ltd

Planet Personnel is a consultancy specialising in the recruitment of candidates for the global apparel, footwear and textile industries.

Planet Personnel Ltd. The Empire, 9 Lord Street, Halifax, West Yorkshire, HX1 5AE

Email: info@planetpersonnel.com   Website: www.planetpersonnel.com

Prestige Recruitment Services

Prestige Recruitment Services is a consultancy recruiting for positions in fashion and retail amongst others in the UK and offshore.

Prestige Recruitment Group. (Head Office) Blue Square House, 24 Bennetts Hill, Birmingham, B2 5QP

Tel: 0121 244 5004

Website: www.prestigerecruitmentservices.co.uk

Quest Search and Selection

Quest Search and Selection have offices in London, Manchester and the Middle East, and work in the retail and consumer goods sector from buying and merchandising to E-commerce and digital, design and technical to procurement, supply chain and logistics. See website for further details.

Quest Search and Selection

Website: www.questsearch.co.uk

Retail Careers

Retail Careers advertised opportunities from operations and retail management, store manager, to visual merchandising, display and POS (point of sale), shop floor and sales assistants, distribution and E-commerce, to wholesale, technical and design. An easy to use website providing lots of information for jobseekers with jobs advertised both by location and career.
Retail Careers.Co.UK. Langstone Technology Park, Langstone Road, Havant, PO9 1SA
Website: www.retailcareers.co.uk

Retail Management Consultants Ltd

Retail Management Consultants Ltd., offer four core services: Insights, Connections, Recruitment and Consultancy. 'They offer market intelligence and feasibility studies, to putting companies in contact with the right people, to recruiting the best talent for business'.
Retail Management Consultants Ltd
Email: info@retailmanagementconsultants.com Website: retailmanagementconsultants.com

RetailMoves.com

RetailMoves.com is a retail job search engine for the retail sector across the UK. The website features many jobs offering an email alert facility, careers advice and guidance.
Retailmoves.com
Website: www.retailmoves.com

ROC Recruitment

A recruitment agency for permanent, contract and temporary staff for a range of organisations, from world-class blue chip companies to elite private individuals across a variety of sectors and job roles including apprentices, administrative, finance and accounts, beauty management, beauty sales and therapists, customer service, education and assessors, executive, facilities, human resources, office management, personal and executive assistants, reception and front of house, retail area/regional managers, retail brand communication, retail buying and merchandising, retail E-commerce, retail executive, retail head office, retail operations, sales and retail store management, retail supply and logistics, retail technical and wholesale. See their website for further details of their Divisions, their current clients and client testimonials, and all services offered.
ROC Recruitment. Moss House, 15-16 Brooks Mews, London, W1K 4DS
Tel: +44 (0)20 7318 1400
Email: reception@roc.co.uk Website: www.roc.co.uk

Style Incorporated

Founded in 1977, Style Incorporated is a London-based recruitment agency works with clients from a range of business sectors including luxury, retail, fashion, travel, leisure and the arts.
Style incorporated
Website: www.styleincorporated.com

Talisman

Talisman Fashion is an international recruitment consultancy working with companies in the fashion, retail, sports and lifestyle sectors. Case studies and testimonials, are available for viewing on their website, along with featured job vacancies located in the UK, Ireland and internationally.
Talisman
Tel: +44 (0) 203 1741 679
Website: www.talismanfashion.com

Temps Online Ltd

Temps Online Ltd., is one of the UK's leading online recruitment agencies offering a cost-effective service to companies and organisations, and catering for every industry sector. For the job seeker, Temps Online Ltd., offers a very easy to use online job search for full time, part-time, freelance, short contract and interim positions. See website for further details.
Temps Online Ltd
Website: http://tempsonline.co.uk

Totaljobs.com

Totaljobs.com is part of Totaljobs Group Ltd; and is an online recruitment company. It also offers careers advice and tools, CV and cover letter templates and the opportunity for you to upload your CV to show case to potential employers, and to receive the latest job alerts.

Totaljobs.com
Website: www.totaljobs.com

U&I Recruitment

U&I Recruitment are global fashion, textiles and retail recruitment specialists across all industry sectors from buying, merchandising, product management, design (from juniors to design directors), E-commerce, technology, production, marketing and PR, to all positions in the retail and sales sector.

U&I Recruitment
Email: info@uandirecruitment.co.uk   Website: www.uandirecruitment.co.uk

Vohs & Co

Vohs & Co are a fashion industry recruitment consultancy working with industry suppliers, high street retailers and fashion brands.

Vohs & Co
Website: www.vohsandco.com

Samples from the Royal Albert Memorial Museum & Art Gallery's large collection of lace
© 2015 Royal Albert Memorial Museum & Art Gallery, Exeter City Council

Trend Forecasting Services and Consultancies

This section presents details of forecasting services and consultancies that offer a range of trend forecasting services and products, from full colour trend publications providing the latest seasonal reports predicting colours, yarns, fabrics and trims to style directions for a range of sectors including printed textiles, interior and product design to lifestyle. Other services offered include the publication of newsletters to highly analytical reports summarising market intelligence involving industry research and business analysis to specialist knowledge of specific markets.

Carlin International/Carlin (UK) Ltd
Carlin International/Carlin (UK) Ltd is a design, style and communication agency, and producers of trend publications for colour, fabrics and yarns, womenswear, menswear, kids, active sportswear, lingerie and lifestyle.
Carlin International. Head Office, 79 Rue de Miromesnil, 75008 Paris, France
Tel : 00 33 1 53 04 42 00
Email: moscrin@carlin-groupe.com Website: www.carlin-international.com

Color Association of the United States (CAUS)
'Founded in 1915, the Color Association of the United States creates and delivers global colour intelligence across industries'. Categories listed include: Interiors, Men's, Women's, Youth and Beauty. See website for details of resources, membership, consultation, education and forecast categories.
Color Association of the United States (CAUS)
Email: info@colorassociation.com   Website: colorassociation.com

Committee for Colour & Trends (CCT)
The Committee for Colour and Trends (CCT) provides colour and trend forecasts for footwear, handbags, jewelry and accessories 12 to 18 months in advance of the selling season.
Committee for Colour & Trend (CCT)
Email: info@Colourandtrends.com   Website: www.colourandtrends.com

Concepts Paris
Concepts Paris offers a resource for lingerie design offering trend books, online trend updates, image galleries and shopping guides. They have offices in Paris, London, New York and Kowloon, Hong Kong.
Concepts Paris
Website: www.conceptsparis.com

Design Options Inc
The only Los Angeles based trend and colour forecasting company Design Options is dedicated to bringing Southern California's aesthetic to the world. See website for full details of product range and forecasting services available, which include 'Young Missy', 'Junior Contemporary', 'young men's' and 'Kidz' along with a 'Customise' service.
Design Options Inc. 110 East 9th Street, Suite B769, Los Angeles, California 90079, USA
Email: DNow@design-options.com   Website: www.design-options.com

The Doneger Group
Founded in 1946, The Doneger Group is a source of global trend intelligence, focused merchandising direction, expert analysis of the retail business and comprehensive market information. Services offered include 'Industry Research and Analysis, Directives West, Trend and Colour Services, Consulting Services and Online Services'
The Doneger Group. New York, USA
Website: www.doneger.com

Drapers

Drapers is key to all UK fashion business featuring the latest news, trends and catwalk reports. Visit Drapers excellent website for details of industry awards and events, top fashion jobs, exclusive sales data, insightful viewpoints, and research and reports on the latest in business and fashion industry news, trend information, jobs, awards, and much more.

Drapers. Telephone House, 69-77 Paul St, London, EC2A 4NQ, UK

Tel: +44 (0)20 3033 2600

Website: www.drapersonline.com

Esp Trendlab

ESP Trendlab is a trend research and consultancy agency in New York, USA, who predict and analyse design trends for over 1000 brands worldwide, from design and lifestyle to consumer mindsets and socio-cultural movements. They offer a subscription website 'Trend Lab', a digital bookshelf to view and much more.

Esp Trendlab. 12 West 37th Street, New York 10018, USA

Email: info@esptrendlab.com   Website: esptrendlab.com

EzTextiles

EzTextiles.com is a royalty-free, online Digital Textile Library offering millions of high resolution (300dpi .tif) production ready images. All the images are colour reduced and full editable in all types of software. Libraries include contemporary and vintage prints, knit, woven plaids and woven stripes. There is also a Product Library that allows the user to instantly visualise, render and download the patterns they choose in a photographic realistic format, graphic silhouette or a classic sketch and or mini-body. See the EzTextiles website for further information.

EzTextiles

Email: john@sanodesignservices.com   Website: www.eztextiles.com

Fashion Forecast Services

Established in 2001, the Fashion Forecast Services offers international reports for colour and trend services to the fashion, homewares and associated industries.

Fashion Forecast Services

Email: info@fashionforecastservices.com   Website: www.fashionforecastservices.com

Fashion Snoops

Based in New York, Fashion Snoops is a global trend research and advisory company. They offer an online subscription-based fashion forecasting service.

Fashion Snoops. 39, W 38th Street, New York, New York 10018, USA

Website: www.fashionsnoops.com

Fashion Trendsetter

Fashion Trendsetter is a design and trend office founded in 2003, and FashionTrendsetter.com is their online fashion and colour forecasting, trend reporting and news e-zine, providing fashion information and news from the major trade fairs, trend reports and fashion forecasts.

Mailing Address: Fashion Trendsetter. Senay Gokcen, 50 Colfax Avenue, Ste Ad8606, Clifton, New Jersey 07013, USA

Website: www.fashiontrendsetter.com

Future Laboratory

Future Laboratory provides trend forecasting, consumer insight and brand innovation, and offers consultancy to 'innovate and inspire'. They also present at conferences, provide In-house trend briefings, and workshops. Publications include: trend and consumer reports.

Future Laboratory

Website: thefuturelaboratory.com

Huepoint Color

Huepoint Color is a Division of the Donegar Group. They publish targeted cross-disciplinary colour seasons for fashion and apparel, home furnishings, and digital design, 18 months in advance of the market. See the website for full details of their services, colour library and publications.

Huepoint Color. 39 W 37th Street, 18th Floor, New York, NY 10018, USA

Website: huepoint.com

International Colour Authority (ICA)

The International Colour Authority (ICA) was founded in 1966 and is a world leading colour forecasting service providing colour trends for interiors, exteriors, fashion and all manufactured coloured products. See the ICA website for further details of services.

Colour Academy Ltd
Email: info@intenationalcolourauthority.org   Website: www.colourforecasting.com

Luminary Colour: K M Associates

Luminary Colour offer trend and colour information, a consultancy service, trend events and presentations. Luminary Colour: K M Associates - KMAUKprojects Ltd t/a K M Associates.
Website: www.kmauk.com

MBF Trend Consulting

Founded in 2001, MBF Trend Consulting is a New York City-based consulting firm that provides clients with trend and design directions, reports and presentations.

MBF Trend Consulting
Email: contact@mbf-trend-consulting.com   Website: www.mbf-trend-consulting.com

Mode Information Ltd

Moda Information are publishers and distributors of trend, colour and forecasting services used by major high street retailers and designers. They produce books, magazines and online services particularly for the areas of textiles, fashion, graphic design, interior, architecture and lifestyle.

Mode Informtaion Ltd. First Floor, Eastgate House, 16-19 Eastcastle Street, W1W 8DA, London, UK
Tel: +44 20 7436 0133
Email: weborder@modeinfo.co.uk   Website: http://modeinfo.co.uk

Nelly Rodi

Established in 1985, Nelly Rodi is a trend forecasting agency for fashion, lifestyle, beauty and media. Services include the development of brand products, seasonal trend books, and Trend Lab publications: Colour Intelligence, Colour Palette, Men's Edition, Women's Edition, Lingerie, Prints, Fabrics, Life and Style, Décor and Atmosphere, and many more.

Nelly Rodi. 28 Avenue de Saint-Ouen, 75018 Paris, France
Email: infos@nellyrodi.com   Website: www.nellyrodi.com

Peclers Paris

Pecler is a worldwide company based in Paris with offices also in New York, Shanghai and Munich. They are a trend, style and innovation consulting agency providing expertise in trends, brand and style strategy, product innovation and seasonal product development.

Peclers Paris. 23 Rue du Mail, 75002 Paris, France
Tel: +33(0)1 40 41 06 06
Email: peclers@peclersparis.com   Website: www.peclersparis.com

Promostyl

Established in 1966, Promostyl is an international trend office providing trends for fashion and design. They also offer a creative consulting service providing bespoke services on branding, design, communication, retail and training. See website for details of services, workshops and trend seminars. Offices are based in Paris (Head Office), Tokyo, New-York, Beijing, Shanghai and Guangzhou.

Promostyl (Head Office). 5 Passage Thiere, 75011 Paris, France
Tel: +33 (0)1 49 23 76 00
Website: www.promostyl.com

Sano Design Services

Sano Design Services is a CAD Textile Service Bureau and a digital fabric printing studio based in New York City. The studio is comprised of skilled artists, CAD and Graphic designers that have over 20 years' experience in the apparel, home, beauty and hard goods industries. Services offered include developing original prints, graphics and illustrations, digital fabric printing, trend, branding, merchandising, product visualisation, tech packs compilation, online resources, illustration and sketches, and overall process consultation.

Sano Design Services. 7 Dey Street, Suite 501, New York, NY 10007, USA
Website: www.sanodesignservices.com

Style.com

Fashion show reviews, trend reports, style notes and shopping guides, people and parties, beauty, videos, and Designer Directory.
Style.com
Website: www.style.com

Style Lens

Style Lens is a fashion trend reporting and forecasting company. See website for details of services and location of global offices in Japan, USA – West Coast, East Coast, Brazil and South America.
Style Lens UK
Email: Info@Stylelens.Com   Website: www.stylelens.com

Stylesight

Stylesight offers fashion trend forecasting and analysis for the style, fashion and design sectors, and has offices in New York and Los Angeles, USA; Brazil; China in partnership with CTIC; Hong Kong and Australia; and contact details for Korea, Taiwan, Japan, India, Turkey, Middle East and Greece.
Stylesight
Tel: 020 7613 6280
Website: www.stylesight.com

Trend Bible

Trend Bible is a 'home and interiors dedicated trend agency that produce a range of trend publications, industry-specific reports and also offer bespoke consultancy services.
Trend Bible. 1 Maling Court, Union Street, Newcastle, NE2 1BP, UK
Tel: 0191 265 0665
Email: enquiries@trendbible.com   Website: www.trendbible.com

TrendPulse Ltd

TrendPulse is the one-stop creative resource dedicated to interiors and home product design and development. It gives insights into global trends in lifestyle and home interior products and is used by retailers, suppliers, buyers, merchandisers and designers working in the lifestyle and home interiors markets worldwide.
TrendPulse Ltd. 90 Sarsfeld Road, London, SW12 8HL, UK
Tel: +44 (0)208 675 7935
Email: info@trendpulse.co.uk   Website: trendpulse.co.uk

Trendstop

Trendstop.com is an online fashion and trend forecasting agency based in London, predicting fashion and lifestyle trends from season to season. Online reports are available covering a diverse range of categories from womenswear colour and style trends to print and graphics, embellishment forecasts, footwear, catwalk prints and materials, buying guides trade show and retail reports.
Trendstop. 28-39 The Quadrant, 135 Salisbury Road, London, NW6 6RJ, UK
Website: www.trendstop.com

trendwatching.com

Established in 2002, trendwatching.com is an independent company providing information and insight reporting into consumer trends and providing business ideas.
trendwatching.com
Email: londonoffice@trendwatching.com   newyorkoffice@trendwatching.com
(See website for details of offices in Singapore, São Paulo Office and Lagos.
Email: londonoffice@trendwatching.com (London Office) Website: http://trendwatching.com

Trends West

Trends West services include consultancy, sample buying, webinars providing trend information and creative direction, photopacks and newsletters.
Trends West. 6399 Wilshire Boulevard Suite 1000, Los Angeles, California 90048, USA
Email: info@trendswest.com   Website: www.trendswest.com

TRENDZINE Fashion Information Media Network
TRENDZOOM: Fashion trend and forecasting service for the fashion and design industries, and founder of Trendzine: the Fashion Information Media Network. Catwalk reports, trend books: colour and style directions for women, men, youth and accessory areas, urban sportswear, street and trend analysis are available.
TRENDZINE Fashion Information Media Network
Website: trendzoom.com

WGSN (Worth Global Style Network)
WGSN (Worth Global Style Network) trend forecasting and analysis cover the spectrum of product design, from range planning, merchandising, marketing and sourcing. They have offices throughout Europe, Asia, North and South America, and the Middle East. Services offered include coverage from global catwalks, inspiration and design tools, a tailored advisory service, a Vogue archive which includes every issue from 1892 to today, retail analytics system, reports and Webinars.
WGSN (Worth Global Network). Greater London House, Hampstead Road, London, NW1 7EJ, UK
Email: sales@4C.wgsn.com   Website: www.wgsn.com

WWD (Women's Wear Daily)
Women's Wear Daily (WWD) is a property of Fairchild Fashion Media, and provides daily reports and are 'the industry voice of authority in the global women's and men's fashion, retail and beauty communities and the consumer media that cover the market'. WWD offers an informative website that provides comprehensive coverage of the latest on fashion trends, runway reports, market features and business news.
WWD (Women's Wear Daily)
Website: www.wwd.com

Zandl Group
Zandl Group is a New York based agency 'dedicated to keeping brands and businesses on-trend and culturally relevant to today's hard-to-reach consumers'. See website for full details of services.
Zandl Group
Email: info@zandlgroup.com   Website: http://zandlgroup.com

Mary Katrantzou's Autumn/Winter 2014 collection where she commissioned Hand & Lock to create 'heaps' of embroidery inspired by jewellery. Image credit: Saoirse Crean.

INDEX

Section 5: Fashion and Textile Information Directory

This section includes all services in alphabetical orders, as listed.

Business Advisory and Support Services

Exhibition Organisers

Fashion, Textile and Associated Exhibitions and Trade Fairs - UK

Grants, Awards, Finance and Funding Opportunities

Legal Support

Museums, Research Centres, Collections and Galleries

Organisations, Guilds, Network and Associations

Recruitment Agencies and Services

Trend Forecasting Services and Consultancies

Websites and Additional Useful Resources

All About Leather
Website: www.all-about-leather.co.uk

The Business of Fashion (BoF)
Website: www.businessoffashion.com

Centre for Fashion Enterprise (CFE)
Website: www.fashion-enterprise.com/

Design Trust
Website: www.thedesigntrust.co.uk

Fashion Monitor
Website: www.fashionmonitor.com

Fashion United
Website: www.fashionunited.co.uk

Innovation Textiles.com
Website: www.innovationintextiles.com

Make it British
Website: http://makeitbritish.co.uk/about

TRAID – (Textile Recycling for Aid and International Development)
Website: www.traid.org.uk/about-traid

All Walks Beyond the Catwalk
Website: www.allwalks.org

Let's Make it Here
Website: www.letsmakeithere.org

Acknowledgements:

I would like to thank everyone who has supported this project. In particular I would like to thank the following for their time, patience and for their contributions to this publication: Boutique Mahali; Bora Aksu; Matthew Andrew - Lecturer in Photography and Practitioner, University of Salford; Gary Assim – Head of Retail and Intellectual Property Group Leader, Shoosmiths; Brad Burton – MD of 4Networking; Francesca Coombs – Lecturer in Fashion Marketing and Promotion, the University of West London; Christine Faulhaber – President and CEO at Faulhaber Communications; Omar Franco – Creative Director, Evocca College, Melbourne Area, Australia; Tom Gillman - Commercial Director at Crafted, Ipswich; James Innes - Founder of CVCentre.co.uk; Matthew Harding – Co-founder of palmer//harding; Gerardine Hemingway(MBE) and Wayne Hemingway (MBE) – Founders of HemingwayDesign; Jaana Jätyri - Founder and CEO of the trend forecasting agency Trendstop; Debbie MacBeattie - Managing Director, ROC Recruitment and Temps-online; Kay Mawer – Managing Director at Clothkits Ltd; Laura Olivia - Printed Textile Designer; Clare Parker – Owner Vintage Vixen; Harriet Sanders – Founder of Harriet Sanders Accessories; Margo Selby – Founder of Margo Selby Design Studio; Levi Palmer – Co-founder of palmer//harding and V.K Wise.

I am also grateful to the many businesses, associations and individuals who have given their support to this project, in particular: Africa Fashion Week, London (AFWL); Anna Marie Benedict – AFWL Press Team; Bankfield Museum; BIS – Department for Business and Innovation Skills; Heather Bostock; Boutique Mahali; British Fashion Council; the British Library Business & IP Centre; Calderdale Museums; Calverton Museum, Nottinghamshire; Abi Carney; Catwalking.com; Gennni Cechini, Marketing and PR at Textile Events; Ciment Pleating Ltd; Angela Clare - Collections Officer, Calderdale Museums Service; Saoirse Crean Photography; the Department of Education and Employment; the Department of Trade and Industry (DTI); Elpeeko Ltd, Lincoln; Ethical Fashion Forum; Mallory Giardino, Membership Director, Source Ethical Fashion Forum; Cecilie Harris; Lucy Hawes - Press Officer, Victoria and Albert Museum, London; Heis Associates; HemingwayDesign; Jan Hicks, Archives and Information Manager, Museum of Science and Industry; Innovate UK; Donna Lambert - Lamb to the Slaughter; London Fashion Weekend; Rob Mackenzie, Marketing Assistant, Royal Albert Memorial Museum and Art Gallery; Robert McCaffrey, Communications Manager, Hand & Lock; Chris Moore Photography; 4Networking; New Designers; Newman College University; Pomegrate Designs; Gareth Pugh - Corporate and Collections Information Officer, Museum of Science and Industry; Nina Sandhaus - Press Office Assistant, Victoria and Albert Museum; Scoop; Technology Strategy Board; Jacqui Turner – 4Networking; Nicola Vanore Tebo – USA, Fashion Agent; Jim Varney; Victoria and Albert Museum, London; Antony Waller - Director ANTWALLER & Co; Matt Weinert, Managing Director, Ciment Pleating Ltd; Steven White, (Enterprise Analysis Team, BIS).

A special thank you to the Editorial Team Jonjanski and Kelly Morris, and to Lesley Purveur, Partner at Larken & Co Solicitors, Newark for legal guidance. Huge thanks go to all the team at Elpeeko Limited, Lincoln, UK, to Clare Griffiths, Art Director and to Steve Turner, Managing Director for their enthusiasm, advice and guidance, and hard work in the design and typesetting; and to the print room team for their care and attention in producing the book.

On a personal note, I would like to thank all my friends and family for their patience, support and encouragement in my work over the years: Ian Baxter; Catherine Burge, Sol Burge; Tricia Clark; Pat Foster; Louise Gravil, Sally Haymes; David and Caroline Gill; Rachael Isaac-Pascoe; Erica Joslyn-Beales; Polly Lancaster, Janie Lismore; Paul Middleton; Mike Saks; Pilar Navarrete Herranz; Catherine Orkney; Carolyn Puzzovio; John James Skinner and most importantly my parents George and Margaret Brown for their continuous love, support and enthusiasm in all that I do.

Picture Credits:

I would like to thank the following businesses and individuals for providing photographic images. Every effort has been made to contact the copyright holders but any have been omitted, Raven House Studios would be pleased to correct them in any subsequent editions of this publication.

p4	Catwalking.com
p6	Matthew Andrew; Heather Bostock; Emma Andrew; Mathew Andrew; Janie Lismore
p28	Cecilie Harris
p32	Courtesy of Cement Pleating, UK. Photo credit Matt Weinert
p34	Cecilie Harris (top left); Mitchel Sams (top right); Fionna Essex (bottom right)
p37	Rebecca Louise Parker
p38 & p39	Courtesy of Margo Selby Textiles
p40 & p 41	Courtesy of Laura Olivia
p44	Janie Lismore – (All images)
p45 & p46	Heather Bostock
p49 & p50	Matt Wreford
p54	Courtesy of Gary Assim
p59	Mitchel Sams
p60	Courtesy of Scoop London
p65	Courtesy of London Textile Fair, Courtesy Textile Events (Top); Courtesy of Ethical Fashion Forum (bottom)
p66 & p67	Courtesy of Brad Burton, 4Networking
p76	Courtesy of Scoop London
p81	Jeff Broudeau
p89	Matthew Andrew
p90	Catwalking.com
p97	Courtesy of Debbie MacBeattie
p99 & p100	Courtesy of Trendstop
p102	Tom Campbell (top); Chris Dadey (bottom)
p103	Catwalking.com
p105	Trevor Leighton (left); Chris Moore (right) Courtesy of HemingwayDesign
p106	Colin Davison (left); Rebecca Reid (right)
p 107	HemingwayDesign
p109	Courtesy of the Museum of Science and Industry
p110	Courtesy of the Victoria and Albert Museum, London
p119	Courtesy of the Museum of Science and Industry
p128	Courtesy of Textile Events
p160	David Garner. Courtesy of the Royal Albert Museum & Gallery, Exeter City Council
p186	Courtesy of Calderdale Museums
p191	David Garner. Courtesy of the Royal Albert Museum & Gallery, Exeter City Council
p196	Saoirse Crean – (Website: www.saoirsecrean.com).Courtesy of Hand & Lock
Back Cover	Fionna Essex

Raven House Studios wishes to thank all the companies, artists, designers, businesses, associations, colleagues, friends and family who have supported the research, development, design and production of this publication.